Massacred By Mother Nature

Exploring The Natural Horror Film

Massacred By Mother Nature

Exploring the Natural Horror Film

by Lee Gambin

Midnight Marquee Press, Inc.
Baltimore, Maryland, USA

Copyright © 2012 by Lee Gambin
Interior layout Gary J. Svehla
Cover design by Susan Svehla

Midnight Marquee Press, Inc., Gary J. Svehla and A. Susan Svehla do not assume any responsibility for the accuracy, completeness, topicality or quality of the information in this book. All views expressed or material contained within are the sole responsibility of the author.

Without limiting the rights under copyright reserved above, no part of this publication may be reproduced, stored in or introduced into a retrieval system, or transmitted, in any form, or by any means (electronic, mechanical, photocopying, recording or otherwise), without the prior written permission of the copyright owner or the publishers of the book.

ISBN 13: 978-1-936168-30-9
Library of Congress Catalog Card Number 2012951005
Manufactured in the United States of America

First Printing by Midnight Marquee Press, Inc., October 2012

Dedication

To Daniel, Michael, Melissa, Adrian and Eileen,
I dedicate this book…
may we always remember the early to mid-'80s
as a time of comfortable, cozy lounge rooms,
readily handy snacks and a healthy dose of horror films.

Table of Contents

Pg 9   Preface

Pg 10   Forewords From Four of The Finest

Pg 15   From Hitchcock's Flock to Girdler's Grizzly: An Introduction to the Natural Horror Film

Pg 24   And A Frog Shall Lead Them: Mother Nature Gets Angry As Humankind Panics

Pg 56   Aquatic Attacks! It's A Matter of Life and Death Under The Sea

Pg 76   (That's When I Fell For) The Leader of the Pack: Bite Worse Than Bark— The Bad Doggies of Cinema

Pg 92   Insectellectual: The Discreet Charm of the Creepy Crawly

Page 114	Children of Kong, Spawn of Godzilla: The Super-Sized Animals of Hollywoodland
Pg 137	The Two of Us Need Look No More: Human Help in the Natural Horror Film
Pg 158	Stock Characters of the Ecological Horror Film: Haunted Loners, Left Over Cowboys, Environmental Sympathizers, Sassy Professionals and Wise Indians
Pg 169	The Animal Kingdom Reigns Supreme: Animal Attack Sequences, Interviews and Other Fun Stuff!
Pg 206	I Do Not Understand The Human Race: An Ode to the Ecologically Evil
Pg 210	Index

PREFACE

Growing up I knew horror movies meant the world to me.

Luckily, as a kid in the suburbs of Melbourne, Australia, this love for horror films was shared by the likes of some of my friends and family. Most notably I'd enjoy watching loads of horror movies nearly every night with my cousins, who were the same age as me. Our mothers were avid fans as well and they'd sometimes watch along with us. We rented every single horror film possible from local video stores, bought videos that became a special treat or made sure we stayed up late enough to see what the networks were playing so we could record it!

We loved all of it—the classic Universal horror movies and the Hammer films, as well as all the modern stuff that was made post-1960; all the stuff that was coming out at the time, our time, that great period, the 1980s! Back then, the TV networks played lots of amazing stuff and they seemed to revel in screening films from the 1970s, a perfect era for horror.

One of my most vivid memories growing up was when I was probably seven or eight and looking through the TV guide and saw that *Grease* was screening on Channel 7. My cousins Melissa, Adrian and Eileen were also very much into all kinds of movies (musicals being no exception) and we were going to have a sleepover and tune in. But on the TV guide I noticed that right after *Grease*, a movie called *Bug* was to be shown; I told the others and they were keen to see it too.

I became obsessed with *Bug* instantly, and that night, after *Grease* finished, I was extremely eager to stay up for it. On this occasion the others all fell asleep and I thought right there and then that perhaps horror movies would forever be more important to me than the other genres ... to everyone else they were good fun and much loved, but to me these celluloid fright-fests were part of my make-up.

Being an avid animal lover it was always satisfying to see beasts of any kind kill humans. Something in that was completely comforting. My cousins loved that stuff too. We became obsessed with *Jaws* and *Cujo* and *King Kong* (both the classic starring Fay Wray and, yes, even the De Laurentiis film with Jessica Lange) and drew the characters and played out scenes from many of these movies using our vivid imaginations. So, to Daniel, Michael, Melissa, Adrian and Eileen, I dedicate this book ... may we always remember the early to mid-eighties as a time of comfortable cozy lounge rooms, readily handy snacks and a healthy dose of horror films.

Forwords From Four of the Finest

A Word from Chris Alexander
Editor-in-Chief For *Fangoria* magazine

Chris Alexander, editor-in-chief of *Fangoria* magazine

How appropriate that Lee Gambin's new book is a love letter to nature unbound, while he himself is a bit of a force of nature in his own right.

Lee beat me to the punch working for *Fangoria*, the little horror rag I have the honor of editing, and he contributes some of our most popular material. Lee had already been scribbling for the magazine, or at least had been embraced by the previous editor Tony Timpone, before I came on board, and after publishing a wonderful two-parter (it didn't start as a two-parter but, hey, Lee is, as Stephen King calls himself, a "putter inner," and the piece was epic enough that it needed to be split) on *The Children of Nightmare on Elm Street* that was lively, cheerful and very intelligent. I loved it; so did my readers.

That's why as of this writing, even though I have not read the final manuscript of *Massacred by Mother Nature: Exploring the Natural Horror Film*, I know that I—and you—are in for a treat. Lee has this uncanny way of taking a subject, no matter how lowbrow, and injecting it with a sort of enthusiasm and reverence that most scribes are afraid, or simply unable, to evoke.

I am a fan.

As will you be, dear reader, once the last few words spill out onto the final pages. So please buckle in and let Lee take you on a trip, a journey into realms of weird cinema where the fuzzier the beast, the bloodier the bite, the calmer the visage, the crueler the wrath—the better! This is nature's revenge, Gambin-style!

A Word from Dee Wallace
Star of *Cujo*

Cujo is a metaphor for the force of nature that was once calm and nurturing but suddenly turns violent and destructive. As a gentle wind can suddenly become a hurricane of mass destruction and terror, Cujo transformed from a loving pet to a murderous monster. As is true of all forces of nature, that shift affects everything in its path—the relationships of key players are all altered and redefined. A marriage that was in trouble finds hope, and the relationship between mother and child reaches new heights of commitment and love. But this can only happen when faced with the horrors that be.

Dee Wallace (from *Cujo*)

Those who are unaware of the force of evil may fall prey to the unfortunate outcome. The world at that ranch is also irrevocably affected, and the lives of all who enter must deal with the fate of their creation.

But the biggest victim is Cujo himself. Once loving and gentle, one act of the cruelty of nature (being bitten by a rabid bat) changes the reality of what he is. That becomes the metaphor for the movie—the innocent caught in the fear and desperation of nature unleashed, and the resulting self-definition and growth that results if we choose to learn the lesson.

A Word From Bert I. Gordon
Director of *Beginning of the End, Food of the Gods* and *Empire of the Ants*

When Lee Gambin told me he was writing *Massacred by Mother Nature: Exploring the Natural Horror Film*, I thought about the animals in some of the movies I had produced/directed that did their share of massacring … giant rats the size of jungle tigers in *Food of the Gods*, huge ants in *Empire of the Ants* and beastly-sized locusts in *Beginning of the End*. The big rats in *Food of the Gods* needed training for them to do their massacring in the movie, and it wasn't easy. We bought three hundred of them from a laboratory that raised rats for medical research. After our principle photography with our human stars on an island off the coast of Vancouver Canada was completed, we started training the rats back in Hollywood for their scenes that would later be combined with the people footage by means of special visual effects. [This is all explained in my autobiography, *The Amazing Colossal Worlds of Mr. Bert I. Gordon*, available at my website bertigordon.com.] The first scene in *Food of the Gods* that we planned on shooting was the one where the rats charge down a long, grassland area towards our hero Marjoe Gortner, with the goal of eating him. As the scene with Gortner was already filmed with him on a grass area, we constructed a small

Bert. I. Gordon (right) on the set of *The Magic Sword*, with Basil Rathbone (left) displaying a prop

set about 12 feet long of miniature grass to simulate the area, with him and the cage of rats on one end, and an empty cage on the other end. We opened the gate of the cage containing the rats and coaxed them with cheese along the grass strip so they would travel toward the empty cage on the other end. After several hours of training, the rats performed perfectly. When we would open the door to their cage, they ran toward the empty cage with the cheese just as the script called for! Then, with the noisy high-speed, 35mm movie camera set up with the two cages out of the scene, and bright lights illuminating the miniature set, I called "Roll 'em," and the cameraman started the camera, and I called "Action!" and the rat cage door was opened ... and the rats didn't move ... they just stayed in the cage! We tried the filming over and over many times, but the results were the same, as if we had never trained them. The rats remained in the cage. With many thousand feet of unexposed film thrown into the garbage, I called it a day. As I tossed and turned during a sleepless night, about three in the morning a possible solution to our rat problem popped into my head. The next day we started training the rats as before, from the beginning, but this time we had the bright lights turned on, and the noisy high-speed, camera running without film. Then, after several hours of training with camera and lights, we put film in the camera and shot the scene with the rats performing beautifully. The answer? When training rats for filming, we had to have the environment similar to when we would film—sound, lights and all.

As for the giant ants in *Empire of the Ants*, we naturally didn't have a training problem, but we had to go into the Panama jungle to film them. It was the only place I could find a species of vicious looking ants that would appear menacing when enlarged into monsters in our movie.

And for the giant grasshoppers for *Beginning of the End*, I found the grasshopper look I wanted in a locust plague in Texas, but the California Agriculture Department wouldn't permit me to bring the grasshoppers into the state to film them because that would introduce a new species to California. After more sleepless nights, I came up with an idea that I presented to the Agriculture

Department. I suggested that we would only bring male grasshoppers into the state. Without any females of the species, they wouldn't be able to propagate, and the officials went for it. I had an entomologist in Texas collect the male grasshoppers and ship them to Los Angeles in locked cages. Upon their arrival, the Agriculture Department people examined every grasshopper to make sure they were all males, before turning them over to us. I forgot to ask the California Agriculture Department entomologists examining our stars from Texas how they could tell a male from a female grasshopper. But not being a grasshopper, I realized it really wasn't that important at all!

A Word from Veronica Cartwright
Star of *The Birds*

In regards to my portrayal of Cathy Brennan in *The Birds,* I saw her as an innocent who lived on an island who couldn't understand the possibility of birds wreaking havoc on the townsfolk of her native Bodega Bay. When Tippi Hedren's character Melanie Daniels brings lovebirds as a gift to my character, I decided to make Cathy be completely unaware and unable to make the connection that these seemingly innocent birds could possibly be involved in the horrors that unfold. I think this was all summed up in my last line in the movies: "Can't we take them with us Mitch, they haven't hurt anyone …"

I loved working with Alfred Hitchcock. He was very kind to me. I was born in the area where his favorite wine cellars were located. During our first meeting,

Veronica Cartwright (right) on the set of *The Birds*, with Tippi Hedren looking on

13

he told me what kinds of wines to get and how to cook a steak, as I would need these skills when I got married. I was only 12 years old at the time! I took him tea, which was prepared by Peggy Robinson, every afternoon at 4:30. During production, he always let me ask questions about how things worked, such as the cardboard cut outs of the crows that sat on the jungle gym. He said your eye sees the movement of the real birds and you assume all the birds are real. Also, in regards to the final scene where we leave the badly damaged house, I asked how it would work if there wasn't a real door to actually open. Hitchcock had Rod Taylor, who played my older brother Mitch, mime and demonstrate the technique. With the use of light, a door appears to be opening, to which Hitchcock coyly added, "Ahh, the magic of movies!"

Several intense scenes needed to be filmed, such as the sequence where the birds come down the chimney in the living room. Something like 15,000 birds had been gathered and put in shafts up the chimney. The set was surrounded by plastic with a hole for the camera lens and air. The crew pulled the shafts and the birds came down and went to the top of the plastic. The birds then fell down when they realized they couldn't go anywhere. They were all scooped up and the production crew would do it all over again. We shot most everything twice, once on location and then again on the set at Universal Studios. The school kids running from the birds at the school was done on a treadmill that was set really fast. That running sequence was then combined with the location background scenery. What an amazing movie to work on! On top of all this, Tippi Hedren was really nice to work with, and because she had a daughter the same age as me (Melanie Griffith), I think she felt comfortable around me.

From Hitchcock's Flock to Girdler's Grizzly: An Introduction to the Natural Horror Film

There is absolutely no need whatsoever to fear genre pictures. Images and words from the Western, the musical, the science fiction movie, film noir of the 1940s and 1950s and, the most resilient and successful of all, the horror film, resonate and have intense longevity. Genre films are escapist fairytales, folkloric analogies that explore themes within structured narrative processes. They utilize familiar formulas to convey meanings of expression far more articulately in a poetically poignant sensibility than some non-genre drama. Non-genre melodramas simply "tell it how it is"; these pictures ignore otherworldly experiences like the romance of the Wild West, the glamour of song and dance or the misunderstood beauty of movie monsters. Instead, they play a "real-life" scenario. Something that defies the mystique of cinema as an art form and really misses the point on many artistic levels. And well-executed artistry most certainly dictates success on all levels; most obviously financial and commercial gain. After all, genre films saved studios. The Western and the gangster movie turned in healthy profits for Warner Bros., the musical and fantasy films helped shape and keep MGM afloat and horror was Universal's most treasured asset. So even when discussing moviemaking as a perpetually working business machine, genre films like Westerns, musicals and horror are ultimately at the core of a successful thriving industry. They exist and procreate, shaping new styles of cinema and giving life to a new line of movie types, something that non-genre melodrama cannot do.

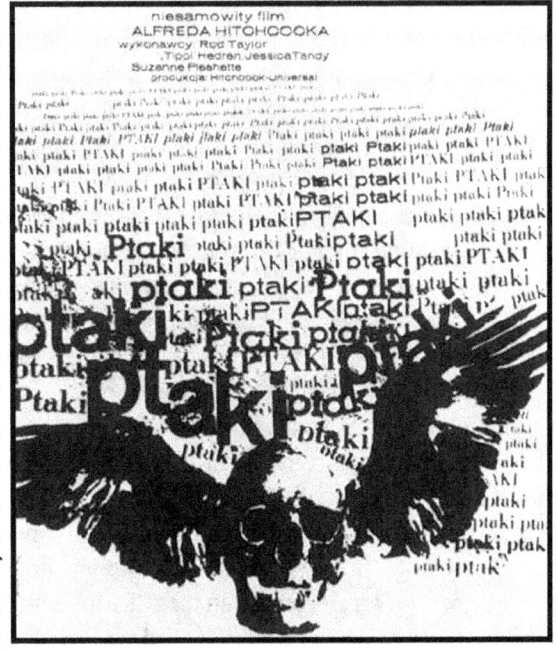

Polish poster for Alfred Hitchcock's *The Birds*

15

Minnie Castavet (Ruth Gordon) is a modern day satanist with a plot brewing for the wide-eyed innocent Rosemary (Mia Farrow), from Roman Polanski's *Rosemary's Baby*.

Westerns, musicals and horror films are capable of giving birth to what one would call a subgenre. That is, something derived from the archetypal model but coming into its own and existing as something on an entirely different plateau, developing its own stock standards, plot devices, character types, etc. Paving the way for future films of that subgenre. The Golden Age Westerns of John Ford and Howard Hawks spawned the ultra-violent spaghetti Westerns of Sergio Leone; the classic movie musicals of Busby Berkley and Vincente Minnelli became a grandparent of the integrated musical, the rock opera and so forth. The horror genre, in all its mass appeal and glorious variety, boasts the most subgenres—from vampire movies, to werewolf films, to mad scientist pictures, to ghost stories, to evil children in cinema, to the hag pictures, to the slasher film and the gore movie. The horror genre—throughout the ages, from the magic that was the birth of cinema right through to today's age of digital hi-tech wizardry—is the busiest mother of them all.

On the topic of motherhood, or more importantly monstrous motherhood, one very important baby was born in 1968 that changed the direction of mainstream horror forever. That baby belonged to Rosemary, and the rise of the satanic-themed/possession film was ushered in. *Rosemary's Baby*, much like *Psycho* before it, carried the horror film out of the decadent Gothic otherworldliness of previous years and landed it smack into the heart of contemporary society. Roman Polanski's film about modern day witches in Manhattan brought with it an extremely successful subgenre, that of the cinema demonica. Coinciding with the notion that God was truly dead, youthful disillusionment, an angry anti-establishment movement and a growing interest in the occult and

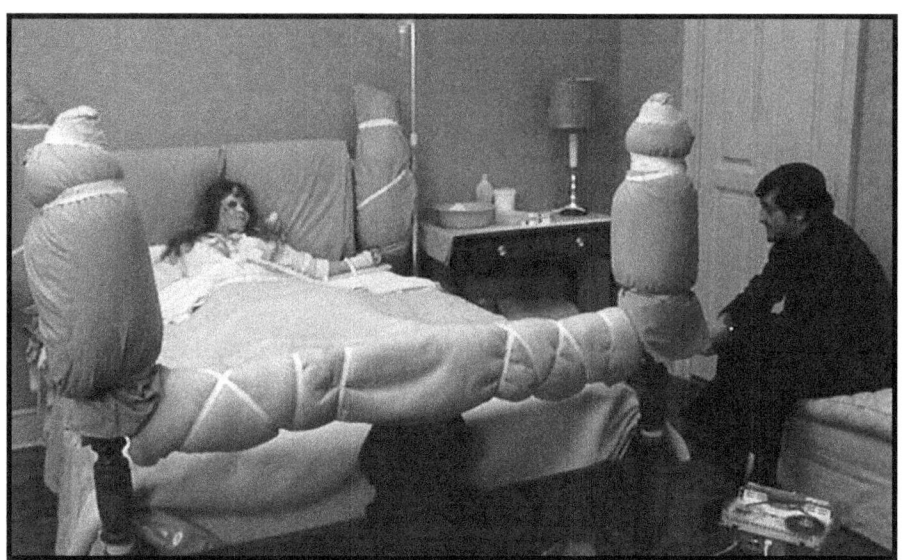

Conversations with the devil: Father Karras (Jason Miller) talks to the possessed Regan (Linda Blair) in the demonic-themed chiller *The Exorcist*.

other religions outside of Christianity, the satanic horror film was extremely popular and was benchmarked by an iconic film called *The Exorcist*. Soon enough two more subgenres of the horror film began to rear their misshapen heads to tag alongside the satanic-themed entries. One looked a lot like the head of a massacred bloodied corpse and the other, a more familiar earthy offering, resembled the head of a bird, or an alligator, or a frog or a great white shark. The two subgenres to take off with great gusto in the 1970s (taking their cue from cinema demonica*)* were the body horror movie and the ecological threat or natural horror film.

The body horror subgenre was a celebration of visceral pleasures, or displeasures. It was a stylistic operatic expression of bloody gore and violence with intense character study and personal growth (or dismemberment) being at the fundamental center of all the films. The works of David Cronenberg, Dario Argento, Wes Craven and Tobe Hooper were not only acutely intelligent and genuinely terrifying but also visually sumptuous, their distinct visual styles all very carefully conceived and remarkably sharp. The body horror subgenre in all its gory glory lead the way for the stalk 'n' slash films of the late 1970s, which got far more excessive in brutality and flamboyant in expressions of violence throughout the 1980s. The stalk 'n' slash movies quickly became the most commercially successful film subgenre of all time. Films like *Halloween* and *Friday the 13th* and their countless sequels (and imitators) made a fortune and became much loved entries in the world of modern horror.

But many audience members, including hardcore horror fans, forget that the third subgenre of the early '70s, the natural-horror film, was born alongside

A by-product of the Atomic Age: *Attack of the Giant Leeches* (with Yvette Vickers)

that of cinema demonica and body horror (as well as the latter's prolific daughter, the stalk 'n' slash film) and was just as successful. Perhaps there weren't as many eco-terror movies as there were masked-psychopaths-on-a-murderous-rampage, but they were plentiful and each contained purpose and ideas. The natural horror film suggests that the real evil that will ultimately destroy us is not from another planet, not at the hands of the devil, not from supernatural beings like ghosts or vampires, not at the mercy of malicious psychopaths like Norman Bates, Leatherface and family, but from nature itself. From the bugs and the bees and the dogs and the cats and the whales and the rats—Mother Nature is not happy, and she will slaughter the human population with the help of her friends, her loyal minions of feather, fur and fin.

In the Atomic Age of the 1950s, supersized animals and insects wreaked havoc on unsuspecting humans in movies like *Earth vs. The Spider, Beginning of the End, Them!, Attack of the Giant Leeches* and *The Killer Shrews* (these gigantic beasts will be the main focal point in a later chapter in this book), preying on the anxieties of a generation of people terrified by nuclear influence and destruction. But it was a portly English auteur that had already made an important mark in Hollywood horror by directing the first-ever slasher film (if you don't count *Peeping Tom*), *Psycho*. Alfred Hitchcock also brought the killer animal movement into the limelight. Ultimately, he turned a subgenre that was founded in a popular generic fear (the Atomic Age, Russian influence and Communism and Cold War fears) into a subgenre dedicated to character and specific objective fears (anxieties, personal demons, relationship woes, et al.).

In 1963, Hitchcock sent forth *The Birds*, a film inspired by the novelette of English author and playwright Daphne du Maurier, that told the story of inexplicable avian attacks off the coast of California. What Hitchcock does with this film is exploit the human traits of his characters and the situations they're in by using the bird attacks as an analogy of human tension that goes unsaid. Seagulls, crows, sparrows and other birds diving to peck out the eyes of the citizens of Bodega Bay are a manifestation of what the characters aren't saying or doing but also a response to what they are feeling. The screenplay,

The panic in Amity Island as seen in *Jaws*

written by Evan Hunter, is loaded with character-driven plot devices and distinct character driven intent, both implicit and explicit, from Tippi Hedren's sexual aggressiveness, to Rod Taylor's coy flirtation, to Suzanne Pleshette's secrecy, to Jessica Tandy's quiet suffrage and so forth. The violent attacks from the birds heighten these complex characteristics and physically embody the interior struggles of the film's human cast. Ultimately, *The Birds* scrutinizes human relationships and slyly delves into the disturbances of sexual frustrations and desires, yet the film on a very simplistic surface level is basically about killer birds.

Twelve years later the attacks didn't come from above, but instead came from the murky depths of the ocean as movie maverick Steven Spielberg unleashed his great white shark on the residents of a New England coastal town in *Jaws*.

Jaws, one of the most successful films ever made and a film that influenced an entire generation of moviemaking moguls, is ultimately a B monster movie in the guise of a slick Hollywood blockbuster. Spielberg's fishy flick is as scary as William Friedkin's *The Exorcist*, which was a huge influence, not only on horror cinema, but cinema in general and it became the landmark of cinema demonica. (The other horror film of the '70s that shaped the way was Tobe Hooper's body horror film, *The Texas Chain Saw Massacre*). But *Jaws* was effective in a completely different way to Friedkin's possession tale. First, *The Exorcist* is a female driven film (both protagonist and mon-

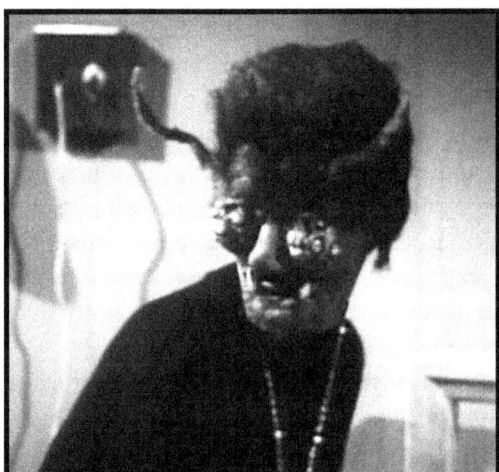
The female monster reigns supreme and is brought to the forefront as depicted in *The Wasp Woman*.

ster are female), and it is a film of fire and brimstone. *Jaws,* on the other hand, is an outdoor adventure buddy movie with males in the leading roles, a rarity for horror films that usually feature women or girls as protagonists, whether they be the non-monstrous lead or the monster herself. When the monster is a female she is usually brought to the foreground (*The Wasp Woman, Dracula's Daughter, Cat People, The Bad Seed, Carrie,* et al.), but it is not at all made clear that the shark in *Jaws* is specifically female. What the shark comes to represent makes us question gender-influenced motivation. Fundamentally the horror genre is specifically a female genre along with the romantic comedy/drama, the musical comedy/drama and the feminine centered fantasy film (i.e. the Disney princess films such as *Cinderella* and *Snow White*), whereas the male genres are the Western, the action movie, the science fiction film and the gangster movie. Hence, this gender play in *Jaws* is a major contributing factor to its success. It poses the question—is the shark in *Jaws* a monstrous feminine; that is, a living, breathing all-consuming vagina dentata? This shark consumes male ego and interrupts strong, male relationships. Late in the movie the shark nudges the boat just when the three male leads are enjoying an intimate moment. Of course, the great white's first victim is the nubile Susan Backlinie, but is this an attack to attract the male gaze? After all, the haunted Chief Brody (played by the always appropriate Roy Scheider) is the first person to act on this attack, and he is someone who has to face his own personal fears (more insecurities plaguing his masculinity) in order to combat this force of nature. Here, the film comes to read like a Western dressed up as a horror film—man conquering the wilderness and defending human masculinity over monstrous feminine animalism.

Tippi Hedren, as Melanie Daniels, is the outsider interrupting the natural order, bringing *The Birds* to Bodega Bay.

Much like *The Birds* and *Jaws,* a lot of the eco-horror movies that came afterwards adopted the notion that the attacks from the animals were a manifestation and/or an extension of character, situation and the complexities of relationships.

For example:

Character—In *The Birds,* Melanie Daniels, as played by Tippi Hedren, inadvertently brings the bird attacks to Bodega Bay. They are forever linked with her coming to the sleepy town. In *Jaws,* the shark is Chief Brody's (Roy Scheider) personal demon, a symbol of his subconscious fear of the unknown.

Situation—Tippi Hedren is new to Bodega Bay in *The Birds*. She is an outside force influencing the environment of an established place. The shark in *Jaws* becomes an enemy of the people, influencing trade and commerce as well as exploiting personal tragedies and loss.

Cold War fears are realized in *Them!*

Relationships—Tippi Hedren is cause of great concern for Jessica Tandy's character. Tandy is the over-protective mother of Rod Taylor and Hedren has her eyes set on him. The rivalry between oppressive mother and out-of-town temptress has been noted (not only by film scholars but by intuitive audience members) as the cause of the birds turning on the human population; whereas in *Jaws*, the shark gleefully toys with the all-male buddy-hood shared between Chief Brody (Scheider), Hooper (Richard Dreyfuss) and Quint (Robert Shaw). Looking at the final act of *Jaws* from the complex perspective of gender interplay, the shark would be the monstrous feminine and the three men her fearful prey. The vaginal mouth of the shark opens baring layers of sharp teeth that feed on the anxieties of men who seem to be far more comfortable in the company of other men rather than in a possible scary heterosexual embrace.

Outside of filmic artistry and the genesis of storytelling, societal factors contributed to the evolution of the natural horror film. Similar to how the paranoid 1950s dealt with a growing concern of radioactive horrors in those films inhabited by gigantic mammoths like the giant ants in *Them!,* by the late 1960s and early '70s the issue of environmental destruction started to offset the anti-war movement, a sub-movement of sorts born from youthful rebellion and student unrest. Environmentalism, much like the anti-war subculture, started to influence not only activists and the newfound socially aware, but also the style and consciousness of the new eco-horror films led by the likes of American International Pictures' *Frogs* and many, many more.

It really wasn't until the very late 1970s and early 1980s that the environmental movement took off and entered the mainstream. Militant animal rights activists and eco-warriors voiced their concern for the sake of their planet, beginning to raise their passionate voices, refusing to remain invisible and forcing a global recognition of the dire straits Mother Earth was in. Like the predecessors of the fight for the oppressed (namely the black civil rights movement, the women's movement and gay liberation), the environmentalists brought ecologically, politically motivated organizations, such as Greenpeace and Animal Liberation, into the public domain. Vegetarianism and veganism were becoming more commonly practiced dietary choices in Western culture. Environmental consciousness was becoming second nature to suburbanites. The impact of the destruction of rainforests, the ozone layer and the oceans were common knowledge that became subject of discussion, not only in the White House, but also in the classroom.

Films like *Frogs*, *The Day of the Animals* and *The Pack* warn us what dire things could happen if the planet is continually raped by pollution or if voiceless, innocent animals are neglected or treated badly at the hands of man. Nature will have her revenge and these horror films reinforce this notion. The impact human beings had on their environment and the rape and eventual destruction of the planet hit a nerve in (and outside) Hollywood during the '70s, and the ecologically aware horror film emerged. Such movies became descendants of a mighty angry Gillman from *Creature from the Black Lagoon,* ready to take his revenge on the people of his dying Earth. These little movies with big hearts proved to be an undeniably powerful force in the history of the horror film.

The father of all natural horror, the Gillman, from *Creature From The Black Lagoon*

The following is a sentimental, heartfelt look at this extremely popular and prolific subgenre. Since Hitchcock initially gave us his frightening flock, the natural horror film is much loved, not only by horror movie fans, but also by cinephiles that revel in great storytelling and enjoy the carnage brought on by the paragon of animals. These films, as popular and highly successful as they've proven, are also seldom discussed or referenced, so I offer an insightful interpretation on numerous angry animal movies I adore. From the electrically-driven evil worms in *Squirm*, to the vengeful killer whale in *Orca* and to the sheer brilliance of the menacing bear in *Grizzly* (a film made by a maverick filmmaker that far too many know nothing about; a genius taken away from us too soon, Mr. William Girdler), this book is to enlighten by offering clear insight into the movies as well as the people involved in making them so memorable. Let me

Although films dealing with monstrous flora will not be covered here, *Little Shop of Horrors* hits all the right notes for killer plant movies.

offer just another quick side note. Before settling in to write this book, a colleague of mine asked if I would be including movies such as *The Day of the Triffids* and *Little Shop of Horrors,* movies that featured plants and all manner of flora that killed human beings or movies that featured disastrous events as a result of chaotic weather (more notably those movies would be considered disaster movies rather than of the horror genre)? Without even blinking I replied, "no," simply because I have a far greater affinity for natural horror films that feature animals as the number one threat. Not to say that I don't love the aforementioned movies, but I just feel that there is so much more ground to cover in movies depicting the animal kingdom causing great distress for mankind. However, just for everyone who loves killer plants, I have a special treat in a later chapter ... but it is a stand alone, as this book is devoted to all things ferociously fauna.

This book will affectionately scrutinize the social and political commentary of these movies, dissect fundamental stock standards as well as offer informative anecdotes relating to the films' creation and production, as well as their distinct and varied narrative devices, analysis of performance, audience appreciation and overall filmmaking. Ultimately, this book is written out of sheer love and a deep respect for these great films, and I do hope that as the reader reads on, he or she will learn to appreciate these fantastic celluloid treasures that have most definitely left a huge print (actually more so a huge paw print) on my heart ... enjoy!

AND A FROG SHALL LEAD THEM: MOTHER NATURE GETS ANGRY AS HUMANKIND PANICS

Revenge is a popular motif in the natural horror film. From the disgruntled dogs who were abandoned by their owners on Seal Island in *The Pack,* to the critters that kill the wealthy humans who contributed to their environment being polluted in *Frogs*, the idea that nature will take care of itself by culling the people population in order to sustain a healthy ecological system was a sure-fire plot device for these popular and diverse movies. But outside of the nature-runs-amok branch of motion picture, revenge movies as a whole became a popular sensation with audiences come the 1970s, and they were an extremely bankable movie type. Rape revenge films such as the *Death Wish* movies starring Charles Bronson were successful action films, Clint Eastwood's *Dirty Harry* series were even more financially successful and critically acclaimed, and then in the horror genre the landmark Brian De Palma film (based on a novella by Stephen King) *Carrie* really proved to outcasts everywhere that revenge is a dish best served in cold blood. Even benign revenge movies that were more in the guise of the rise-of-the-underdog-against-all-odds catalogue (as depicted in films like *Rocky*) struck a nerve with audiences, who at the time were at the tail end of a war, disillusioned with their government and in socio-economic woe. A film like *Rocky* uplifted people who were almost always at the bottom of the barrel, their revenge warranted against the man, the oppressor, the guy who's always at the top. With the natural horror film frenzy coming into full swing during the 1970s, revenge was a key plot motive—harmful, abusive, ignorant and self-involved human beings will pay at the hands of Mother Nature, this idea becoming a strong element that made these horror films work. Many of the human characters were represented as unsympathetic louts who got served violent deaths and this always makes for good fun.

Brian De Palma's *Carrie*, starring Sissy Spacek, becomes the ultimate in revenge-themed horror.

Ultimately the audience doesn't care if someone of ill repute is having his/her comeuppance at the mercy of angry animals, animals whose anger is completely warranted. And with burgeoning animal rights groups coming into action and environmental causes taking shape and making a noise in public arenas, many audience members smiled when animals of all kinds massacred their human oppressors, possibly the same audiences who secretly cheered when Sissy Spacek used her telekinesis to kill her high school tormentors in 1976.

Showmanship plus! The American International logo lets the audience know they'll be in for a good time (from *Frogs*).

Nearly a decade after Hitchcock gave us *The Birds*, independent American International Pictures (headed by moguls James H. Nicholson and the charismatic Samuel Z. Arkoff) decided to tap into the enviro-monster movie market with their sleeper hit *Frogs*. The genius of American International Pictures was that they were an unpretentious, thrifty and extremely intelligent business-minded film company that always favored showmanship as its number one principal, understanding what audiences wanted and delivering great entertainment that satisfied.

The other major factor that made the company so successful was that American International Pictures reveled in cinematic crazes and fads. They were the company responsible for beach blanket movies usually starring the perky Annette Funicello and Frankie Avalon, films that were rock 'n' roll-centric featuring the likes of glamour girls such as the lovely Mamie Van Doren, the blaxploitation movement that really lampooned the careers of great actors Pam Grier and William Marshall, movies that featured giant creatures (much loved by film auteur Bert I. Gordon) and yes, even the Mother Nature goes crazy subgenre.

Frogs (1972) was the staple creature feature for AIP and a response to the expanding environmental movement. Plus it is a throwback to Alfred Hitchcock's feathered masterpiece. (Film critic and essayist Fran Lebowitz said *Frogs* was one of her favorite films and very much likened it to Hitchcock's much loved movie.)

Frogs forces us to comprehend the possibility of the natural world turning on us. What would happen to the human race if the creatures that populate this Earth decided to sting, bite, claw, swallow and gnaw away at us, leaving humankind for compost? After all, the animals, birds and insects of this planet are far more in

One of the amphibians, quietly observing, is ready to do some damage in *Frogs*.

tune with the natural order of the environment itself, so if they decided to wreak havoc, it is scientifically accurate to assume humankind would be at a total loss. Not to mention the fact that there are billions more species of insect than any mammal here on Earth. A film like *Frogs* exploits the notion that humans have truly lost touch with the natural world and poses an over-reliance on man-made creations/abominations that dictate and shape the way in which one is to live. These man-made devices commit damage in the natural horror film and this warrants nature's vengeance. The notion of man conquering the wilderness as seen in many an adventure film and Western is a staple in many a creature feature. If trampling on the fauna and flora that surrounds us means making a livelihood for our human protagonists, then so be it. But there are consequences and these consequences act as the major focal point of *Frogs* and other eco-horror movies that would follow. Ultimately *Frogs* warns us: Don't mess with nature or nature will mess with you!

These movies also play on the fear of the natural world itself as a tangible, monstrous entity. It exploits the physical repulsion and phobias that may exist in our species in regards to the sliminess of snakes, frogs and turtles, the furriness of tarantulas, bats, dogs and so forth. The otherworldliness of normally mundane creatures is exploited to tap into human uneasiness. But what if audiences aren't scared of such creatures? Does a film like *Frogs* work? Of course it does! It works as an enjoyable ride in what ultimately I like to call a comfort horror movie. Comfort horror movies, as far as I am concerned, are films that fundamentally serve to satisfy one's love of the genre, a safe and fun ride that horror film aficionados can enjoy. But if audiences are genuinely queasy when it comes to the animal attackers in these motion pictures, then the movies work in the same way as someone scared of the devil would be emotionally stirred while watching a satanic-themed horror movie like *The Exorcist,* or someone who is scared of being stalked and torn to shreds at the hands of some psychopath would feel watching numerous slasher films such as *The Burning* or *Happy Birthday To Me*. In essence, it is all objective as nobody really *sees* the same movie. When looking at these natural horror films or creature features, one must question whether the beast running amok is scary to an audience.

However, in the realm of cinema, animals such as the common rat can be presented as extremely terrifying. Cinema, that great fabricator of the truth, can absolutely heighten the horror a rat can evoke. Perhaps one rat on its own may not cause great alarm, but if the rats came in mass numbers as depicted in movies such as *Willard* and *Deadly Eyes,* then they may be fear inducing. If they are mammoth in size much like the rodents in *The Food of the Gods* and *Altered Species,* then that may prove even more horrific. Animals such as frogs, turtles, butterflies and lizards take on a monstrous role in a film like AIP's *Frogs*; they are mankind's most natural enemy and most well equipped. Ecological horror films show us that the real terror is not from outer space, not from a Gothic nether region, not from ancient fears of the devil and of curses—but rather from planet Earth itself; Mother Nature's minions become her foot soldiers of fury.

An uninvited dinner guest slithers on the scene in *Frogs* (Sam Elliot at center).

The story of *Frogs* involves a wealthy family, the Crocketts, who live in a huge manor that is located just by the swamplands in the very green, sweltering southern countryside of Florida. Ray Milland plays the cantankerous patriarch of the family, Jason Crockett, who proudly proclaims, "We are the ugly rich!" to his mess of a family. His misfit clan includes a bickering married couple comprised of an alcoholic wife and a grouchy ex-jock, their neglected kids, a spoiled fey lackey, a sleazy photographer and his noble but ditsy model girlfriend, a dotty aunt and a lascivious driver. Also, a maid and butler who are leftover black servants from a by-gone time. Milland is nature's formidable enemy. He is the reason why his environment is in dire straits. He is the cause of great pollution and this results in the natural world having to take care of its own. Entering the world of the Crocketts is outsider Sam Elliot who plays Pickett Smith, an environmentalist photographer. As soon as Elliot comes into contact with the Crockett family, things start shifting and the film exploits the marvelous who's-gonna-die-next motif!

The opening of *Frogs* really sets us straight: Elliot is seen paddling his canoe through the swamplands and taking snapshots of local fauna. However, interrupting such beautifully captivating naturalism is garbage. Polluted lagoons, plastic bags wrapped around greenery and non-degradable bi-products contaminate the normally lush Florida swamplands. Elliot is quickly involved in a boat accident where the very attractive Joan Van Ark, who plays Karen Crockett, rescues and invites him to at least get a change of clothes and stay for dinner at her estate. He is introduced to the family and the honorary guests but forms a solid genuine bond with Van Ark, who increasingly becomes attracted to the often-shirtless Elliot. (*Frogs* really exploited a shirtless Sam Elliot, which led him to make *Lifeguard*, the film that got him a lot more worldwide attention).

Although Sam Elliot's character is a naturalist and environmentalist photojournalist, he plays the role like a rogue cowboy (even his name Pickett Smith evokes imagery of a Republic Pictures Western gunslinger). His swagger is overtly sexual and yet understated, his deep low voice always kept at a calm level, almost always conveying a sense of tough machismo. But his character is completely fused with a healthy dose of sensitive understanding. A clear example of this quiet-man understanding is seen during the low-key scenes he shares with the beautiful Van Ark, who, looking pretty as a picture, captures the essence of being the true black sheep of this messed up upper-class family. She ultimately is the outsider on the inside and this makes the romance blossoming between Elliot and her all the more organic in its evolution.

The "ugly rich" in *Frogs*: Ray Milland, the patriarch, far right (in wheelchair); the outsider on the inside, Joan Van Ark (in the middle); and the environmental sympathizer Sam Elliot (seen standing)

Frogs really does its job perfectly. Having telepathic amphibians communicate to the other animals to do their bidding is a stroke of genius. Lizards spill harmful chemicals in an enclosed greenhouse to get rid of one of the human costars, an angry snapping turtle chews the leg off a woman and a wild-eyed gator snaps his way through a screaming man demonstrating Mother Nature running amok at her best!

I remember reading an old issue of *Famous Monsters of Filmland* where a young reader wrote a letter to Editor-in-Chief Forrest J Ackerman complaining about the title of the movie. It read:

> "Why is the movie even called *Frogs*? The frogs don't even do anything throughout the whole thing!"

Sure, the frogs may just hop around and croak like crazy, their big black eyes starring right into camera, but their actual physical involvement in the death of Ray Milland's character is a wonderful pay off and a slimy sadistic finale! Milland has come to realize through the help of Elliot and Van Ark, and through the multiple deaths that have occurred, that his rape of nature has come to bite him on the ass! In a final act of neglect avoiding the situation, Milland turns on his phonograph playing crackling ragtime records and sinks into his booze. Frogs start appearing outside the window and soon enough inside his den—a den decked out with the heads of boars, tigers and deer, animals that have died at the hands of the reckless creature-fearer/animal-hater Milland! He is tormented by these frogs and succumbs to their wrath. The shot of a large toad rotating on a spinning LP is one of the film's most glorious images—the cycle of nature made literal.

Unpretentious, intelligent and beautifully made, *Frogs* is a staple in the ecological warfare venture and it set the mold, post-*The Birds,* for the natural world being the featured monster. It also most certainly paved the way for animal attackers being driven by revenge as seen in later films like *The Pack* and *Orca,* rather than the more commonly featured animals and insects who are inexplicably malevolent as depicted in such treats as *Rattlers, Nightwing* and *Jaws.*

Steven Spielberg's massive hit, borrowing from Henric Ibsen's *Enemy of the People,* Thomas Hobbes's *Leviathan* and Universal's classic *Creature from the Black Lagoon,* may have struck a nerve with audiences everywhere, making *Jaws* the benchmark of all natural horror movies. But a director who really deserves

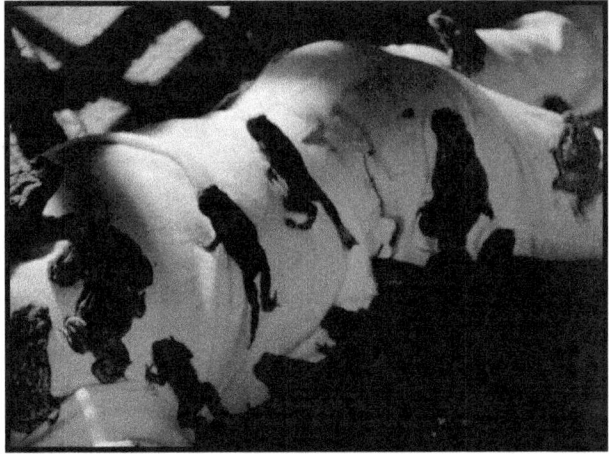

The frogs have their revenge on Ray Milland in the chaotic finale of *Frogs.*

a noteworthy mention in this book is a contemporary of Spielberg, someone who created two of the greatest eco-horror treats to come out of the 1970s. In my humble opinion these two movies are quite honestly just as important as that great white shark gem. The two movies are *Grizzly* and *The Day of the Animals,* and the director's name is William Girdler.

Girdler (who died tragically in a helicopter accident in the Philippines while on location for a film that was never finished) was a maverick filmmaker with a sharp sense of style and a keen eye for visual sumptuousness. Girdler's eco-sensitive horror gems, possessing not only great intensity and strong narrative flow, are also made with such heart that they are easy to compare to the works of Spielberg. In the span of seven years, from 1972 through to 1978, William Girdler made nine feature films in the horror and action genres. In that same period, Spielberg directed four movies—two major box-office hits including *Jaws* and *Close Encounters of the Third Kind*, as well as the critically acclaimed *The Sugarland Express* starring Goldie Hawn and William Atherton and a seldom seen made-for-TV *Exorcist* rip-off called *Something Evil,* starring Sandy Dennis. An *Exorcist* rip-off was on the cards for Mr. Girdler also, but first a few stops occurred before we get to that clever urban entry in the cinema demonica.

Safe for a moment from the giant man-eating bear in *Grizzly*

Born in Louisville, Kentucky, William Girdler started his own production company, Studio One Productions, while only in his early twenties, and his first major film effort was a gory slasher film called *Three On A Meathook,* which was a film loosely based on the life of serial killer Ed Gein (who also prompted Robert Bloch to pen his horror classic *Psycho*). Next Girdler directed three blaxploitation films. First was a vehicle for the subgenre's regular sassy hot star Pam Grier, *Sheba, Baby*; second was a gritty urban thriller called *The Zebra Killer* and finally was the ingenious, aforementioned *Exorcist* rip-off that belongs both to the cinema demonica and blaxploitation subgenres, *Abby.* The film starred thespian William "*Blacula*" Marshall as a jive talking, no-nonsense exorcist. The film also starred Oscar nominee Juanita Moore (who was nominated for her role in the remake of the heartbreaking *Imitation of Life*). Girdler also reigned in Tony Curtis and Susan Strasberg for a superb horror film, *The Manitou,* which explored American Indian curses and retribution. But it is the two natural horror films that really stand out as Girdler's finest works—the gory glory that is *Grizzly* and the frenzy that is *The Day of the Animals*!

Grizzly (1976) was a hugely triumphant film; it was Girdler's most financially successful and critics praised the film for its strong script, beautiful cinematography and genuinely scary sequences involving a mammoth grizzly bear. Although the film was continually compared to *Jaws,* with some journalists reviewing it as "Jaws With Claws," much like *Orca* (another film that copped the *Jaws*-clone syndrome), the film definitely stands on its own furry feet and has its own distinct style.

The mighty roar from the monstrous bear in *Grizzly*

Producer and writer Harvey Flaxman's encounter with a bear during a camping trip supposedly inspired the screenplay. David Sheldon, a writer and co-producer, thought the concept would make a great movie, and seeing that *Jaws* did so ridiculously well at the box-office, perhaps a killer bear film may do just as well. Within weeks, director William Girdler had acquired $750,000 from independent company Film Ventures International and production went underway.

The first attack in *Grizzly* is terrifyingly terrific! Two young women are breaking camp in a national park and one of them has her arm torn off by an 18-foot man-eating grizzly bear! The other woman races away and finds very brief refuge in a nearby cabin, but the beast tears down the walls and she too is brutally mauled to death. The brute strength and sheer hunger of this bear is unstoppable, and it is up to heroes Christopher George, Joan McCall, Andrew Prine, Richard Jaeckal and Joe Dorsey to save the day—and the national park! The film has some wonderful moments and some great action sequences involving the large bouncing bear. The bear herself was nicknamed Teddy and was in actual fact an Alaskan Kodiak bear (she is also the mother of Bart the Bear who went on to be in many hit movies throughout the '80s). Teddy's "performance" is astounding and proves to be a genuinely frightening foe to the likes of the male leads (George, Prince and Jaeckel) who, incidentally, all appeared in the John Wayne Western *Chisum*. With luscious locations (the film was shot in Clayton, Georgia), sweeping cinematography (a lot of beautiful helicopter work masterfully executed) and nicely conducted and well-scoped scenes involv-

[left to right]: Andrew Prine, Richard Jaeckel and Christopher George as the three human adversaries of the dangerous, rampaging bear in *Grizzly*

ing the bear in all her gargantuan glory, *Grizzly* is a perfect example of action meeting horror and joining hand-to-paw in perfect harmony. Much like *Jaws* tapping in on the action-adventure motif and marrying it to the horror movie world (the third act of *Jaws* is *Moby Dick*, both becoming an outdoor high seas adventure romp), *Grizzly* does much the same with the bear being combated in an action-adventure format. A large explosion ultimately kills the bear.

As I stated earlier, on the initial release of *Grizzly*, critics compared it to *Jaws*. Is this fair? Of course it is and, when looking at the two films, they do share some similarities, similarities that really don't undermine either movie. In both movies the male leads are each in a sense impotent to their taking on the natural menace, the shark in *Jaws* and the bear in *Grizzly*. They need to enlist help of some kind in order to combat their natural monsters. Christopher George's character is a skilled chief ranger but has no idea about bears, whereas Roy Scheider's Chief Brody is a police officer that has no understanding about sharks. Of course this may prove to be a slight plot hole in the script of *Grizzly*—why wouldn't a park ranger know everything about bears? Aren't rangers meant to fully understand the environment they govern? Even Ranger Smith knows all there is to know about Yogi Bear, does he not? It makes sense that Scheider/Brody doesn't have a clue about sharks. After all he is from New York and a police officer that generally deals with very human crimes, not natural disasters caused by wild beasts. But let's not let this minor detail and slight flaw in the script of *Grizzly* get in the way of a great movie. George's character may never have had any personal experiences with bears prior to what happens at the beginning of the film. Both Scheider and George have to enlist outside help from a cocksure specialist as seen in Richard Dreyfuss in *Jaws* and Richard Jaeckel in *Grizzly*. These two men are a rarity in the subgenre, as male helpers are seldom seen in the eco-horror universe. Usually the specialist/expert at hand is a woman (Charlotte Rampling in *Orca*, Katherine Ross in *They Only*

Kill Their Masters, Kate McNeil in *Monkey Shines,* et al.), which makes for a clearer sense of woman being closer to nature than men (more on this subject in a later chapter). Also making the assistant male emphasizes the introduction of the action/adventure mold inside the very female-orientated world of horror— a merging that is really put on show here in *Jaws* and *Grizzly,* making these two movies stand out from other eco-horror movies of the time. Other similar traits in both films have officials refusing to listen to the horrific happenings. In *Grizzly* Christopher George's supervisor refuses to close the national park and, in *Jaws,* Murray Hamilton (who plays Amity Island's mayor) refuses to shut down the beaches, both putting the campers and beach goers in great jeopardy. A bounty is put on the bear and the shark leading to chaotic happenings. In *Jaws* the fishing enthusiasts and shark catchers-to-be over crowd the docking area in Amity, while in *Grizzly* the hunters shoot at anything they see in the thickets of the forest. Also, Andrew Prine, in *Grizzly,* and Robert Shaw, in *Jaws,* both play veterans of war and captains of boats and planes.

In the same way *Grizzly* was compared to *Jaws,* so were the two directors compared. It is much noted that if Girdler had not passed away in that tragic accident, he might have made just as many wonderful movies as Hollywood's hugely successful and influential Spielberg.

Actress Joan McCall penned a screenplay for a sequel to *Grizzly* called *Grizzly 2: The Predator.* The film featured newcomers George Clooney, Charlie Sheen and a pre-*Mask* Laura Dern. Some scenes were shot involving a giant grizzly bear attacking a rock concert,

The bear's grisly handiwork in *Grizzly*

but the film was pulled and never completed because of issues with funding a giant mechanical bear that was to be used in close-ups. Reports exist that this film may be re-cut and released but nothing has surfaced as of yet.

Girdler's follow up was not a sequel to his man-eating bear wonder but instead a movie that is completely perfect in every way—his cinematic treasure *The Day of the Animals* (1977). Put simply, *The Day of the Animals* is a masterpiece. Not only does it unfold beautifully with a solid script, fantastic performances and animal actors that are just simply divine, the movie is a clear indication that William Girdler was a master craftsman. The film is a well-

As big as a chopper! The exciting climax of *Grizzly*

mounted, visually breathtaking scary ride and the message is as crystal clear as the crisp skies Girdler captures with his Todd-AO lenses. Mother Nature is angry and she shall have her revenge. The film tells the story of a group of nature adventurers all going along on a hike up the Californian mountains, each for individual reasons and under the guidance of Christopher George (a favorite of Girdler's). Boasting an all-star cast, a superbly loathsome Leslie Neilsen appears in one of his most ruthlessly repulsive roles ever. On board too is the breathy brilliance of Ruth Roman. Also appearing is Richard Jaeckel (once again) and the magnificent Lynda Day George, who sizzles with both sexy spunk and unnatural *natural* beauty. *The Day of the Animals* is a wonderful example of William Girdler's maverick filmmaking that would have easily paved the way for more of his genius!

The opening titles feature stunning images of all the animals we are soon to encounter—as we too go on the hiking expedition with the cast. Girdler's eye is as sharp as one of the hawks he captures in his film. The framing of the animals is just breathtaking. We see a cougar stroll by and, to the upper left hand side of the frame, a bald eagle lands at her nest. In the meantime, right up close and to the bottom of the screen, a furry tarantula crawls past. A coyote shares frame with a great big brown bear as a rattler shimmies across the dusty plains. This is movie making at its most stylized and yet charmingly naturalistic.

Lalo Schifrin's score is a nicely concocted piece of music. His compositions are always interesting, respectful of narrative situation as well as character. When a composer is able to nail the content of a film and create his or her own story in music, the composer has not only done his or her job, but also surpassed expectations. He has contributed to the storytelling, not just completed the task at hand in post-production for a director who liked their previous work. Besides his music for *The Day of the Animals*, Shifrin's later score for AIP's *The Amityville Horror* is just as hauntingly beautiful. Yet far more effective is his music for the prequel, *Amityville II: The Possession*. His use of odd, sharp-jarring tones juxtaposed with sweeping musical motifs and a John Williams-esque sense of urgency make the score for *The Day of the Animals* simply splendid. The music really does become an animal of sorts, and one of the most brilliant things Schifrin does is know when not to score a scene. Silences (especially most noted where the lawyer and the little girl finally make it to a road, free from the dangers of the mountains, and stumble across the now desolate ghost town) are exceptionally effective and really do play on isolative fears and anxieties. It also helps the natural sounds of the agitated animals voice their anger—the hissing of rattlers, the growling of a dog—all of these sounds made far more dynamic when Schifrin's masterful command of music comes into play (and non-play).

In *The Day of the Animals* the ongoing depletion of the Earth's ozone layer has caused a chemical imbalance in the natural world. All the animals that live above 5,000 feet (and that is all of them since this film is set in the highlands of North California) have been affected, causing them to become aggressive and violent. Their natural response to this rape of their environment is to kill the culprit, that being humankind. The film opens with rolling text actually stating that this may one day actually happen and who is to argue with the movies? Not me!

The human characters are an assortment of archetypes with built-in character development. Ruth Roman is constantly in a state of disapproval as she is an upper class New Yorker who has no time for nature. She is also an oppressor to her henpecked son who just longs for a strong male role model. He finds this in the ailing ex-football star and the wise Navaho Indian. Wise Native American Indians find themselves as staple stock characters in many an eco-horror film and it is this Navaho who is the first to notice the change in the animals' behavior. The young teenage working class lovers are naturalists who have a healthy understanding of the environment, while their middle-aged, middle-class counterparts (a lawyer and his wife) constantly bicker, a nice parallel to sit in the middle of the imbalances of nature. The stunning Susan Backlinie,

In William Girdler's *Day of the Animals*, birds of prey attack Susan Backlinie.

who played Chrissie (the first victim) in Spielberg's *Jaws,* plays the bickering wife in Girdler's film and she is also the first victim. Hers is a wonderfully staged and terrifying death sequence, which harkens back to Hitchcock's *The Birds.* Early in the piece she is attacked by a coyote and decides to leave the camp. Her husband joins her but they get lost—perhaps a bi-product of their constant arguing—as a flock of large birds of prey swoop and peck at Backlinie as she tumbles off a cliff to her death. Her husband, alienated from the group, has to fend for himself but comes into the company of a little girl lost (her parents killed by angry animals), hence plotting him into a forced fatherhood situation with fatherhood being something the character has chosen to avoid. *The Day of the Animals* intelligently explores the notion that nature itself will shape the very essence of what we are, always changing us, as characters are forced to play the cards dealt.

Leslie Nielsen's character is by far the most repulsive. He starts off as a capitalist with a solid disrespect for nature. He is not only horribly offensive and racist but also misogynist and selfish. He is an

Humans become more animalistic when pitted against the natural world in *Day of the Animals*. Leslie Neilsen turns violent and the exhausted Kathleen Bracken is soon to become his latest conquest.

advertising executive, looking for land to exploit for his new campaign, and he is instantly disliked by many of the other hikers. Nielsen's repugnant behavior comes to full blossom when he turns into a horrendous potential rapist lunging at the young teenage girl. "And right now I want that!" he snarls as he corners the cowering lass. The girl's boyfriend defends her but is killed by Nielsen. Thankfully, this awful character is then mauled to death by a large grizzly bear that tears him apart.

The death sequences are unique and cleverly executed. There is never a feeling of repetition in this film, and Girdler's handling of the small border town becoming an abandoned wasteland is just perfect. The evacuation led by the military is done with style. Here, once again, a connection to the movies of Spielberg comes into play. In Spielberg films like *Close Encounters of the Third Kind* and *E.T.: The Extra-Terrestrial* (both released after *The Day of the Animals*), government officials move civilians from their homes or come to investigate unnatural goings on. Here, birds of all kinds—vultures, buzzards, eagles and condors—

and snakes, rats, bears, cougars, mountain lions, bobcats, wolves, dogs, coyotes, etc. have caused mankind great stress and it takes the military to defend the human population from complete extinction.

Girdler truly understands character, plot, violence and sheer terror in his films. All these aspects are carefully structured so that the human dynamics within the story organically extend what the monstrosities in nature actually command. In Girdler's movies, humankind can be a nasty abomination, but Earth-dwelling creatures, be they birds, bears, cougars or dogs, are just doing what comes naturally.

Due to the chemical imbalance in the atmosphere, a mass evacuation is organized in *Day of the Animals*.

Another movie that relies heavily on the imbalance of nature, becoming an extension of human inner violence, is an Australian natural horror film called *Long Weekend*. It tells the story of a city-slicker couple who come to the wild lands of Outback Australia in an attempt to fix a damaged relationship, but they find that all the creatures that inhabit the surroundings (possums, dingoes, kangaroos, et al.) are not quite accommodating. These two out-of-touch bickering humans are forced to get along in order to fend off the natural angry world. Released in 1978 (a year after *The Day of the Animals*), *Long Weekend* slowly became a cult classic Ozploitation genre piece (it took filmmaker Quentin Tarantino to bring it to the attention of American audiences years after its initial release) that truly captures the alien inner-space of the hazardous and foreboding Outback.

However, the most commercially successful and popular of Australian creature features is a wonderfully lit genre entry known as *Razorback*. *Razorback*, made in 1984, is a visually stunning movie. Electrifying colors make this cult hit exciting to watch. The actual boar himself is an amazing creation, a huge marauding beast that audiences can almost smell in the thick heat of the Australian Outback. Stylistic and sharp, the wild pig movie became the most popular of Oz horror films next to the very different genre feature, Peter Weir's *Picnic At Hanging Rock*. *Razorback* makes a subtle connection between the sweaty piggish behavior of not only the boar but also the yokels that roam around the vast desert lands. Following a sequence where the aforementioned yokels sexually harass the American wildlife reporter who has come to Australia to do a story

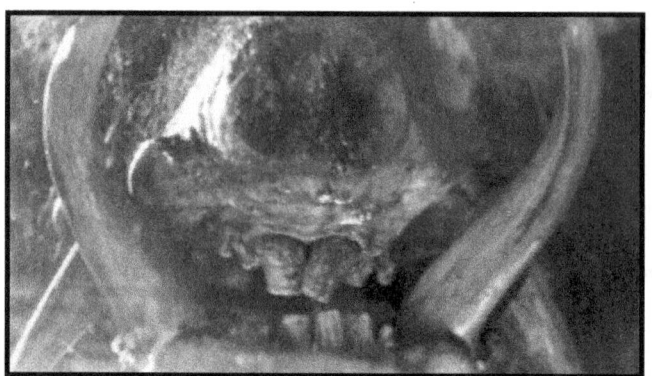

The hideous tusks of the grinning, wild pig in *Razorback*, waiting outside a hapless victim's car.

on native wildlife being used for pet food (the outsider coming into a foreign world), the terrifying pig terrorizes her car, and her death is a grueling and truly heart-stopping moment in the picture. The sick behavior of uneducated local creeps is nothing compared to the unstoppable force that is the wild boar. *Razorback* draws from the two prickly characteristics and makes us clearly understand the damaging results of both.

Once again here in *Razorback* an outsider comes into a new world and, from the onset, things in the natural environment change. Or, in the case of *Razorback*, something evil, an ancient monster, wakes up. This theme returned once again in yet another Australian eco-horror movie released years later, *Rogue,* where an American travel journalist visits the badlands of the Northern Territory only to deal with a large crocodile hell-bent on devouring him and fellow humans!

Something that doesn't pop up in any of the above mentioned Australian natural horror films (strikingly strange yet possibly reasonable at the same time) is a wise elder of an Aboriginal tribe explaining the "reasoning" behind the monstrous animal attacks, or an elder offering some kind of ancient folkloric legend in reference to wild pigs and the like. Natives and original rightful owners of the land are more than often depicted in these films as the closest relative to Mother Earth and most definitely the human link to the natural order of the universe. They understand why the beast is angry and have an all too clear understanding of the wrath of nature. Albeit these natives are usually secondary characters and their roles recede once their job (that is giving the right information used or ignored by the white stars of the films) is done. They are much like the gypsies that

Gregory Harrison is the American outsider pitted against the ancient evil of the Australian Outback in *Razorback*.

offered help in classic Universal monster movies (Maria Ouspenskaya in *The Wolf Man*) or the scholars of the occult that understood old-time ghosts haunting the problematic contemporary world (Zelda Rubinstein in *Poltergeist*). The natives in the natural horror film usually don't leave as great an impression as the aforementioned ladies of *The Wolf Man* and *Poltergeist*.

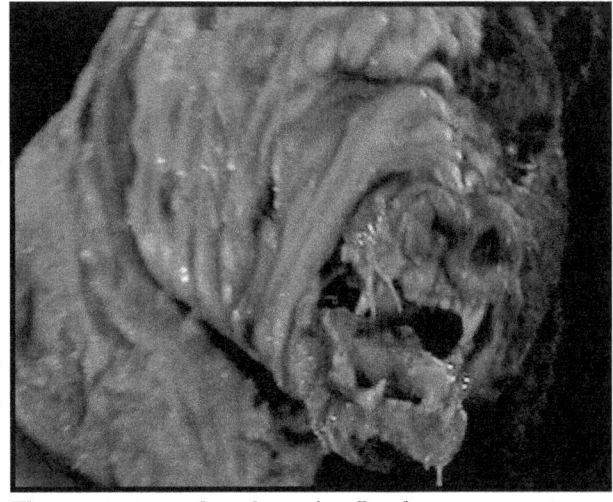
The mutant mother bear in *Prophecy* represents an environment in turmoil.

However, two films of the eco-horror subgenre bring the native wise elders to the foreground—*Nightwing*, which I will discuss more so in a later chapter dealing with stock characters in the natural horror film, and *Prophecy*, which really does make the eternal struggle of the Native American the main focal point of the story.

John Frankenheimer's *Prophecy* (1979) is a great movie and often seen as one of the most important of the eco-horror films, as it is distinctly about environmental pollution and the monstrous results it can cause. The film also handles the concept of commerce and trade versus nature and environmental wellbeing without pretension or becoming overtly preachy. Because the writing is so smartly conceived and the direction so acute, the film becomes much more than a canvas for a "green is good and industry is bad" mantra.

Robert Foxworth plays a doctor in public health that specializes in dealing with the underprivileged. We first see him tending to a baby who has been severely bitten by rats in a black ghetto in Washington, D.C. An earlier sequence in the film depicts the black ghetto juxtaposed with images from a rally involving Native Americans demanding respect and the reclamation of their land. This narrative-driven theme of two worlds completely ruined by industry, greed and racial oppression will soon spill over into the second and last act of *Prophecy*.

Foxworth's wife, played by Talia Shire, is a classical musician (she plays the cello, the most mournful of instruments) and has just found out that she is having a baby. We learn fast that she doesn't want to let Foxworth know that she is pregnant, so she keeps her newfound condition a secret. Foxworth's character has strong political views about over-population and is completely opposed to becoming a father. Shire, however, wants the baby and cannot bring herself to have an abortion.

Early on, Foxworth is offered a job in Maine where political unrest exists involving two opposing sides—mill workers and loggers who run a large paper mill and local Native American tribes who are angry at the destruction of their forest. To the Indians, the forest is their life and they have a clear dependence on the natural greenery and waterways. They are described as a "fishing people" and clean, healthy water is essential to their livelihood, something the paper mill has been responsible for polluting for some time. Mercury poisons the water and Foxworth investigates what has been happening to local Opies (O.P.—original people), who are becoming sick, mentally ill and losing babies as a result. The issues arising in Washington regarding the destruction of not only the forests, waters and land of the Native Americans but their actual claim to be rightful owners of America are but part of a tricking down effect of what is happening in the deep green forests of Maine. We learn quickly that the mill is to blame for the ill health of many of the native tribes as well as the mutations within the forest. Fish have become oversized, tadpoles are as big as dogs and raccoons without rabies are attacking people without mercy. But a large mutant creature (unseen for most of the first two-thirds of the picture) is the most feared and is doing mighty damage around the forest.

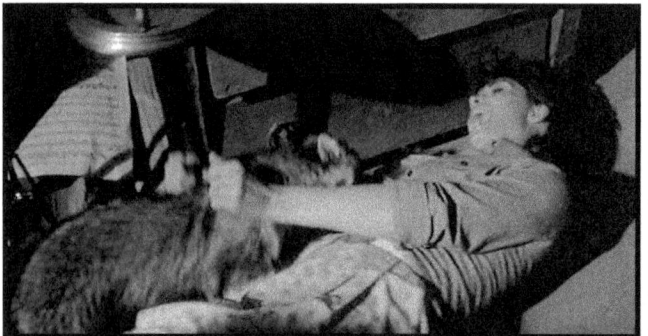

In *Prophecy*, pregnant Talia Shire is attacked by a raccoon driven crazy by the effects of pollution in the forests of Maine.

She is a mutant bear and is talked about as an Native American legend called the Katahdin. A Native American elder says that she has awakened to protect the people and that she is made up of many parts of all of God's creations. However, when the mutant comes face to face with the ill-fated old man, she tears him apart and swallows him whole. The film suggests that even folklore and ancient legend has no chance against mutations created by science—science completely at the servitude of corporate demand. The mutant bear is a great work of puppetry and SFX wizardry, with her skinless snout oozing bloody gore and her claws extending from masses of red raw flesh. She races through the thickets of the forest with great ease and precision.

But it is Shire's characterization as the haunted, pregnant cellist that is the most quietly interesting. She is shy and retiring but strong in her own strange way. During a romantic moment with Foxworth, she explains that she admires the daughter of the aforementioned elder because the young Native American

Yet another hideous mutation from *Prophecy*

woman remained strong even when scared in the face of adversity. But Shire's character is just as powerful as she develops her strength through understanding the condition of the forest. Shire's character is almost analogous with the forest as both Shire and the forest harbor secrets—Shire's being an unborn baby and the forest's being the mutant bear. Also, both are mothering something unnatural and potentially destructive. Shire learns a horrifying truth about the condition of her unborn baby. She has eaten fish from the polluted waterways that will in fact contaminate her embryo and mutate her infant, making her more in tune with the forest, which becomes home to mutant beasts and a poisoned water supply.

A superbly subtle scene that captures Shire's understanding of what is to come is when she looks with great sympathy at a mutant bear cub she and Foxworth have found. Much like Mia Farrow in *Rosemary's Baby* giving in to her maternal instincts and soothing her crying, demonic baby ("Aren't you his mother Rosemary?"), so will Shire have to contend with a deformed, skinless, bloody mass of a child who may look just like the mutant bear cub.

Foxworth's character, however, a man completely uninterested in the trappings of parental responsibilities, has to battle this beast, has to slay the dragon, before he can tend to the nest. Much like the character of Michael Myers being an embodiment of Laurie Strode's (Jamie Lee Curtis) anxiety and panic of giving into romance and sexual desires in *Halloween*, the mutant mother bear in *Prophecy* may be a physical manifestation of Foxworth's fear of fatherhood. The bear is relentless in the last 20 minutes of the film, running down the surviving cast members. In the end, Foxworth overcomes the monster and slays her, stabbing her repeatedly, conquering the violent mutation as well as his fear of becoming a father.

Prophecy is a beautiful, smart gem with lots of heart and doesn't compromise to give us a happy ending. Consequences linger long after the credits roll. Also, the final shot employs the *Carrie* gag that many horror movies of the '70s and '80s enjoyed. That final shot sets up the audience, appearing serene and harmonious, until the "boo" happens and the monster leaps up in frame scaring the bejeezus out of the audience. In *Prophecy*'s case, a large mutant raccoon or some other kind of creature pops its head out to offer a final old-fashioned squeal—the next creature to wreak havoc on the forestlands of Maine!

Of course revenge doesn't have to be a direct response to nature being mistreated. The human characters that populate these animal-themed horror movies may also be deserving of sweet revenge and beasts of all kinds can help out in the best way possible.

The Uncanny (1977) is a portmanteau movie from Britain's Rank Organization, although it could be mistaken for a film produced by Amicus. Horror movie legends Peter Cushing, Donald Pleasance and Ray Milland star in this creepy, sharply written film. Cushing plays a frazzled writer who visits his publisher one evening to discuss his new book about the inherent evil of cats. He explains that he truly believes that cats are demonic beings, supernatural foot soldiers for Satan and he tells his publisher three horror stories dealing with the devilish malice of the feline kind. The first story deals with an elderly wealthy woman who decides to rewrite her will leaving her fortunes to her many pet cats, rather than her snotty nephew. Her nephew, however, has ulterior motives. He is dating his aunt's maid and gets the domestic to steal the will so it can be changed before it goes to the lawyers. His aunt sees the maid do this, but the aunt is killed, smothered by the young lady who used to serve her tea. The cats witness this travesty

A cat attack from *The Uncanny*

and kill the maid and the nephew, avenging their late mistress's death. The second story involves a young girl who, after her parents are killed in a plane crash, goes to live with her aunt and uncle. She brings her beloved cat Wellington along with her, but her horrible cousin insists her parents get rid of him. The young girl, whose mother was a practitioner of witchcraft, uses her old spell book to get her revenge by shrinking her spiteful cousin to the size of a church mouse. Wellington has a new game to play. In the last story, Donald Pleasance plays an actor bored with his actress wife and plots her death in order to make way for his new mistress. His wife's devoted cat avenges her murder.

The opening credits for *The Uncanny* are set to sublime, gaudy colors and strange etchings of cats that would make Saul Bass proud. Fueled on the revenge motif, each story in this wonderful anthology movie reads like an old American E.C. horror comic where wrongdoers get their comeuppance— and it is the household cat that serves up the bloody demise of these ill-fated characters.

Churchill, the resurrected zombie cat, from the Stephen King adaptation of *Pet Sematary*

Of course the cats in this film are simply acting out of loyalty, that is, their owner or human companion has been wronged so they feel obliged to fix matters the best way they can, using their claws and sharp teeth. It is to be noted that the cats in *The Uncanny* are never at the command of their owners like the snakes are in *Jennifer* or the rats are in *Willard*. (Human commanders of their animal foot soldiers will be discussed in a later chapter.)

Cats also feature in the 1988 horror film *Uninvited,* where one is infected with a genetically engineered virus and comes aboard a cruise ship causing gory distress for all those on board. In the terrific *Pet Sematary,* directed by Mary Lambert and based on the best selling novel by Stephen King, Churchill is the family cat who, after being hit by a truck, is interred in a local Micmac Native American burial ground, only to resurrect but not quite right. He is sickly sinister, a zombie cat that acts as a catalyst to the lead's descent into desperation, with depressingly devastating results. In two other King adaptations, *Sleepwalkers* and *Cat's Eye,* cats also feature as creatures possessing mystical powers beyond human comprehension. And in cult movie mogul Ted V. Mikels's wonderful grindhouse gem *The Corpse Grinders*, desperate cat food company owners decide to put human meat into their product to boost business. What happens, however, is that the cats that eat this food soon develop a taste for human flesh and start tearing out the throats of every human they see!

Of course the living ancestors of the domestic house cat, that being lions and tigers and other big cats, would prove far more terrifying adversaries for the human race simply because they are larger in scale and can devour a human the same way one of these majestic beasts would catch, kill and eat an antelope or zebra. Lions feature in movies like *Roar,* directed by Noel Marshall, starring Tippi Hedren (18 years after she survived *The Birds*) and co-written by the man who

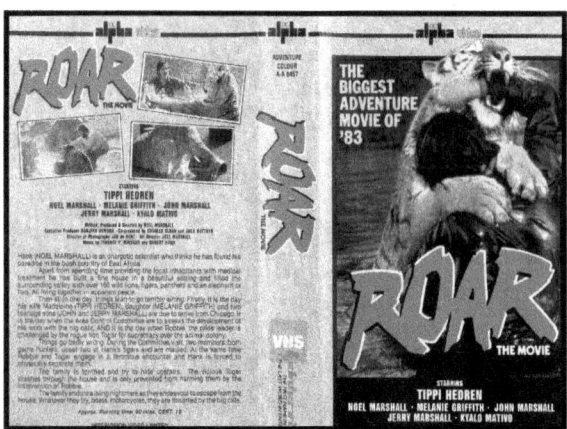

The Alpha VHS cover art for *Roar*—marketed as an adventure romp, although it was a terrifying excursion.

played Lurch from television's *The Addams Family*, Ted Cassidy, and *The Ghost and the Darkness,* written by talented screenwriter William Goldman, starring Michael Douglas and Val Kilmer.

A film like *Roar* (1981) examines human interaction and interplay with wild, untamed beasts. It poses the question: Can two very different species coexist without any dilemma? The lions in *Roar* are ultimately wild animals; nothing can stop them from tearing the living daylights out of their human co-stars. The film chronicles the life of a white man living in the savannah of Africa with his hundred or so pet lions, tigers, leopards and cheetahs. When his family, including Hedren and Hedren's real life daughter Melanie Griffith, come to stay, the entire human cast is at the mercy of these wild cats. All seems to be fine in the beginning of the film as the movie plays out like a live-action Disney romp in the vein of *The Swiss Family Robinson,* but this mood soon shifts and these ferocious lions and cats start to fight for supremacy within the household and attack the people who have raised them. They chase the humans into tight corners, tear down the wood panel walls of the jungle shack, snarling and biting, to pin down their human friends. What results is quite a frightening descent as the natural world denies the help of human interest. *Roar* captures this beautifully. The genius of this movie is its shift from family adventure of a lighthearted style to ruthless, relentless attacks from these animals that look mighty hungry and angry. By the end of the movie, the film reunites the human principles, the lions and other big cats. They come to live in harmony by the final reel.

The numerous mishaps in production of this film are many and belong to the annals of Hollywood legend. *Roar* began shooting in 1970 and wrapped up in 1981, costing a reported $17 million and only making $2 million on its release. During production Noel Marshall, Melanie Griffith and cinematographer Jan de Bont were all brutally mauled by lions. De Bont (who later went on to do his best work in Lewis Teague's adaptation of Stephen King's *Cujo*) was actually scalped by one of the ferocious lions during the development of this film, while Marshall's face, arm and chest were torn to shreds and he was instantly hospitalized before any more shooting could take place. But much good came from *Roar*, mainly due to the glamorous star of the picture, Tippi Hedren.

The compassionate Hedren is an avid animal rights supporter and founder of a lion sanctuary at the Shambala Preserve. She is a strong advocate for the rights of wild cats and her experience on the set of *Roar*, working with the animals used in the movie, really led the way for her to be extremely vocal in preserving the natural habitat for her feline friends. It paved the

The Shambala Reserve, a sanctuary for big cats, was made possible because of the movie *Roar* and the devoted animal rights activism of actress Tippi Hedren.

way for her to write the book *Cats of Shambala* and make several documentaries about lions and other big cats. Although *Roar* didn't make nearly enough money at the box-office to cover expenses, the final gross earnings went to fund the Shambala Preserve (located just on the edge of the Mojave Desert in Acton, California) and get it started as one of the greatest wildlife preservations in North America. It should be noted that Hedren actually rescued a lion that was kept by Church of Satan leader Anton LaVey, who was told by the State of California that he could not keep a lion as a house pet in the suburbs of San Francisco.

Roar is a visually gorgeous film and the lion attacks are extremely terrifying. A very thin line exists between what is staged and what is actually happening, and judging from some lion-on-human contact within the film, it is hard to distinguish what is real and what has been conceived for show. The scary truth of the matter is that this is exactly what the movie is suggesting. Lions are wild and therefore untamable; humans are too trusting or stupid but think they could condition lions to live as domestic pets.

However, Hedren's wonderful work in and out of *Roar* should be celebrated, as it is an admirable thing that stars of such magnitude bring animal rights to the limelight. Hedren joins a long list of avid animal rights activists who are all associated in the movie-making business—Doris Day, Raquel Welch, Brigitte Bardot, Linda Blair, Cassandra "Elvira" Peterson, Pamela Anderson, Betty White and so forth. Such active participation really does make a statement about the connection between Hollywood women and their love/dedication to the animal kingdom. This is something this writer believes wholeheartedly should be trea-

A rogue male lion devours an unfortunate railway worker in *The Ghost and the Darkness*.

sured and honored, despite *Roar*'s ill fate at the box-office and on-set misfortunes. The seldom seen *Roar* really does let the audience know that humans out there do care. This is the lasting legacy *Roar* has left.

Lions are given the William Goldman treatment in *The Ghost and the Darkness* from 1996, and, the critically acclaimed Oscar winning screenwriter, whose credits include *Misery, The Stepford Wives, Magic* and *Marathon Man,* penned an exciting action-adventure horror thriller set in the depths of the Tsavo grasslands in Kenya. The film's plot involves a malicious attack where two lions killed workers who were busy building the African Uganda to Mombasa railway back in the late 1800s. The lively script and captivating imagery work hand-in-hand, the lion attacks are photographed beautifully and, despite Val Kilmer's insipid characterization of the film's hero, the rest of the cast does a good job. Goldman's screenplay is loosely based on a book called *The Man-Eaters of Tsavo* by Lieutenant Colonel John Henry Patterson (characterized by Kilmer), but Goldman's main contribution, leading to a complete fictionalizing of Patterson's account of lion attacks, was the introduction of a fictional game hunter named Charles Remington, played by the gruff and rough Michael Douglas. Douglas's character is a stock standard in the eco-horror fare. Much like the Quint character as portrayed by Robert Shaw in *Jaws*, Douglas embodies to perfection the haunted hunter. He bears the scars both inside and out in regard to his encounters with man-eating lions. His story during the middle of the second act is much like Quint's recount of the Indianapolis in Spielberg's movie (more about this in the following chapter), and it sets the mood for what is to come. Douglas is as scary as the lions themselves; he is untamed, without regret and accursed—he lives for the hunt.

In *The Ghost and the Darkness*, William Goldman manages to write a taut script that breathes new life into a simple idea. He recreates a folkloric campfire story in the body of a reported incident that may or may not have happened at the turn of the century. What could have been another memoir in the vein of Lieutenant Colonel John Henry Patterson's book becomes something far more appealing and compelling. Goldman is a master storyteller and this is his imagined ghost story involving animals that are all too real for the likes of the residents and workers in Tsavo.

Upon the movie's initial release, *The Ghost and the Darkness* was instantly compared to *Jaws,* as was *Grizzly.* The media called it "Jaws in the jungle," and although *Lawrence of Arabia* was the other point of inspiration, according to Goldman in his book *Which Lie Did I Tell?,* the movie utilized many of the similar devices plotted by Spielberg's shark opus. However, these devices should never be harnessed to simply one movie (or a movie that, yes, is a benchmark classic; yes, was critically and financially successful; and yes, changed the shape of movie making) but instead to many other films that employ the formula of humankind facing adversity in the shape of the natural world.

Something that really sets *The Ghost and the Darkness* apart from other creature features is its steady handling of displacement and the importance of Africa as the setting. The film is completely obsessed with displacement (Kilmer's character and his wife are but fish out of water) but the theme does not distract audience attention. Africa is a perfect place for an Anglo-Irishman to lose his bearings when faced with the terrors that lurk in the grasslands of the Kenyan plains. Africa, in the end, serves as a wonderful setting for such a scary ride, but strangely enough, the place is seldom used! It makes one question why more pictures of this subgenre aren't made in the beautiful yet savage lands of the Dark Continent?

Val Kilmer's nightmare of his wife (Emily Mortimer) being attacked by rogue lions occurs in *The Ghost and the Darkness.*

Of course exceptions exist and one of them is *In the Shadow of Kilimanjaro.* Much like *Roar,* this stellar movie is seldom seen, set in a dustbowl African village where a drought has caused thousands of local baboons to go insane. The gore comes aplenty and the grittiness is necessary for such a bleak vision of an environment under great stress. In this monkey fiasco, nature's turn against itself (an intensely damaging drought) causes great distress, not only for the native animals, but also for the humans that occupy the story. They are at the mercy of the wild baboons that have been denied water, and therefore, they will have blood as a readily available alternative. We as an audience genuinely don't feel for the thirsty simians; instead, we fret for the humans caught in their battle to survive. This is because no one has mistreated the baboons; it's just nature at its cruelest. During *In the Shadow of Kilimanjaro,* both man and ape are victims to the perils of nature.

These terrified and terrifying baboons attack Damien and his mother as they drive through the London Zoo, from *The Omen*.

Baboons play an integral role in Richard Donner's *The Omen*. In the demonic classic chiller, the baboons are not acting out of rage, anger or revenge; instead, they are lashing out in fear. Lee Remick is driving through the London zoo with little Harvey Stephens, who of course plays Damien, the anti-Christ himself. The animal kingdom as a whole understands the true nature of Damien's demonic malevolence and, even though the youngster has no full comprehension of the evil he represents, the baboons make it no secret that they are terrified of him. In fear they attack Remick's car and cause great distress for mother and unholy son.

The link between man and monkey is one that has been exploited time and time again throughout cinema history. From the very beginning movies such as the forever glamorous *King Kong,* right through the Disney retelling/remodeling of *Mighty Joe Young*, man and monkey have been forever connected, not only by science and evolution, but also by thought patterns and interpersonal character attributes. Even movies such as *King Kong,* movies featuring gorillas/apes/chimps presented as fantastical, mammoth beasts, wild giants driven by lust, desire, rage, defense, vengeance or pure fear, create a lineage from bestial behemoth to civilized man. At the center lies truth and deep-rooted understanding between the raw id of a beast and the intricate intellect and super ego of man.

Because humans are after all descendents of apes, it makes sense that monkeys would prominently feature in the subgenre of ecological horror, and two noteworthy entries are *Link* from 1986 and the brilliant *Monkey Shines,* directed by George A. Romero, from 1988.

The manipulative and shifty orangutan in *Link*

Link tells the story of highly evolved chimps and orangutans trained by a wealthy scientist played by Terence Stamp. Elizabeth Shue, a young anthropology student, comes to stay at the large English manor where Stamp and his many monkeys live, and she is astounded by the genius of these creatures. Most notably intelligent is Link, the dutiful butler. But once Stamp disappears off the scene, Link starts to act strangely. He gets overly protective and possessive of young Shue and turns on his fellow monkeys, who live similarly as Link does. Soon enough, Shue has to fight for her survival from this menacing primate. Much like *Roar*, *Link* focuses on man's involvement and interference with animal behavior, and this conditioning almost always leads to disastrous results.

Ella, the capuchin monkey, is about to electrify a potential threat in *Monkey Shines*.

But it is George A. Romero's *Monkey Shines* that really is the top banana when it comes to sinister simians and their human victims. One of the main reasons this film succeeds is because it relies heavily on character development and the real horror growing from the alienation, anxiety, paranoia and obsessions of the characters in question.

George A. Romero is one of the horror genre's most acclaimed directors. Much has been written about his career. His *Living Dead* series headed by the landmark horror opus *Night of the Living Dead* from 1968 changed the way filmmaking in general (not only horror cinema) was perceived. With the sequel *Dawn of the Dead*, Romero was completely embraced as a socially aware filmmaker and his political agenda shone through in his zombie masterpieces. His movies meant something not only to genre fans but also to cinephiles everywhere. The third in his *Living Dead* trilogy, *Day of the Dead*, a film clever and solid in its equal delivery of gore and social commentary, was plagued with studio compromise. Romero, a normally independent filmmaker, was subtly shifted into the studio system and with that came abiding by certain rules. Level Entertainment was in charge of *Day of the Dead* and Romero ceased his involvement with them, wanting to tackle another project. This project was *Monkey Shines*.

Handling the syringe filled with the serum that turned her into such a demon, Ella intends to use the serum on her human perpetrator, in *Monkey Shines*.

Monkey Shines would be Romero's first book adaptation, and from the get-go, Romero changed the setting from the U.K. to his hometown of Pittsburgh, PA.

The movie is a wonderful examination of repressed violent desires and wish fulfillment gone horribly wrong. It tells the story of Alan Mann (even his name is suggestive of the importance of his species) played by muscularly handsome Jason Beghe. Beghe's Mann is a young healthy athlete studying law (an over-achiever obviously, someone both obsessed with physical prowess as well as academic excellence) who one morning is hit by a car on a routine jog. Romero manages to tell us so much about Beghe's character in the first five minutes of the movie, and the director captures the tragedy and painful reality of his accident masterfully, solid bricks crashing onto the hard concrete smash into pieces. Such imagery becomes a clear representation of Beghe's broken body and eventual broken psyche.

His complex operation is headed by Dr. Wiseman (Stanley Tucci), who is instantly established as a sleazy, repugnant cretin and who, as we later find out, is having an affair with Beghe's girlfriend, Linda (Janine Turner). The operation goes wrong (we discover later that this malpractice is intentional, a ploy Tucci's character uses to get Beghe out of the picture in order to pursue his involvement with Linda) and Beghe is rendered a paraplegic.

Beghe's friend Geoff (John Pankow), a researcher in craniotomy, enters the scene. Pankow's character is completely devoted to his work, and although he is first introduced as a benign character, he ends up being a demented Victor Frankenstein of sorts (ultimately suffering at the hands/paws of his "monster"). At a Pittsburgh university, Geoff is experimenting with capuchin monkeys and the human brain. He injects himself with serums that keep him awake (a sick devotion to his work) while at the same time injecting his number one test monkey (that he calls Number Six, a name devoid of any interpersonal connection) with a formula that is derived from a brain that was donated by a Jane Doe. This highly "evolved" monkey, a creature with a chemical imprint of the human psyche in her bloodstream, will eventually be the connection that protagonist Beghe has with the surrounding characters that try to "help" him.

As the story gracefully moves forward, Beghe's character is somewhat plagued with two more characters that want to control him rather than help him—his mother Dorothy (Joyce Van Pattern) and a somewhat neurotic older, live-in nurse Maryanne (Christine Forrest). Increasingly frustrated, Beghe becomes hard to deal with for these two women, and finally, Pankow suggests an alternative to help out his friend in need.

Pankow goes to visit a halcyon sanctuary where helper-monkeys are trained to assist the disabled. Headed by the lovely Dr. Melanie Parker (Kate McNeil)—who in turn becomes Beghe's saving grace—Pankow offers to donate Number Six to her sanctuary to be trained as a helper capuchin monkey. He explains that his monkey is highly intelligent and will be easy to teach. Pankow has ulterior motives however; he is donating Number Six to McNeil's sanctuary out of fear, as his experiments have been deemed dangerous by the dean at the university. By giving Number Six to McNeil, who will eventually train and hand her over to Beghe, Pankow may see the results of his experiments outside of public scrutiny. This humanistic monkey will showcase her newfound abilities in the home of an invalid. Number Six is quickly renamed Ella and brought to Beghe's house by McNeil, who teaches the human how to instruct this very dutiful simian. What unfolds, however, is a tale of obsession and sickly desires. The horrors of very human conditions are brought to the limelight through Ella the primate, who quite simply becomes an extension of these horrors. She is a genie in a lamp for Beghe, but at the same time she becomes a demonic force that will eventually turn on him.

Ella becomes specifically linked to all the characters surrounding Beghe. She is at first a helper, a role that is already occupied by the live-in nurse. Because Ella's growing affections/obsession with Beghe become deadly, the nurse packs up and leaves. Secondly, Ella wants to be Beghe's girlfriend, so twisted bestiality is explored in this film with so much intelligence that it becomes plausible. Ella turns on the woman who scorned Beghe, his ex-girlfriend, the one who was cheating on him.

During the darkest moments of this film, Beghe buys into this madness, and even though his character starts off as a calm, patient man, he descends into becoming a malicious, violent menace. As his condition

Ella makes friends with her paaraplegic friend (Jason Beghe) in *Monkey Shines.*

In *Monkey Shines* the bond between Jason Beghe and Ella is a twisted, pseudo-sexual one, plagued by sickly obsession that has disastrous results.

grows more frustrating and Ella's influence through the "shine" they share becomes aggressive, he subliminally wishes for his faithful monkey to go out and burn down the cabin that is host to his cheating ex-girlfriend and her new-found love, the same doctor who caused Beghe's paraplegia. Ella does so, killing them both in a blazing fire.

Also, of note, much like Rod Taylor's relationship with his oppressive mother Jessica Tandy in *The Birds*, Beghe has a quiet resentment towards his mother, who seems to revel in his newly found infantile state. Mother smothers him. In the scene where she is bathing him much to his disgust, Beghe explodes into a hateful rage. He shares his disdain for his mother that eventually grows into a distrust and resentment toward Ella. Thus, Ella is linked to Beghe's mother in the same way Ella was also linked to his maid and eventually his "girlfriend." She is Beghe's connection to those that surround him. But Ella doesn't like to be put in the same category as the likes of Beghe's oppressive mother, so she kills her, dropping an electrical device into her bathtub. Ella forces herself onto Beghe as his one true companion, one who will control him in the end and drive him to madness.

Only when McNeil's character is in jeopardy (Ella's furious jealousy over the blossoming romance developing between Beghe and the nurturing animal trainer) does Beghe's connection with Ella cease. McNeil ultimately saves the day (and Beghe physically, emotionally and psychologically) while Ella succumbs to the pent up rage of this broken man, resulting in a violent and terrifying death.

Monkey Shines examines the link between man and monkey as told through a nightmarishly tightly wound tapestry. It suggests that even benign creatures—if mistreated, experimented upon, rejected, refused love or denied a place of importance—may turn out to be as vengeful as young Ella.

Monkeys also prove to be deadly in *Congo* from 1995 and *BloodMonkey* from 2007. Contemporary filmmakers have no qualms making evil monkey movies or other ecologically themed horror films as such films prove successful whether they are theatrically released or released straight to DVD/Blu-ray. Recent natural horror films made in the last 10 or so years have proved to be rather successful: *Snakes on a Plane, Anaconda, Pighunt, Lake Placid* and many more. However, it does make sense that the subgenre really flourished in a decade that was becoming completely aware of the state of the environment, discovering the results of pollution, ecological waste and the torment of the planet. Films like *Frogs* and *The Day of the Animals* are most definitely products of the 1970s. They are concerned with biological warfare and an environment in peril as a result of the negligence of the human race, and it is during this decade that exploitation cinema

BloodMonkey was released as part of a series of direct-to-DVD films under the umbrella of the Maneater Series.

was in its heyday. Ecological monster movies like *Frogs* were considered exploitation by most film authorities because they tapped the fear of the growing incited anxieties concerning the condition of the Earth. On the flip side of exploitation films like *Grizzly*, we have hugely successful major studio releases like Spielberg's *Jaws* that made a killing at the box-office by informing audiences that if they liked a killer shark movie, well, they may even like a movie about a killer bear. Some went in an even more direct homage to films like *Jaws* by being specifically oceanic-centric like the internationally produced *Great White* and *Tintorera*. There was even a movie, *Blood Beach*, where the actual shore killed holidaying beach bunnies. The ethos of this kind of moviemaking and marketing was on par with the laws of the circus—loud, brash and in your face, entertaining and fronted by carnies whose religion was showmanship. These movies are entertaining, exploitation gems that either tap into a current trend or increasing fears of the natural world.

Nothing was subtle about many of the movies made outside of the Hollywood studio system and this is all clearly established from the initial outset in the advertising. These movies are marketed in the same way an ice-cream van blaring a slightly off-key rendition of "Greensleeves" cruises down the streets of some unsuspecting suburb (and I mean that with absolute respect).

Famed comic book artist Neal Adams' beautiful postser for *Grizzly*

The taglines are to the point and extremely well written, the titles capture the very essence of the commonly used term lighting-in-a-bottle, the artwork for the posters are vividly visceral masterpieces that stay with audiences long after seeing the picture (just think of comic artist Neal Adams's beautiful *Grizzly* poster or the skull covered in earthworms used for *Squrim*) and the trailers are cut with such gusto that they really prick up one's ears. Ecological horror films made outside of the major studios (and most of them were) boasted a cavalcade of wonderful marketing in their inventive campaigns—from the press releases, to the press books, to the lobby cards, to the 8-by-10 promotional photos. These films were more than often successful due to the fact that the artistry (artistry outside of the actual film itself) really helped sell tickets and generate attention. Independent film companies like American International Pictures made an effort to get promotional art out as fast as they could, sometimes even before a writer sat down to pen the script. This kind of thinking really paved the way for these inspired horror movies to do extremely well, cementing careers and securing starving artists who, for a long time, worked hard to get where they wanted and needed to go.

Ultimately low-budget marketing doesn't really differ from marketing big budget Hollywood movies that are peddling the same shtick. If we compare the poster of something like *The Exorcist* to one of its imitators, such as *Beyond the Door*, an absolute contrast in style and concept exists. The poster for *The Exorcist* is ambiguous, serene—only a suggestion of the foreboding is hinted. However, the movie itself is an intense character study that turns into a vicious magic show. The poster for *Beyond the Door* is extremely warts'n'all; nothing is left to the imagination here (the actual movie monster's face depicted in all her horrific glory for all to see) and yet the two films are pretty much selling the same product. Different methods of sales marketing are evident, but they are both movies about demonic possession. Stripped of its critical acclaim and arty tone, *The Exorcist* is also just another horror movie (much like many of the low-budget exploitation movies of previous years, made around the same time) featuring someone in extremely heavy make-up to make them grotesque.

A stunning poster for *Piranha*

And this is something that should be celebrated! Independent companies like AIP, De Laurentiis and the Roger Corman-owned Concorde Pictures and New World Pictures reveled in rubber monsters and special character make-ups. Such companies were phenomenal at churning out what audiences wanted to see. If they noticed the masses of people turning up in droves to line up for *The Exorcist* and *The Omen*, they cashed in on the demonic craze and made films like *Abby* and *The Mephisto Waltz*. If *Jaws* captured the attention of millions of people worldwide, then why shouldn't *Piranha*, *Orca* and *Tentacles* do the same?

Aquatic Attacks!
It's A Matter of Life and Death
Under the Sea

The ocean has always been associated with mood and the depths of the subconscious. Movies that dealt with underwater dwelling creatures exploited the demons that haunt both the psyche and the spirit. Just like the sinister monsters lurking in the deepest, darkest recesses of our minds, underwater dwelling creatures like piranha, killer whales, octopi and sharks lurk beneath the surface waiting to strike. Many of these aquatic horrors may owe a lot to films like *Creature from the Black Lagoon* and the science fiction hit *Voyage to the Bottom of the Sea,* but it is the much discussed *Jaws* that really got things moving as far as seaside horror movies go.

Killer sharks and ferocious fish come to represent the hidden anxieties and fears hiding within the ocean of our subconscious mind. Roy Scheider as Chief Brody in *Jaws* has a deep fear of the water and no real reason exists why he is scared. Perhaps it is just that he doesn't want to face his inner demons. Much like Jason Miller as Father Karras in *The Exorcist*, Scheider's personal demons come to surface when faced with a direct threat. For Jason Miller it was the possessed Regan and for Scheider it was the leviathan in the shape of a great white shark

Jaws is a spectacular adventure film but given the tone of a horror movie, and it will be forever remembered as a benchmark in the changing face of cinema. When *Jaws* opened the world watched and Hollywood changed forever; it ushered in the era of the blockbuster, but more importantly, it ushered in a

Robert Shaw is about to be devoured by the symbol of the vagina dentata that is the killer shark in *Jaws*.

The startling moment in *Jaws* that prompts Roy Scheider to suggest that his team is "gonna need a bigger boat!"

somewhat short-lived era of the smart blockbuster. Entertaining, intelligent and razor sharp in visual style and content, *Jaws* was and remains a superlative piece of maverick movie making.

Roy Scheider is the epitome of the haunted hero, the lone ranger hell-bent on discovering the truth about the isolated, strange deaths occurring around Amity Island. He is also forced to confront his inner demons by physically venturing out to face a very tangible monster, that of a great white shark that is turning swimmers into hearty meals. In order to conquer his demons embodied in the man-eating shark, Scheider's Brody must rise up against commerce, harmonious community and family values as embodied by the mayor of Amity, played by Murray Hamilton. Brody's strange detachment from his wife Ellen (Lorraine Gary) and his two children are clear indicators that this shark is consuming him metaphorically and possibly (hopefully for the shark) physically. He finds two supporters in the last sea-bound act of the movie, rich kid oceanographer Hooper (Richard Dreyfuss) who is as much a fish out of water as Scheider is and hardened Seabee (in the vein of *Moby Dick*'s eternal hunter Ishmail) Quint, beautifully played by a snarling Robert Shaw.

Lorraine Gary (in a performance that is subtle and perfect in every way) confesses to Scheider that Shaw's gruff Quint scares her. She expresses this fear in the final scene of the second act, right before we are subjected to a beautiful, poignant zoom-in shot of the tattered old ship carrying our three male heroes out to sea. This banged up old sea vessel called the Orca is seen through gleaming white jaws hung up over a window at the Quint household (a souvenir of Quint's conquering of the wild). This is a great foreshadowing of what the third act will entail and a brilliant condensation of what the film is ultimately about—the shark, even symbolized by its massive threatening jaws, is an all-consuming leviathan from the deep and man is its prey. Lorraine Gary's comment about Shaw's character evokes the possibility of the madness and scariness of

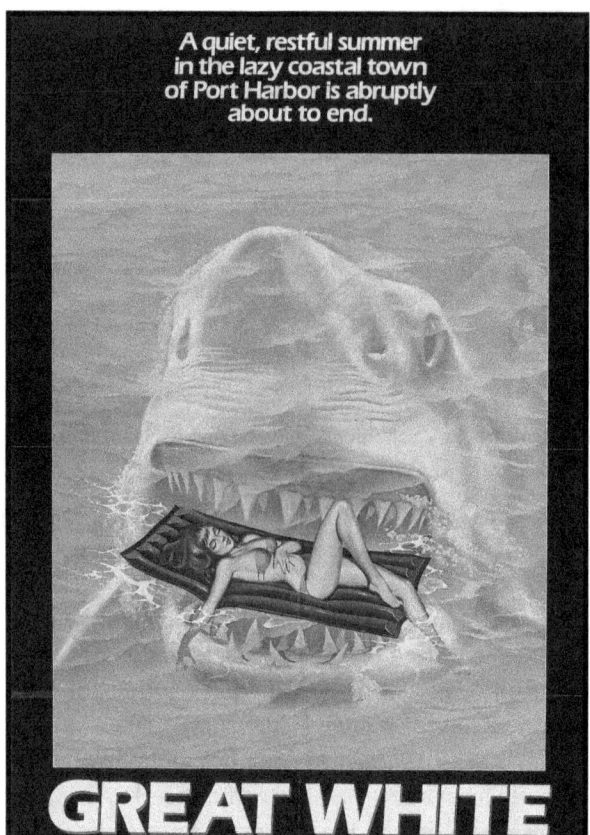

The controversial *Jaws* rip-off *Great White* was pulled from theaters on its initial release.

men (most notably men who are haunted and/or hunted). The visual of the mounted jaws enveloping the little tugboat going out to a potential watery grave suggests the magnificent power of the animal and the insignificance of man.

Just as *The Exorcist* spawned dozens of imitators, *Jaws* did the same. Some were great, and some were not so great. But most contained unique storytelling devices, distinct characterizations and personal flair. These movies, the spawn of Spielberg's big fish tale, really did capture the imaginations of not only moviegoers everywhere but also young up-and-coming filmmakers ushering in a new wave of popcorn monster movie fun. The blueprint had been set and it was time for the aqua-dwelling leviathans to reign supreme, at least for a little while.

Direct rip-offs of *Jaws* (i.e. movies that use sharks as the monster and were released around the same time when the hype and popularity of Spielberg's movie was at its peak) include Italian movies *Monster Shark* and *Great White* (aka, *The Last Shark*), a Mexican/British hybrid in *Tintorera* and *Mako: The Jaws of Death,* which really needs discussion in a later chapter.

Great White suffered greatly when the copycat movie was released seven years after *Jaws* played theaters. Universal Studios sued the American distributor of *Great White* claiming the film was plagiaristic, and despite a very brief North American run from Film Ventures International, *Great White* was pulled from theaters after Universal won its case. *Great White,* however, is a fun treat featuring lots of shark attacks, albeit none possessing real tension or suspense as seen in Spielberg's film. But this relentlessness makes it a fast paced and enjoyable romp for those wanting to see some underwater carnage!

The low-budget *Tintorera* has its own distinct style and works quite well. Its style and story are both very basic—a killer shark becomes a very genuine threat to a romantic relationship that has blossomed into a *ménage a trois*. Susan George stars as a beautiful young English tourist visiting a Mexican fishing resort, becoming involved with a traveling businessman and a womanizing swimming instructor. George is far more endearing in her performance here than she was in Sam Peckinpah's rape revenge *Straw Dogs* six years earlier, and even though *Tintorera* comes across as a highly stylized Mexican soap opera, mixed with straight out bisexual pornography, the shark attacks are vital to the story (making a statement on carnal desires and sexual aggression) and relatively impressive.

Mako: The Jaws of Death (aka *The Jaws of Death*) used the human help motif, a staple in eco-horror cinema.

My third example of direct *Jaws* rip-offs is the wonderful *Mako: The Jaws of Death*. The reason this writer feels the film is wonderful is that it strayed from being yet another movie about inexplicable attacks (not to say that inexplicable attacks are not warranted as brilliant subject matter), but it is good to see something else outside of this mold. What makes this film different is that actor Richard Jaeckel stars as a man obsessed with sharks who develops a spiritual connection with them. He becomes alien to his own society, rejecting his fellow man in favor of living for his beloved sharks. At the same time, his fishy friends are getting a bad rap for themselves and are subject to poaching. As the film moves forward, Jaeckel develops a telepathic connection to his sharks and communicates with them, eventually using them to kill off anybody that comes into his world who he sees as a threat. This film shares many similarities with

One of the frightening *Piranha* as built by SFX extraordinaire Rob Bottin.

the terrific *Stanley,* where the protagonist has a similar connection to snakes (the film actually belongs to a later chapter where I will be discussing animals that help their human friends (*Pigs, Jennifer, Willard,* et al.), but because the movie still relied heavily on motifs and storytelling devices used in Spielberg's monster shark hit, its inclusion here alongside its fishy brethren is warranted.

Communication between humans and underwater creatures is explored once again in *The Day of the Dolphin*, where George C. Scott trains his beloved dolphins, Alpha and Beta, to share open discussions with he and his wife. Unfortunately, these brilliant dolphins are kidnapped by sinister folk who want to get these lovely creatures to carry out a political assassination, by bearing an explosive near a yacht carrying the President of the United States.

Dolphins feature not as a threat but as an aide in the second *Jaws* sequel, *Jaws 3D* (a flawed but fun movie), but more on that later as we come back and have an in-depth look at the legitimate sequels to Spielberg's sensational 1975 blockbuster.

Sharks seem to pop up in many other movies as cold-blooded killing machines, such as *Red Water*, *Open Water* and *Deep Blue Sea*, but three of the best *Jaws* clones didn't feature great whites or any kind of shark as the menace. In fact these three movies are far cries from being dubbed simply as imitators, despite what some lazy critics might say. Some may even argue that these films are just as good, if not better, than Universal's huge hit. To get to the point, these movies are the satirically smart *Piranha,* the snappy, subversive *Alligator* and the beautifully composed, melancholy masterpiece *Orca*.

One of the best tributes to *Jaws* was director Joe Dante's superb *Piranha*. Adept in delivering social satire and being extremely well directed, acted and plotted, *Piranha* is a great example of B-movie ingenuity, political critique and viscerally effective parlor tricks. The opening reads much like a slasher film, which were becoming increasingly popular with the critical acclaim accorded films such as *Halloween* and the earlier *Black Christmas*. Two nubile, horny teenagers decide to take a swim in what seems to be a swimming pool connected to a military installation. They are both brutally devoured by unseen critters from the murky depths, and as their blood surfaces, we are lead into the opening titles.

Heather Menzies (all grown up since playing Louisa Von Trapp in *The Sound of Music,* and of course she was the leading lady in another eco-horror hit, *Sssssssss*) plays a determined, zealous insurance investigator who is sent to find out what has happened to these two teens. She hires a local to be her tour guide. Eco-horror regular Bradford Dillman (who has starred in many natural horror movies, such as the marvelous *Bug* and *The Swarm*) is an alcoholic loner living in the deep thickets of the forest, and he makes for one reluctant guide. His supposed harmonious existence is interrupted by intrepid, sassy Menzies, but ultimately she helps him get out of his drunken stupor leading him to re-establish his strained relationship with his young daughter, who is spending her summer at a camp headed by Joe Dante regulars Belinda Balaski, Melody Thomas Scott and Paul Bartel (in a typical deliciously darkly comic performance).

Menzies and Dillman discover that the compound where the two teens went missing was formerly a fish hatchery prior to being used by the U.S. military. They

Director Joe Dante regular Belinda Balaski is about to become fish food in *Piranha.*

soon find bizarre specimens in jars as a sneaky Ray Harryhausen-like creature parades around, hiding from our two leads. Something is afoot, and as soon as a disheveled Kevin McCarthy is discovered, the truth begins to surface about the teenagers' deaths. McCarthy (a wonderful character actor and the lead in the classic *Invasion of the Body Snatchers*) is a lead scientist who was commissioned to work on a Vietnam War project called Operation Razorteeth, where the U.S. government wanted to engineer killer piranha fish to survive the cold waters of Vietnam in order to inhibit the Viet Cong movement. However, these piranha have escaped from the military compound and been released into the main waterways of the town. Their first stop—the summer camp!

With make-up artist extraordinaire Rob Bottin (his following ventures *The Howling* and *The Thing* will prove far more amazing) at the helm of making

Ramon, the huge 'gator, emerges from the sewers to take on the impoverished ghettos of Chicago in *Alligator*.

the piranha tangibly effective monstrosities, serving up plenty of excessive gore and bloody carnage, *Piranha* really does make a statement about the media's coverage of the Vietnam War. These violent fish massacre locals and hundreds of tourists, but the treatment of this terror is swept under the carpet and kept in the shadowy realms of denial by media and government officials alike. Political commentary is clearly important to a director like Joe Dante, and it works splendidly in context. Complete with wonderful performances by Joe Dante favorite, Dick Miller, and queen of horror Barbara Steele as a sinister government agent, *Piranha* is a perfect film. Alongside *The Howling,* screenwriters everywhere should study John Sayles' script to learn how to write entertaining and extremely sharp, socially aware genre fare.

Also written by John Sayles is Lewis Teague's *Alligator* (1980), a brilliant example of the post-*Jaws* eco-horror subgenre where a natural (albeit genetically enhanced) threat becomes the enemy of the people. In Teague's film we have the urban legend of alligators living in sewers coming to life in a smart, sophisticated fashion. Everything about this film is pure gold, as all the elements come together to make for one of the wittiest creature features of the 1980s.

The story begins at a tourist trap featuring live 'gator shows where a young reptile enthusiast purchases a baby alligator to keep as a pet. Her animal-phobic father decides to flush the poor reptile down the toilet, letting it loose into the catacombs of an underground Chicago sewer system. Years later, severed body parts keep turning up in local waterways and the little girl, now a grown up herpetologist played by Robin Riker, helps local Chicago police officer David Maddison (Robert Forster) uncover the sinister reasoning behind this malicious bloodbath of multiple deaths. What they soon realize is that a wealthy tycoon in cahoots with the town mayor is behind a series of growth hormone experiments to tackle the world's food shortage problem. This tycoon has his top scientists experiment on dogs, and once an experiment is complete, the canine carcasses are thrown into the sewers only to be devoured by one hungry 'gator. What results is a massive reptilian mutation with an endless bloodlust that only Forster and Riker can tackle.

John Sayles' script is a witty, 90-paged monster masterpiece that masterfully comments on environmental decay, the dangers of science and social class resentment. Sayles has his alligator (named Ramon) start off attacking the people in the urban ghetto, then it creeps up on the working class, then slithers its way to chomp on the middle class, ultimately reaching the upper class, where the monster is finally in clear sight, thus making a wonderfully acute commentary on how a class-conscious society fails to "see" the problem until it hits the wealthy elite. Some may say this could be a critical response to the U.S. government's denial of the AIDS epidemic, which was beginning to make headlines at the time of *Alligator*'s release. Along with this socially aware critique, Sayles clearly has fun with the genre and is always armed with a clever joke to tail end each scene. An example of the script's ingenuity is noting the great establishing point where the bomb that is eventually used to destroy the pesky oversized alligator is also the same bomb that earlier in the film is used by a delusional but rather harmless schizophrenic to threaten the Chicago police department. The scene with the potential bomber is played for laughs—a comic relief moment in a movie that is played very straight when involving the alligator's murderous rampage. In regards to the inclusion of the bomb and the mad bomber, the movie suggests that something good and worthwhile (the killing of the 'gator) in the long run could arise from what is played as a silly situation (the bombing attempt at the police headquarters). This is a perfect statement made by Sayles addressing an audience that may not wish to see a movie about a huge killer alligator. In turn, the film is telling its audience to stick around and look beyond its exploitative window dressings.

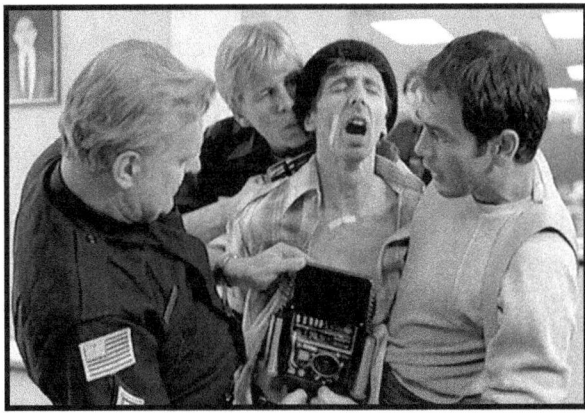

Robert Forster and fellow officers apprehend a mad bomber-to-be in *Alligator*.

A John Sayles trademark of sorts is also used in this film where much of the information about the alligator's path of destruction is given to the audience and main protagonists from news coverage in choppy, sharp segments. This device is used in *Piranha* and *The Howling*; it's a commentary on the role of the media and the monstrosity it can be and also spawn. Sayles epitomizes all this in a scene where eager to make a buck Chicago-dwelling entrepreneurs quickly peddle alligator-themed souvenirs, while townsfolk are being eaten alive.

Eating the sinister rich in *Alligator*

The cast does a great job with their unpretentious and dynamic performances. Led by Robert Forster as the no-nonsense tough Chicago cop with a tortured past (he can't shake off the memory of his old partner who was shot down back in St. Louis) and Robin Riker as sassy, feisty herpetologist Marissa, the film boasts some great character actors to make the killer alligator romp more fun. Sydney Lassick (the unsympathetic English teacher who got electrocuted in *Carrie*) plays a dodgy pet shop owner who makes shifty deals with the scientists experimenting with growth hormones, and Henry Silva plays a sleazy bounty hunter, Col. Brock. Both meet their bloody fates at different points in the movie.

The kills are beautifully bloody and raucously unapologetic. A neighborhood baseball game is interrupted by a savage attack where our pal the 'gator tears a police officer apart. At a children's dress-up party a young boy is forced by his peers to leap off the backyard diving board and our scaly friend is hiding in the pool. A SWAT team takes to the water ready to shoot down the hungry beast, to no success, as the 'gator shreds the boy's legs off. The best sequence of them all is where the rampaging beast eats the rich. The beast crashes the wedding of the daughter of the tycoon responsible for the alligator's mutated state and munches his way through the guests. The tycoon and the mayor (another red-handed culprit) are served the best death sequences—the tycoon is crushed within his limousine while the mayor, in the grasp of the mighty jaws of the alligator, is bashed against the same vehicle. The alligator is a masterpiece of a hybrid invention—one part a mechanical nightmare that chomps unfortunates into pieces and then uses its mammoth tail to thrash folks about. The alligator's presence is awesome in size, and the mechanical model is juxtaposed against actual footage of a grotesque live 'gator, in all its scaly splendor.

To the untrained ear and eye, this movie may seem to be nothing more than yet another monster-mutant-on-a-rampage fare to add to the popcorn junk pile, but it is most definitely not junk and commands respect. Like his wonderfully superlative *Cujo*, Teague, along with the snappy writing of Sayles, has come up with a tightly written and intelligent film that will always be a classic to fans of the genre. John Sayles' writing is just so splendidly sharp that sadly the sequel

Alligator 2: The Mutation missed out on his fine craftsmanship, although it did get horror regular Dee Wallace as its star.

Alligators and crocodiles pop up in many other movies and have been seen even in recent times. In *Lake Placid* (1999) a giant 30-foot long, man-eating alligator terrorizes a misfit group made up of Bridget Fonda, Philip Seymour Hoffman, Bill Pullman and Kevin Bacon, who try to capture it while Betty White stars as a friendly local lady who is somehow responsible for the mayhem in that she's a surrogate mother to this ferocious 'gator. The film was a tongue-in-cheek buddy movie with plenty of humor as a counterpart to the shocks and thrills. It proved to be far more successful than its predecessor *Anaconda,*

Tongue-in-cheek or not, a 30-foot alligator is always terrifying (DVD cover from *Lake Placid*).

which featured a giant snake as its monster and also spawned two sequels, rejuvenating the subgenre of killer animal movies for a while, ushering the way for movies like *Primeval, Blood Surf* and Australian movies *Black Water* and the brilliant *Rogue,* directed by Greg McLean, who had a previous hit with the grisly and cynical *Wolf Creek.*

Piranha and *Alligator* really put director Joe Dante and writer John Sayles on the map as major talents, who not only delivered great stories, but also injected them with socially aware commentary and subversive intellect. The superlative lycanthropic venture *The Howling,* a perfect film about werewolves in therapy, would bring these two together again and is a perfect example of their masterful control of excellence in story telling. It is to be noted that before he got John Sayles on board to start writing *The Howling,* Joe Dante was set to direct a film called *Jaws 3: People 0* for Universal, which was to be a horror spoof produced by the same folk that brought audiences the extremely successful *Flying High* and a movie that at the time was to be called *Orca: The Killer Whale*. Dante produced his werewolf opus, which not only became an extremely critical and box-office success, but also a favorite of genre fans (in my opinion its Dante's best film and one of the greatest horror movies to come out of the 1980s). It led him to make his most commercially successful movie ever, the yuletide monster gem *Gremlins. Orca,* however, was left for someone else to take charge, someone

Much more than a *Jaws* rip-off, *Orca* celebrates revenge-fueled ecological horror.

to give it life, grace and elegance. That someone was an Italian maestro of moviemaking, someone in the vein of a Samuel Z. Arkoff or a William Girdler, Mr. Dino DeLaurentiis.

Orca (1977) is a revenge film. Just like *Carrie* is a revenge-fueled horror movie, *Orca* is much the same. The monster of the piece (a killer whale) is first seen as a graceful, elegant beast gliding through the ocean alongside his mate, and it is this opening sequence that establishes this movie monster's heart. Our killer whale is a romantic. He is a loving and compassionate husband to his pregnant bride.

Richard Harris stars as a disheveled sailor who heads an expedition of seafaring men, along with the lovely Bo Derek (in her very first movie role) looking the most beautiful she ever has. The crew are responsible for the death of the killer whale's mate, and in her bloody abduction from the sea, the female has her fetus fall to its death. Watching from the depths is her angry companion, his eyes burning with hatred as Ennio Morricone's sumptuous score turns from angelic and sweepingly romantic to menacing and unforgiving. This killer whale wants his revenge and he shall have it. He scouts and memorizes every human on board the ship that took down his bride and unborn calf, and one by one he sets out to kill them, the captain (Richard Harris) set up for the ultimate death.

Harris, in all his usual gruff hyper-masculine glory, becomes an Ahab of sorts, sets out to capture this Moby Dick of killer whales. The intensity of the whale's rage, Harris's desire and obsession in conquering the untamed wild (once again a Western motif used in a horror film) and the eventual showdown between man and beast is extremely captivating and intelligent, slowly building tension. This movie is powerful and endlessly engaging.

Actress Charlotte Rampling joins the cast as the stoic, strong-willed whale specialist, and she is simply perfect. She embodies everything that is brave, compassionate and sensitive in what is a staple in this subgenre, playing the female lead of the natural horror film. On top of that, Rampling oozes sensuality and glamour. A perfect example of this is in a scene where Rampling's sleep is interrupted by a phone call and she turns on the bedroom light, where it is revealed that she in fact sleeps in a full face of perfectly applied make-up. Sensuality and glamour are two must haves for a woman in the eco-horror film, as sensuality is likened to naturalism and glamour is forever important as a staple in escapist movie fare.

Rampling's voice-over narration as the scientist documenting the state of affairs concerning the killer whale and the equally scary Richard Harris works beautifully in *Orca*. Unlike many other films that rely on voice-over narration, the device is not a lazy tool here. It actually benefits the way the story is told; her no-nonsense tone and delivery manage to tie together the already tightly plotted scenes efficiently, but it also helps the audience understand her very complex character. Rampling on one hand is a sympathetic scientist who cares for the killer whale in question, but she is also someone that, through her narration, makes us understand what attraction (if not a sexual one then an emotional one) she has for Richard Harris. She admires his honesty, his earthy swagger and openly comfortable ignorance. This paints a very interesting character study. Harris is gruff and of a bygone era, while Rampling is a progressive intellectual caught in an age-old emotional turmoil. The whale is driven by vengeance and will slaughter those who were responsible for his beloved's demise.

Orca also stars Will Sampson (Hollywood's most used Native American of the 1970s) as the wise and all-knowing spiritualist who acts as an extension to Rampling's plea for understanding of the untamed beast. He explains to Harris that the killer whale is a spirit of unashamed fury, while Rampling offers a more scientific understanding of the nature of this creature. However, Rampling and Sampson are both equally sympathetic to the whale. Harris, however, is only interested in protecting his life and reigning supreme, but this does not mean he hasn't a sense of guilt about killing the whale's pregnant mate, a guilt born out of fear. This is fundamentally explored in a great scene where Harris seeks counsel with a local priest asking about the spirituality and souls of animals, thus suggesting that the killer whale has validity in his bone to pick with the grim sailor.

The whale is a brilliant creation, the beautiful close-ups of his eyes emoting such complexity and rage. Some spectacular scenes in *Orca* are to be found and one of the most vividly striking is where the killer whale, in all his methodical thinking and quiet fury, sets the coastal town aflame. He is seen leaping with joy as he watches a portion of the once halcyon village burn to

The killer whale's pregnant mate is hung out to dry by Richard Harris and his team, from *Orca*.

the ground. Ennio Morricone's glorious score complements the killer whale's triumphant water ballet and cry of satisfaction (incidentally, out of all of the famed Italian composer's musical scores, *Orca* is my all time favorite). Another memorable scene involves Bo Derek's leg amputation, where the whale trashes the seaside cabin in which she is staying and tilts it toward his mighty jaws. It is a gory gem as we watch Derek's leg being chomped away by the mightily pissed-off whale. Derek's boyfriend screams in terror as he hopelessly watches his gal attacked by the black and white death-bringer, the orca's bittersweet valediction: "You stole my beloved, so I'll take yours!" The final showdown between killer whale and Harris is something that belongs to the mythic. In the white blazing glory of icebergs and freezing cold barren Arctic space, the whale traps Harris, and with a mighty blow from his tail, the doomed Seabee is flipped into the water and left to drown. The killer whale reigns triumphant (a rarity for the eco-horror movie, where the animal in question not only survives but kills the hero/anti-hero).

Accompanied by Ennio Morricone's sumptuous score, the killer whale celebrates his destruction of a village, from *Orca*.

Orca is a spectacle with lots of heart and, in my humble opinion, shares as much importance in this writer's world as Spielberg's legendary hit from two years earlier. From its grandiose dramatics to its lush settings filmed in Malta, *Orca* is a great example of Italian-American co-productions that were becoming exceptionally popular during the 1970s and beyond (a byproduct of the successful and critically loved Giallo films of auteurs like Dario Argento and Mario Bava). Two more fishy fright features were co-produced by Italian filmmakers in the years to come, one was a smart crime thriller with menacing underwater critters and the other was an unofficial sequel to Joe Dante's masterpiece.

Killer Fish (1979) is more an adventure film or a heist movie than a fully-fledged horror film. However, it has some slick tense moments and some nice fishy action late in the movie. Genre regular Karen Black is joined by Lee Majors in this movie involving thieves trying to find lost jewels, which it is said, have been located in the deep dark sea. The problem for these thieves is that these waters are piranha infested. The movie takes a long time to get to aquatic attacks, but it is viewable namely for the snappy dialogue and great chemistry between Black and Majors. Panned by critics as a lukewarm rip-off of the very intelligent, fun ride that was *Piranha* (which incidentally opened the same year), *Killer Fish* does have fun with the genre mergings.

Joe Dante's frightening fish flick however got the sequel treatment, an unapologetically gore-fueled horror fest that was entertaining. It was the directorial debut of a Roger Corman-affiliate who would go on to make one of the highest grossing movies ever made, another oceanic disaster pic (one that may have benefited from killer sharks, seals or turtles), the much beloved (and equally hated) *Titanic*.

If the first *Piranha* satirized the media's involvement with

The poster for *Killer Fish* compared the plight of opportunist humans with fish doing what comes naturally.

the coverage of the Vietnam War and the shifty dealings that happen between government and capitalist enterprise, then its sequel (an unofficial sequel more or less) *Piranha 2: The Spawning* (1981) has nothing really political to say, but it's a fun ride nonetheless. Directed by James Cameron who went on of course to give us great sci-fi/horror landmarks *The Terminator* and *Aliens*, *Piranha 2: The Spawning* is a gory and satisfying exploitation picture with Lance Henriksen heading the cast. The film is loaded with cheesy dialogue, mainly one-liners that are written with tongue firmly planted in cheek. These one-liners come as the coda of each scene, ending them quickly and rather abruptly. There are plenty of bare breasts on board and the violence is masterfully handled, bloody and excessive, exactly what audiences want from a film about killer flying fish. Yes, the piranha develop wings and fly through the air, mauling tourists, but this is an exploitation film, remember.

Fish, being slimy and quick but, most significantly, prominently unseen, make for good creature feature fodder and to this day they are used as malevo-

The unapologetically gory *Piranha 2: The Spawning* had malevolent fish develop wings and come onto land.

lent foils for the human cast members. A hugely successful recent hit is *Piranha 3D* (2010). Not at all associated with Dante's movie, this film is a hedonistic celebration of breasts, blood and basics. Everything about the film is fun, fishy fun. The film plays out like a laundry list from the B brigade: Tits? Check! Gore? Check! Funny party guy who has a great line to deliver while bleeding to death? Check! The movie is surprisingly well thought out and seamlessly looks as though these great fundamentals are secondary to what the filmmakers intended. In other words, the film doesn't strike us as ultimately planned schlock. Instead, it's silly super-fun with brains.

A movie that is just sheer silly and lacking brains is American International Pictures' production *Tentacles* (1977). As much as it is a woeful movie, it is also something of an enigma as it boasts an amazingly stellar cast.

Tentacles was unapologetically made to cash in on the success of *Jaws*. A year later an equally atrocious *Jaws* rip-off *Barracuda* (yes about killer barracuda, well, kind of) was released to drive-ins everywhere. Namely because of its lack of fishy ferocity it did woefully and was pulled quite suddenly from exhibition. However, *Tentacles*, on its initial release, did quite okay box-office and I strongly believe that would have to do with Shelley Winters, Bo Hopkins, John Huston and Henry Fonda heading the cast.

The wonderful Shelley Winters is wasted in this movie only because she shares most of her scenes with insipid children. Her breathy Miss Piggy-esque sex appeal exists and yet it is lost because she has to mother the boy playing her son and his shy, socially awkward friend. Nothing exists for her to say or do. Winters looks as though she has stepped off *The Love Boat* and into this surprisingly slow movie with her pastel

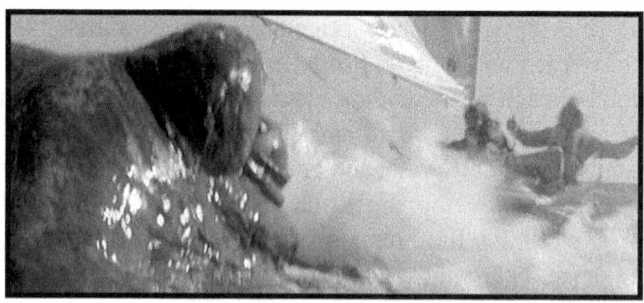

The rubber octopus prepares to take on a sailboat in *Tentacles*.

The poster for *Tentacles* is even better than the movie.

make-ups and flowing cheesecloth gowns that cover her plump stature. Her weight is fodder for jokes made by other characters more than once in this film, but her meaty presence is the best thing in it. It does however come across that the director counts himself exceptionally lucky to have a star like Winters in his little low-budget Italian co-production and this is clear because, when Winters fumbles her lines and appears inarticulate at times, it doesn't matter. The grateful director makes it sound natural and true to the character she's playing, which is a sloppy, slightly flighty drunk who goes through life with the grace of a pregnant elephant.

The only snappy dialogue in this movie is shared between John Huston and Shelley Winters. These two Hollywood legends play an aging brother and sister team who, because of many failed marriages, have decided to spend their senior years living in their childhood home just by the ocean. In a tiny scene we get to know a lot about the two of them. Huston's character is crotchety, a bit depressed, he needs something to wake him up, whereas Winters is lively, energetic, full of lustful desires and happy to be a single older woman who enjoys the occasional man and drink. This scene is written with great ease and you can tell from their performances that these two seasoned pros would have nailed it in one take. More of this would make *Tentacles* bearable!

It Came From Beneath The Sea, employing inspirational stop-motion animation by Ray Harryhausen, featured a lovely octopus terrorizing San Francisco's Golden Gate Bridge.

The score is one of the most annoying pieces of music in cinema history. The musical motif for the monstrous octopus is an electronic harpsichord or accordion that plays the same five notes over and over again, making it not only annoying but also totally out of place with the sometimes atmospheric shots alluding to the creature lurking just under the surface. When we finally get to see the octopus, it is a big old rubber head that looks as though it is being jet-propelled underwater, so it zooms along looking menacing. This is all fine and good, but we could have gotten to see the man-eating octopus earlier. Instead, most of the film obsesses over uninteresting dialogue, generated by Henry Fonda and Bo Hopkins about this "monstrous unknown creature".

An octopus is given a far more interesting role and much more respect in the 1955 horror/science fiction classic *It Came From Beneath The Sea*. Here the inspiring, beautiful work of legendary animator Ray Harryhausen is in full form—a giant octopus terrorizes San Francisco! Its massive tentacles tear down the Golden Gate Bridge as Kenneth Tobey and Faith Domergue look on.

The so-called *Jaws* rip-offs were plentiful but the film itself did spawn a number of legitimate sequels, and the first of them (and most definitely the best) came along with one of the most imitable, memorable and quotable tag lines ever conceived in modern movie campaigns: "Just when you thought it was safe to go back in the water."

Jaws 2—with its superlative script, wondrous musical score by maestro John Williams and amazing cast lead by Roy Scheider, Lorraine Gary and Murray Hamilton, all reprising their roles from the first outing—is a genuinely scary and slick sequel. What made it even more interesting was that it adopted the current trend in the horror genre at the time—it embraced the teen-orientated slasher picture. By the late '70s and early '80s, the slasher film was on the rise. In 1960 *Psycho* set the standard and was the granddaddy or, more appropriately, the mother of all slasher films. By the mid '70s low-budget yet stylish stalk 'n' slash movies like the Canadian gem *Black Christmas* and the landmark opus *The Texas Chain Saw Massacre* lead the way for hugely popular and critically acclaimed films like *Last House on the Left*, *The Hills Have Eyes* and the remarkably bloodless *Halloween,* which interestingly became the blueprint for a long line of extremely popular and increasingly violent gore-fueled slasher films like *Madman, Girls Nite Out, Slumber Party Massacre* and many, many more.

Healthy, young and attractive nubile teens are up for shark feed in *Jaws 2*.

The much discussed and studied formula of the slasher film usually consists of a combination of elements—an event that happened long ago that will influence the course of action in the present; a group of teenagers oblivious to danger that will become victims of the bloody body count; and the one sole survivor, almost always a girl, who is not distracted by the things that "blind" the other teens (coined as the Final Girl by feminist film scholar Carol Clover, who authored the wonderful *Men, Women and Chainsaws: Gender in the Modern Horror Film*). It is the Final Girl who ultimately combats the killer and defeats him or her (at least for the one film before an imminent sequel), a psychotic killer who is usually masked or hidden from view until the very end, the bloody, creative, violent deaths usually occurring after or in cahoots with orgasm. Thus, such movies literally linking violence with sex. The eco-horror subgenre (although not adopting this fad as often as one would think) was happy to jump on the bandwagon of this current and extremely successful trend and *Jaws 2* was one of these films.

Here, an all-powerful leviathan stalks a group of attractive teenagers radiating good health and normalcy (not unlike the Camp Crystal Lake camp counselors of the *Friday the 13th* films). The monster was not a crazy old woman avenging her son's death as seen in *Friday the 13th* or the boogey man stalking babysitters in the Midwest as seen by Michael My-

Roy Scheider faces his demons once more—head to head in a final showdown in *Jaws 2*.

ers in *Halloween*. But here an all-powerful oceanic (and disfigured) Great White shark becomes the monstrosity.

In *Jaws 2* the shark's face is burnt during an attack on a motorboat; it's flesh gray and blackened as it is singed. This affliction adds to the horror of the unstoppable beast much the same way Freddy Krueger's or Cropsey's burnt skin adds to the ugliness and scariness of their presence in *A Nightmare on Elm Street* and *The Burning*. This evokes more terror by showcasing scar tissue and exposed tendons. The shark in *Jaws 2* is no longer an unseen mysterious, hidden demon lurking just under the surface of a usually stoic man's subconscious. Instead, it is a horrible serial killer marked with grotesque injuries and hungry for young flesh.

One of cinema's most famous taglines occurs on the teaser poster for *Jaws 2*.

Jaws 2 has some wonderful moments and most of them come from the excitingly exhilarating sequences following the young teens setting out on their boats for a day of fun in the sun. The teenagers in this film are all completely likeable and their plight is dramatically strong. The stress levels and group dynamics make for wonderful screen time and the shark attacks are beautifully staged and disturbingly terrifying. A poignant moment that is a clear example of the film's effectiveness comes just after one of these ferocious sharks attacks, where the group starts bickering, arguing as to what should be done about this perilous situation. Suddenly one of the group realizes that their yelling at each other is not going to be helpful at all, and one of the girls is heard whispering a prayer to a God she has more than likely never ever prayed to before in her life. A musical sting at the masterful command of John Williams hits and the camera pulls back to reveal the disheveled mess that are the remaining shattered ships which carry our teenage shark bait across the vast deep dark blue sea.

Thankfully, the major players are given lots to work with here. Scheider's Brody is once again the heroic but haunted loner, once again under great scrutiny by Murray Hamilton's mayor, who now has the entire community backing his every decision, jeopardizing Scheider's job as police chief.

Director Jeannot Szwarc (who also directed the brilliant *Bug*) does a remarkable job at carefully not repeating what has already been seen in the original *Jaws* film. He manages to weave a tight tapestry that is both rousingly energetic and well balanced. The audience doesn't feel cheated by having too much teen action and not enough Roy Scheider, or vice versa. The film remains captivating from the first sequence involving the deep-dive discovery of the Orca wreckage from the previous movie right through to Scheider cleverly electrocuting the great white menace.

The second *Jaws* sequel, *Jaws 3D*, is an enjoyable romp and here the animal kingdom is truly embraced as something that we humans should respect. The leading players

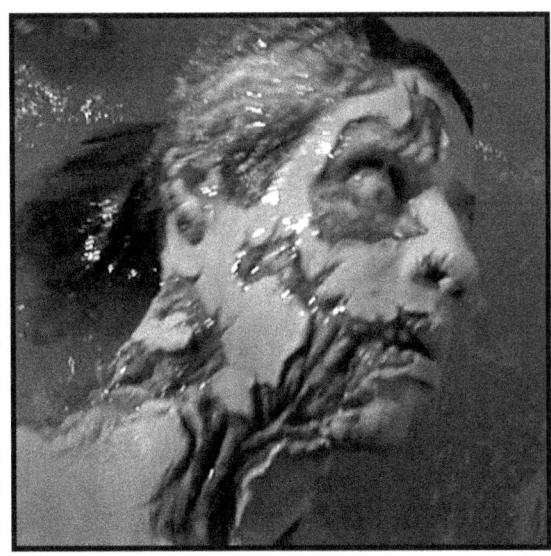
A bloody corpse emerges from a watery grave in Joe Dante's *Piranha*.

in *Jaws 3D* have a beautiful relationship with their trained dolphins, and the dolphins are integrant in the fight against the even larger, hungrier killer shark. The 3D effects are effective and fun and the film has some marvelous stuff in there. It tells the story of a shark causing havoc at a water theme park. The great white terrorizes water skiers, vacationing patrons and park employees, and its messages of ecological preservation and conservation aren't too heavy handed. Unfortunately, the brilliance and genuine terror of *Jaws 2* and the fun and facts of *Jaws 3D* were not replicated in the truly terrible *Jaws 4: The Revenge* where the lovely Lorraine Gary, a great actress who shines in the first two entries as Ellen Brody, is wasted in this starring role as a woman tormented by a shark that has killed her husband and son. The usually wonderful Michael Caine is also wasted in this film that really has not one redeemable feature other than being a movie about a killer shark!

The ocean and its dark ominous depths make for a truly scary movie ride, and when filmmakers add an all-consuming, driven, killing machine, the film becomes even more frightening. This is why films like *Jaws*, *Piranha* and *Orca* have endured; these are films that play on the fears of the inner-space of the ocean which will forever be a place foreign and alien to the likes of land dwelling mammals known as humans. But what if the monster was a creature not from the depths of the sea or a wild animal not normally in the company of mankind like a bear or a lion, what if the monster was a creature that stood by the human race as a faithful companion? What if this loyal dutiful critter that once looked at you with loving eyes suddenly turned on you—yes, I talk of man's (and woman's) best friend, the domestic dog...

(That's When I Fell For) The Leader Of The Pack: Bite Worse Than Bark— The Bad Doggies Of Cinema

Doggy demolition is alive and well; mauling mutts have graced our screen for many years. A snow team dog is the first host to the shape-shifting alien invader in John Carpenter's re-imagining of *The Thing*. Various breeds of dogs do massive amounts of damage alongside other beasts of the Earth in William Girdler's eco-horror frenzy *Day of the Animals*. Samuel Fuller made a strong political statement tackling the issue of racism head-on with his controversial *White Dog*, which features a severely misguided mongrel that has been trained to attack African Americans. Genetically altered pooches have gone on murderous rampages in *Man's Best Friend, Rottweiler*, the Wes Craven produced *The Breed* and *Monster Dog,* starring rock 'n' roll horror icon Alice Cooper, which balanced the werewolf tradition with regular canine carnage quite nicely.

Dogs have also proven to be the loyal disciples of evildoer owners. A Rottweiler is the protector of the young anti-Christ in Richard Donner's seminal classic *The Omen*. In Mario Bava's masterpiece *Black Sunday*, horror legend Barbara Steele is well protected by demonic doggies that she keeps by her side at all times. And in the grand tradition of poodles being associated with effete men, Precious is the pampered pooch of psychopathic serial killer Jame Gumb, aka Buffalo Bill (Ted Levine), in *The Silence of the Lambs.* However, many movies featured menacing mongrels as the number one threat, bringing them to the foreground and letting them off the leash to wreak havoc on their masters and other unfortunates. These movies include the wonderful *Dogs, The Pack, Zoltan: Hound of Dracula* and the most notorious of all, *Cujo*!

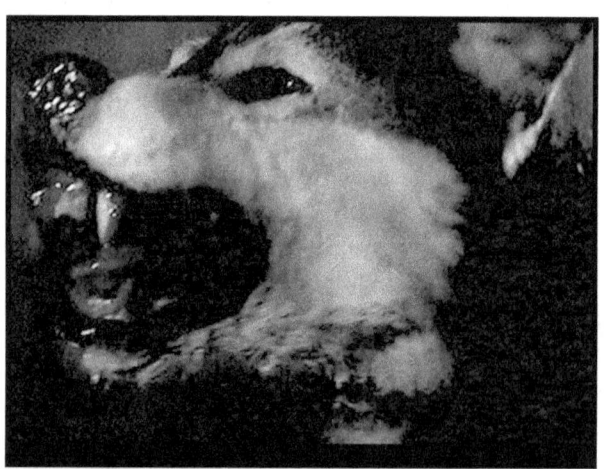

The bloodied shell of a Husky is the first host of John Carpenter's *The Thing.*

Of course, not all dogs of horror are sinister, bloodthirsty, snarling critters; some obediently stand by their owners and prove to be faithful companions. Elvira's (Cassandra Peterson) best buddy Gunk appeared in the horror/comedy *Elvira: Mistress of the Dark*. E-Buzz,

In *Elvira: Mistress of the Dark*, the lovely Elvira (Cassandra Peterson) can always rely on her precious punk rock pooch, Gunk.

the Golden Retriever, loves waffles but is terrified of the ghostly TV people in Tobe Hooper's *Poltergeist*. Nanook, the Siberian Husky, does his best at destroying Peter Pan wannabes with vampiric intentions in *The Lost Boys*. Beauty and Beast, two German Shepherds, protect the victimized family from the cannibalistic mountain folk in *The Hills Have Eyes*. But folks, we are here to talk of the dogs that have done some downright dirty damage in the world of natural horror—so back to your kennels helpful hounds, and let's go for a run with those violently, viciously, crazed canines of cinema.

Sherlock Holmes is a name that seldom comes up in the discussion of horror films. And his creator Sir Arthur Conan Doyle is yet another name that never really pops up. The mystery/crime genre is so clearly separate from the world of ghouls and monsters, so when the two meet it makes for something deliciously different and exciting. Doyle's novel *The Hound of the Baskervilles* has been adapted for screen many times, but it is the original 1939 motion picture that truly gets the heart pumping, making for a good, old-fashioned scary ride. Director Sidney Lanfield's *The Hound of the Baskervilles* stars the classy Basil Rathbone as the intrepid detective, along with horror regulars Lionel Atwill and John Carradine. The movie is a spellbinding Gothic chiller with all the decadence and glamour that one can only get from Hollywood's Golden Age. The film tells the famous story of the Baskerville family and a supposed family curse involving a demonic dog that terrorizes an aristocratic family, hunting each member down. With its sleek style and subtle tone, the film is a great hybrid of the horror and the crime/mystery genre, and the most exciting part of this film involves the flashback sequence featuring the dreaded hound killing the Ralph Forbes character, a very innovative sequence for the time (highly stylized flashbacks were seldom seen during this period of filmmaking).

Even in the 1939 *The Hound of The Baskervilles*, dogs were viewed as the enemy and became the subject of family curses.

Doyle's dynamic story *The Hound of the Baskervilles* was cinematically told over 10 times throughout the years and cemented canine carnage of the celluloid kind for good. Years later, after Sidney Lanfield's 1939 spooky classic, dogs got the horror treatment and became number one enemy of the people in several eco-horror delights made throughout the 1970s and early 1980s.

In 1977 a movie about killer dogs was released through Warner Bros. and did great business, as well as garnering praise from critics. Its original title was *The Long Dark Night* and its equally ambiguous one-sheet features a dirty, disheveled piece of paper that looks as though it was a bloodstained note pleading for help. Such graphics only hinted that the film was actually about rampaging pooches. When the title was changed to *The Pack*, Warner Bros. decided to change the poster to a great design (with far more obvious imagery) involving a simple cut out line drawing of a pack of vicious dogs on the run. The tagline read: "They're not pets anymore!"

The film, set on Seal Island, tells the story of domestic dogs of many breeds who have been abandoned by holidaying visitors. These selfish, neglectful humans have brought their pets with them, and for a number of reasons (namely they can't be bothered to look after them when they return to their hometowns) leave the dogs to fend for themselves in the marshlands of this remote and usually cold, wet island. The dogs have become feral, formed a pack and are violently hungry. Anybody that gets in their way better be prepared for a malicious attack.

A newly formed family are looking forward to coming to the island where, following their decision to move there, they are building a house. This family consists of a marine biologist played by Joe Don Baker, his new wife played by Hope Alexander-Willis and their two young sons (one his, one hers). Another group has decided to move to Seal Island at the same time; this gaggle is made up of an older married couple, their adult sexless son and a young bimbette played by the very sweet Sherry Miles, who seems to be a live-in cook for the older couple (but in fact seems to be more of a set up as a potential mate for their dateless, pathetic man-boy; his father is seen continually agonizing over his son's inability to be aroused by the playfully sexual Sherry Miles).

After a violent curtain raiser where the said pack of dogs brutally attack a horse, an early scene features a vacationing family leaving their whimpering sad-eyed pooch tied to a tree as they pack up from their holiday house

The leader of the wild dogs abandoned by their owners welcomes the latest victim of human negligence in *The Pack*.

and set out to go back home. This poor darling, left out in the cold, manages to break free from the rope and races off to find shelter. The shelter he finds is a dingy, dark, old abandoned shack where he comes across a group of grungy dogs in residence. A terrifying, mangy, golden-haired mongrel seems to be the leader that welcomes the young dog wholeheartedly, making him the newest member of the pack. The only difference here is that this new member is not yet as angry or as feral as the others and, although he stays close to the pack, he lingers in the background when the ferocious group go hunting. Ultimately this dog is the one that can be rehabilitated by the end of the picture.

Some spectacular scenes in this great movie include Hope Alexander-Willis trapped in her car while the dogs attack, clawing their way through the

The angry snarl of the leader of *The Pack*

leather roof and gnawing at the car doors. Other sequences show the hopeless young (sexless) man being chased through the woodlands where he falls off a large cliff to his death; a more graphic and extremely violent scene is where the dogs maul an old blind man and tear him to shreds; another shows the dogs cornering a hapless victim on a pier, and so forth. This film, wonderfully paced, is full of great scenes.

Joe Don Baker does a fine job as the marine biologist trapped with his family and the

In *The Pack*, the dogs are not pets anymore. Here, they have claimed yet another victim on Seal Island.

other unfortunates on Seal Island. His character is a hybrid of sorts, a left over cowboy for a new age. Baker is not only tough and no-nonsense, but also he is sensitive and nurturing; he understands the children, his wife and the ways of nature. His relationship with his own German Shepherd is a touchingly beautiful one, and when his dog is attacked by the aggressive leader of the pack, he instantly ensures his dog is treated and looked after, nursing him back to health straight away. Baker's character is in tune and ultimately sympathizes with the threatening animals (a character trait usually left for the female protagonist of the natural horror film), and through this intuitive sympathy, he can manage to get his family out of dire straits.

The Pack pits man against dog in a very ferocious bloody battle, but it also makes a great point about human relations in comparison to a canine collective. If we look at the relationships inside the Joe Don Baker family—the over protective mother in Hope Alexander-Willis, who fusses over her boy; the stoic, somewhat distant relationship between Baker and his own son; the very real, loving romance between Baker and Willis, which is almost always interrupted throughout the film—we will see they parallel the ways in which the dogs attack. And these parallels are also seen in the relationships between the older couple, their socially awkward son and the bubbly nymphet Sherry Miles. *The Pack* also makes a statement about how these dogs and their dire condition may be reflective of how the human cast members think and act. When the humans become smaller in number and desperate to survive, they suddenly turn as aggressive as the wild dogs.

A nice connection is made between the newest dog in the pack and the Sherry Miles character. Miles races through the woods after she is separated from her

A man and man's best friend reclaim their union by the end of *The Pack*.

frigid friend and finds shelter in the same place the dog found shelter earlier on—that dirty old shack. She hides, covered in blood and mud, and huddles herself into a dark corner. She seeks refuge from the horrors outside, namely being lost in a strange place, but when the dogs find her she is not accepted and they maul her to death. The connection between Miles and the dog from the beginning who seeks a new home is that both are/were in desperate need for compassion, companionship and acceptance. Sherry Miles is genuinely interested in the sexually inept man-boy (she finds it endearing that he'd rather just talk than want to have sex with her), but the man-boy is not interested in her at all and explains that being nice to her (talking to her) was only to please his father. Whereas the dog from the start of the film is in need of some kindness too, but the dog finds it in aggressively, bloodthirsty, canine comrades. Both are in need of something meaningful; there is hope for the dog, but unfortunately, this is not the case for Miles; although the most sympathetic character in the film, she too is killed. Her crime is being human. After all, it's the people who abandoned these angry dogs. Revenge is such a surefire motif for this kind of film and *The Pack* is a perfect example. These dogs have a right to hate people and their unashamed hatred has turned into violent malice.

    The closing scene is a gentle coda to the frenzy that has occupied the last act of the movie. Captured in a freeze-frame for the closing credits is the image of Joe Don Baker and the dog from the beginning, the newest member of the pack. The man extends his arm, reaching out to show compassion, and the dog gradually comes to understand this compassion. Hurt and shunned by mankind, the canine is now ready to re-enter the world of domesticity. It sums up the core theme of the film perfectly—respect the domestic dog and the domestic dog will respect you. Loyalty and unconditional love had been put on the back burner as the year-old relationship man has had with neglected canines on the island is put to the test for the last time. Here a man reaches out to the dog with compassion and that makes all the difference. All round, this is top viewing and a perfect example of the natural horror film that is revenge centric.

A year before *The Pack*, director Burt Brinckerhoff unleashed the aptly titled *Dogs*, a very clever piece boasting an acutely intelligent screenplay with biting charm and an ingenious visual style that complements the storytelling. The film is set in a secluded Californian university and its surrounding rural town. This is the kind of place where suburbia meets vast desert land head-on—large manors overlook dried out barley crops, blue collar tract housing sits across the road from thistle-riddled vacant lots, etc. *Dogs*, much like *The Pack* and other ecological horror films, alienates its characters for the sake of heightening the horror. In a small community town, death and destruction is more intensely personal and worrisome than if the course of action had occurred in the big city. The university itself is smack in the center of nowhere land and is the home to numerous experiments dealing with pheromones and other biological factors that contribute to the misbehavior of mammals, birds and insects, who turn malicious when in the company of fellow mammals, birds and insects of the same species. What is suggested in *Dogs* is that when one animal is in the company of another one of its kind, aggression builds. Not among each other but toward a completely different species entirely. Hence the more the same species gang up, the worse it will become for their chosen target. In this film, of course, the experiments are conducted on dogs, and their prey is humankind.

The gorgeously exploitative title sequence for *Dogs*

The film opens with a canine point-of-view shot. The first visual we're subjected to is that of a grinning human bent over patting the p.o.v. pooch's head. The dog is a Ginger Retriever mix, and it is the pet of the president of said university. The president busily strolls through a dull party in progress loaded with university professors and investors. The dog races out of the large wealthy estate and runs free into the streets where he is greeted by other dogs of various breeds. They form a pack and race down the streets with the golden sun setting in the distance. This opening sequence (the actual title sequence of the movie) sums up everything the audience is about to witness as the foundation of this movie—dogs are going to be packing up and moving forward, influencing each other by forming a bond that will not be easily broken and will soon prove deadly for their human co-stars. In *Dogs*, company alliance and a sense of community are turned into a violent reaction against people. What happens in this film is very similar to what happens in *Jaws*—superiors will turn a blind eye and rebel loners who understand the nature of the beast will be blue in the face trying to explain that something has to be done. David McCallum is the rebel loner here, an English man stuck in a supposedly idyllic American suburb. His displacement and introversion is probably the reason why he has a major drinking problem, which is established very early on and puts a strain on his tumultuous relationship with his girlfriend. He is also completely uninterested in the politics of where the university is going and how it is to be run; McCallum is a doer, not a procrastinator, and even though he is well respected by some of the faculty, he doesn't gel well with the heads of the university's governing body. McCallum is a cowboy, an English cowboy, dirty, stained with the red earth and solemn—his hysteria grows when the situation gets out of hand.

Even cute, fluffy dogs turn vicious and become violently opposed to human oppressors in *Dogs*.

Situation and character are all established very quickly in the film, demonstrating that the script is tightly woven and strong. Some clever dog-related dialogue is interspersed throughout the film, much like John Sayles' treatment of his screenplay for Joe Dante's *The Howling*. A quick example occurs where the vampy Linda Gray shows an interest in David McCallum, and her superior says, "Down Miss Engel," a command usually associated with controlling a disobedient dog. The juxtaposition of the dogs forming a pack and brutally killing people while the townsfolk fall apart is a perfect analogy of how the human condition can quickly worsen and become loose when conflicting attitudes and responses occur within a community. The film subliminally poses a question: If dogs can all agree and have one fixed motive, why can't we?

The theme of student unrest at the winding down of the Vietnam War is explored in *Dogs*, where slacker students and hippies are torn to shreds by angry canines.

Some of the betterscenes are just masterful; a dog show involving children becomes deadly when the pampered pooches turn on their owners and race after them, snarling and biting; one standout scene is where a Doberman sneakily enters the house of Linda Gray and tears her apart in the shower; another wonderful sequence involves the university students being violently mauled by angry dogs. Here the blood and gore goes full throttle, as dogs smash through windows, tear down walls and tear into the flesh of young 20-somethings. The attack at the university campus is a highlight of the movie as angry dogs, hell-bent on ripping into human oppressors, leap through glass doors and terrorize slacker students and hippies. The film consistently lets the audience know that once the dogs pack up and join forces the violence will be aplenty; here the film may also suggest that all mob mentality (be it animal or human) is potentially evil. The pack mentality may be as destructive as it can be positive. Made during a time where student unrest was readily covered by the media, *Dogs* is a great analogy showing the results of youth rebellion and the belief that when one questions authority things may change. *Dogs* is a wonderful film, intelligent and brutal, nicely paced and visually lovely; the Californian sunsets look especially good.

Dogs become subject to great scrutiny in several movies dealing with violent attacks, and the blurry merging of humankind and canine is explored in films like *Mongrel* (1982) and *They Only Kill Their Master* (1972). In *Mongrel*, a young man with bizarre psychological problems cages a vicious dog and starts to kill off fellow tenants at a Texan boarding house. His psychosis confuses people who examine the motives of these bloody deaths. The question remains, which is most guilty—man or dog? This theme is better explored in *They Only Kill Their Masters* where Katherine Ross plays a vet who is sympathetic to dogs and is convinced that Murphy (a Doberman who is supposedly responsible for the death of a woman) is innocent. When joined by police officer James Garner, initially not a fan of dogs at all, Ross has to reconsider her relationship with the animals. Through Garner, Ross has to realize that her thoughts on the canines may be somewhat questionable. However, all this is completely stunted and eventually aborted when it is soon discovered that the actual culprit in this potboiler is a secretly psychotic June Allyson (far from her days in the MGM musicals of Arthur Freed). A strange connection can be made here to the Universal horror picture *She-Wolf of London* (a great werewolf movie without featuring any werewolves) where a young June Lockhart (who we all remember from *Lost in Space* and *Lassie*) thinks she has lycanthropy. In both *They Only Kill Their Masters* and this Universal monster movie the violent actions of woman and beast are made inseparable and painted in a cloudy blur.

Katharine Ross and James Garner take a possible murderer out for a walk in *They Only Kill Their Masters.*

Zoltan: Hound of Dracula, aka *Dracula's Dog* (1978), is a fun if not awkward ride and its number one asset is that it stars one of the most interesting character actors ever to grace the silver screen. Reggie Nalder is a truly unique looking man. With his piercing beady eyes, his gaunt face, his creepy scarification and long thin stature, he made a wonderful career out of playing sinister Nazis, cold blooded villains and Mr. Barlow, the age-old vampire, from the magnificent TV mini-series *Salem's Lot,* based on the classic novel by Stephen King.

Here in *Zoltan: Hound of Dracula*, Nalder plays a Russian innkeeper bitten centuries ago by his vampiric dog Zoltan. As we find out in a flashback, Zoltan heroically tried to save a young peasant woman from being attacked by a bat. The bat was of course secretly Dracula in his most common of disguises and, in an act of anger, Dracula attacked Zoltan, turning the doomed pooch into one of the undead. Fast-forward to the present time—a Russian road crew accidentally opens a subterranean crypt, two coffins emerge and out of them come a well-rested Reggie Nalder and his vampire dog Zoltan!

In the United States, Michael Drake (played by Michael Pataki) is set to go on a vacation with his wife, children and pet dogs. Pataki's Drake is the last ever living descendent of Dracula (I don't know how this can be since he has chil-

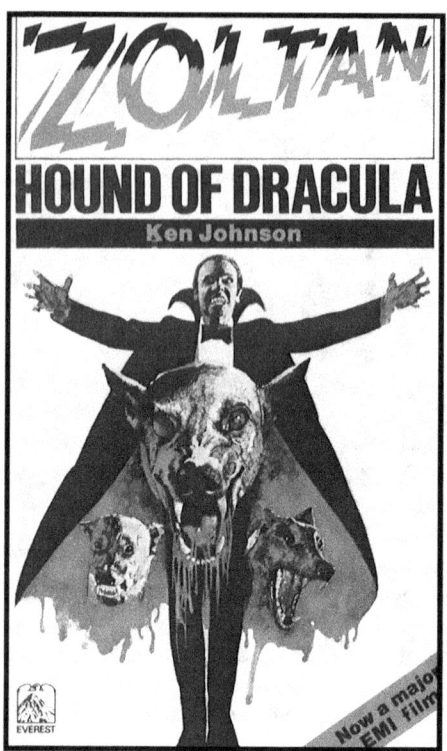

The highly collectible paperback novelization of *Zoltan: Hound of Dracula*

dren!) and Nalder and pooch have their dead hearts set on him. The vampires make their way to America, hunt them down and turn Pataki's pet dogs into vampiric menaces. This is a silly romp that has no real tension or anything truly interesting to say, but to have vampire dogs as the film's number one threat is good enough for this writer!

An equally lighthearted evil dog tale is the made-for-TV movie *Devil Dog: Hound of Hell* (1978), directed by the very talented and very influential Curtis Harrington. Harrington had directed many great horror movies including the wonderful hag pictures *Whoever Slew Auntie Roo?* and *What's The Matter With Helen?*—both starring the fabulous Shelley Winters. Another great psychopathic old lady movie mixed with a touch of the possession-themed film, *Ruby,* was another Harrington standout, with a post-*Carrie* Piper Laurie performance that shines. He also single handedly saved the print for James Whale's Gothic masterpiece *The Old Dark House* and was an advisor on the brilliant biopic about the openly gay James Whale, *Gods and Monsters.*

Devil Dog: Hound of Hell is a great movie. As much as Harrington had many issues concerning its production, the film holds up as satisfying supernatural fun. Harrington, however, was very vocal in later years about not having had a good experience at all making this satanic-themed doggy dozy. He claimed that the producer Louie Morheim interfered in the production and made far too many demands. The look of the satanic pooch, the amount of violence allowed for a made-for-TV movie, the casting choices and so forth caused Harrington major stress. The issue of the movie being made for TV was a challenge for Harrington who had thoughts about making the film a far more interesting and scarier ride had it been financed for a cinematic release. Morheim, however, wanted to hang on to the purse strings and kept explaining to Harrington that films that were made for television at the time were just as good as movies released to theaters (even films that were getting nods from the Academy). He told the disgruntled Harrington that a film like *Kramer vs. Kramer* really could have been a TV movie, as it was low-key, low budget and dealt with social issues (parental separation and single fatherhood) that were key ingredients in films made for television movie fare. The only difference is that it had two in vogue A-listers (Dustin Hoffman and Meryl Streep) in the starring roles, which upped the budget. Harrington decided to continue to make his demonic dog film but decided to omit any social commentary or relevance that were so important to televised feature films. The result was *Devil Dog: Hound of Hell*, a straightforward natural horror film set in the mold of cinema demonica.

Martine Beswick (who made quite a splash in the Hammer-produced horror gender-bender *Dr. Jekyll and Sister Hyde*) appears for two scenes in the beginning of the film as the head of a satanic cult. She purchases a dog, a healthy female that already had previous litters. This dog

The Dutch VHS cover art for *Devil Dog: Hound of Hell*

will prove to become the mother of demonic puppies. Beswick's performance is exactly what you'd expect it to be—brash, loud and over the top—and it's all fantastic! She co-stars alongside R.G. Armstrong, who was doing lots of bit roles during this period (including horror fare such as *The Children of the Corn* and the aforementioned *The Pack*) and he chews up the scenery in his one standout scene where he persuades the young children to adopt a demonic pup. These two character actors really add to the film's dimensions and make it a far more enjoyable experience for the uber-talented Harrington.

But of all the devilish dogs of cinema, none has been more notorious than that slobbering, salivating, sadistic, unstoppable force that is *Cujo* (1983). Born from the mind of prolific horror novelist Stephen King, this rabid beast on a rampage has proved that his bite is far worse than his bark. Lewis Teague's filmic adaptation of *Cujo* is a sublime example of how simplicity and good old-fashioned storytelling can also be intelligent and complex as well. Not only is *Cujo* a beautifully executed scary ride, it is also a clever character study and an acute commentary of a family in turmoil.

The film really differentiates between two major forces of horror—the real and the imagined. The real fears are tangible and easily relatable—infidelity, financial insecurity and the dark—whereas the imagined fears such as becoming invisible, losing loved ones and monsters dwelling in closets are secret fears that are seldom discussed. But Stephen King forces us to deal with these fears. His characters are beautifully painted and fully realized people with real problems.

The adultress (Dee Wallace) left out in the metamorphic storm desperately tries to save her child Tad (Danny Pintauro) from the monster lurking outside their car in *Cujo*.

Masterfully, King puts all these fears (however major or trivial) into perspective when a ferocious in-your-face threat—that of a rabid 200 hundred pound St. Bernard ready to tear you apart—is introduced. As soon as the malicious dog appears foaming at the mouth and barking angrily at the beat up Pinto, the film's protagonist Donna Trenton (beautifully played by horror regular Dee Wallace) puts aside all anxieties and the inner turmoil brought on by her extra-marital affair—her emotional sadness, personal isolation and desperation—in order to save her dehydrated child (another great performance from child actor Danny Pintauro) from being killed by the rabid dog or dying from the oppressive heat.

The novel and subsequent film is one of those rare Stephen King works that doesn't involve supernatural horror (*Misery* is another one that comes to mind) and yet the film and book are somehow told as a fable, parable or even fairytale. The novel opens with, "Once upon a time …" and this really does set the tone for the film. It is a contemporary American Gothic tale set in a very real situation. The realism of the drama gives *Cujo* its teeth, but ultimately, just under the surface, a deep mythic quality exists that pits flawed maiden against lumbering beast.

Opening with a picturesque prologue that features a playful, healthy St. Bernard chasing a rabbit through the Maine countryside, this Disney-esque curtain raiser soon turns ugly as this unfortunate dog comes into contact with rabid bats. He is bitten and in turn contracts the deadly neurological disease. From this opening sequence, a major theme of the film is summed up—what seems to be a happy, peaceful picture ultimately has underlying horror, impending doom and consequential sadness. Later we continually hear the adage, "Nope. Nothing wrong here!" which vocally summarizes this same theme.

The film follows the lives of two families, the white collar Trentons and the working class Cambers. Vic Trenton (Daniel Hugh Kelly) is an advertising executive facing financial worry, while his wife Donna (Dee Wallace) is a bored, lonely and desperate woman who, in fear of growing old and useless, has started an affair with local furniture stripper Steve Kemp (Christopher Stone). Stone's Kemp is also a friend of Kelly's Vic and his character not only strips the Trenton's furniture but also strips Wallace's Donna of her humanity. The couple also has a young son Tad (Danny Pintauro) who imagines monsters in his closet (an imagined fear that will suddenly materialize in the third act). The film doesn't agonizingly scrutinize these characters' personal anxieties be they real or imagined (financial security, growing alone and ordinary, or snarling invisible beasts in one's closet); instead, it clearly states them as fact and we are left with domestic unrest and personal conflict. Juxtaposed to the Trenton's lives are the Cambers, who consist of Joe (Ed Lauter), a drunken abusive mechanic; his downtrodden wife Charity (Kaiulani Lee) and their son Brett (Bill Jacoby), whose best friend is the 200-pound St. Bernard Cujo.

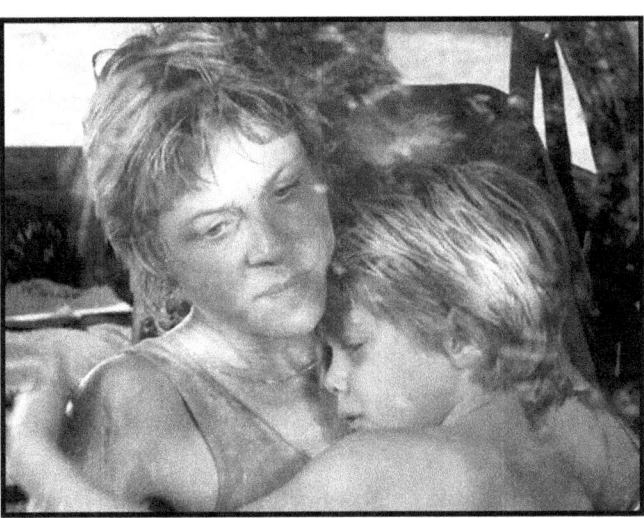

Dee Wallace tries to convince Danny Pintauro that no real monsters exist in *Cujo*.

Stephen King is a master at exploring the dark side of American institutions such as the intricacies of the family, and this becomes the focal point of the story of *Cujo*. King excels at cleverly turning normalcy into pure malevolence. The high school prom becomes a nightmarish hell on earth in *Carrie*, America's love affair with the automobile proves deadly in *Christine*, sinister secrecy in small-town America is examined in *Salem's Lot* and here the family pet (in this case the beloved dog) becomes a monstrous manifestation of the breakdown of domestic bliss.

As Cujo's condition worsens (his rabies taking hold of him physically and psychologically, causing the dog to descend into a vortex of sadistic horrors), the Trenton family suffers and a shift occurs in the Camber household. Daniel Hugh Kelly finds out about Dee Wallace's affair and Kaiulani Lee decides to pack up and leave Ed Lauter. Soon enough, with the help of smooth writing which sets

Bill Jacoby as Brett Camber introduces his dog Cujo to little Tad in *Cujo*.

up circumstances that move our tale forward ever so effortlessly, we reach an intense climactic showdown between a mother trapped inside her broken down Pinto, trying to protect her severely dehydrated son, while an angry, rabid canine foaming at the mouth waits outside. Here the classic archetypal story of the adulterous woman being left out in the storm is played out in a viciously violent, blood-soaked finale. Dee Wallace truly delivers what simply is a *tour de force* role written for a woman, and this film magnificently showcases her great talents as an actress.

Cujo has many transcendent moments, both in the realm of action-packed horror and in subliminal metaphoric subtleties—Dee Wallace roaring with rage after she shatters the glass window of her car trying desperately to get her son to safety; the murderous, crazed, bloodied dog frantically pushing at the busted up Pinto, tearing off the door handles and thrusting his mighty snout through a slight gap in the window; Wallace and Daniel Hugh Kelly's tortured marriage as seen through the innocent eyes of an angelic Danny Pintauro; the satisfying death of Ed Lauter as he realizes his world has crumbled to dust when faced with a menacing rabid dog; and the last moment of Cujo's sanity as he tilts his head toward his friend Brett (Bill Jacoby) and disappears into the foreboding Maine fog. This film is just perfect all round.

Editing, scoring, cinematography and performances (superlative, especially by the always amazing Dee Wallace, the raw energy of little Danny Pintauro and the phenomenal talents of the many St. Bernards used to create the one scary Cujo) give the writing of this tight horror gem the much-deserved lift it needs. This is a Stephen King adaptation at its best—faithful to the novel while still necessarily trimming the fat to ensure the delivery of a solid fable. Ultimately, *Cujo* is filmmaking and storytelling at its best and the rabid St. Bernard must reign as king (pun intended) of monster dogs of film land!

Something the horror film does wonderfully is force us to question the nature of what we consider being safe, normal and/or comfortable. For example, the genteelness and innocuous warmth of the elderly is turned grotesque and monstrous in such films as *Whatever Happened to Baby Jane?*, *Rosemary's Baby* and *The Nanny*. And children who are supposed to be the epitome of innocence and purity suddenly turn sinister in *The Bad Seed*, *The Innocents* and *The Village of the Damned*. In more contemporary times old women and children are still deadly psychopaths in films like *Misery*, *Flowers in the Attic*, *The Brood*, *Bloody Birthday* and *The Children of the Corn*. Dogs are very similar. They have always been seen as domestic Earth angels who love their human friends, but the horror film shifts that perception.

Dogs make for wonderful, scary movie monsters with their snarling snouts, their swift fast movements and ability to hunt and kill victims. But what makes them even more terrifying is the fact that they have been associated with humankind as loyal companions for centuries; dutiful, faithful and loving animals who would do anything for their master. However, in the natural horror film, this sweet connection between dog and human is flipped and the result is a baring of teeth of angst. In these films, dogs become a menace (be it on their own accord or by circumstance) and a formidable foe to the human race.

No rabid St. Bernard appears on the one-sheet poster for *Cujo*. Instead the blood-smeared white picket fence becomes the perfect subliminal image of the breakdown of the American family.

There goes an old saying that "if you lie down with dogs you'll soon get fleas," and this may be true, but can fleas really be all that bad? Sure they may make you scratch like crazy and interrupt good solid sleep, but are they truly that evil? Well, come the next chapter we shall take to the microscope and have an in depth look at all things creepy crawly, as bugs of all kind are scrutinized and analyzed—worms, roaches, flies and bees.

Insectellectual:
The Discreet Charm of
the Creepy Crawly

A shift in horror occurred during the 1950s. Long gone were the days of Gothic nether regions where foreboding castles overlooked peasant villages and a monstrous abomination of nature preyed on the likes of fair maidens. Instead, the fears now were more close to home. With building anxieties of Communist infiltration in the United States growing out of control and influencing not only domesticity but also huge institutions such as Hollywood itself, Cold War fears became an integral influence on monster movie making and storytelling. During this time, the Atomic Age ushered in a new cinematic threat, that of the giant bug invasion (more of this in the next chapter)!

A product of the Atomic Age, Bert I. Gordon's *The Beginning of the End* featured a plague of giant grasshoppers attacking tiny human beings.

Massive insects became an unnatural, scientifically engineered threat to the moral majority. Giant ants and spiders were made the focal point in films subliminally dealing with Cold War fears and paranoia bought on by Russian warfare and socialist leanings (this can be seen in such classic horror and science fiction outings as *Them!*, *Beginning of the End* and *Tarantula*). However, as popular as these mammoth insects were during this period in America's history, come the 1970s, the idea of insects being the featured movie monster was still happening but in a less grandiose way. Come the Age of Aquarius, the creepy crawlies that once could tear down an entire house in one mighty blow were now naturally small in size. They became miniscule, malevolent menaces that now attacked slowly, more methodically and in secret. Bugs in their natural state got under your skin and ate you alive. These insects were forerunners to a new wave of motion picture horror, casually borrowing from the body horror subgenre where one's own flesh becomes our number one enemy and also taking some advice from films dealing with apocalyptic catastrophe, where the end of the world is near. Such insect cinema also embraced a brand new kind of subgenre that was making huge business at the box-office—that of the disaster picture.

Spiders, ants, wasps, bees, bugs and worms all feature in gloriously gory and viscerally exciting movies of the 1970s and 1980s. The dynamics of man pitted against insect is something that requires masterful handling and interesting plot devices. Tangible gross-out concepts like worms squirming into your skin, wriggling around your face and tearing away at your flesh as seen in Jeff Lieberman's amazing *Squirm* make for great body horror disgust, but as *Squirm* so successfully accomplishes, more has to be established and said to make for great genre movie fare.

In William Friedkin's *Bug*, ex-marine Michael Shannon convinces lonely bartender Ashley Judd that insects are rsponsible for every social and governmental conspiracy.

In films like the William Castle-produced *Bug* (1975) and William Friedkin's *Bug* (2006) (both extremely different movies), cockroaches and aphids (imagined or real) come to represent New Age fears and problems. In Castle's film *Bug*, directed by Jeannot Szwarc, Bradford Dillman, Patty McCormack and company are terrorized by bugs that come to represent societal disillusionment and the breakdown of once stoic institutions like the education system and Christian-centric community. Whereas in Friedkin's film *Bug*, bugs come to provide a detailed paranoid account of government mishandlings, corruption within America's involvement in the Gulf War and a terrifying connection to be made between psychology and how the world appears from the mind of an unhinged ex-marine (played by Michael Shannon).

These tiny insects of cinema initially came around to scare audiences in the early '70s, about the same time shady government conspiracies surfaced such as the Watergate scandal. Insects also made their cinematic debut at the same time the drug culture came out of the closet and became a topic of discussion on TV talk shows and in the news. Bugs became a cinematic symbol for all the leaks in once well-contained information, as well as collective ruthlessness as seen in societal dystopia and inter-personal distrust. Bugs also reared their alien-like heads embodying an analogy for youth drug experimentation and eventual dependence. And decades after the 1970s, as proven in William Friedkin's adaptation of the

William Shatner under attack by deadly tarantulas in *Kingdom of the Spiders*

play *Bug* by Tracy Letts, insects of all kinds are still horrifying extensions of a world perpetually controlled by the calculative sinister.

Of all the insects in the world, the spider has been noted as the most terrifying. With their swift movement, their furry long legs and their power to evoke creeping terror (even their cobwebs are so iconic in many horror movies), spiders feature in great ecologically themed horror movies that truly embrace an ideology of a society in deep turmoil. Two very different takes on a world turned upside down by spiders are the stunningly sophisticated *Kingdom of the Spiders* (1977), starring the always-wonderful William Shatner, and the Steven Spielberg produced horror comedy hybrid, *Arachnophobia* (1990).

Kingdom of the Spiders is a marvel to behold and on its initial release was praised by critics as being one of the best nature-runs-amok movies released at the time. This was noted mainly because these critics were extremely impressed that they got to see these rather large and genuinely horrifying tarantulas attack the cast in breathtakingly beautiful bright light. Many cinephiles (including fans of this subgenre), when discussing movies that concern animals killing the human population, would complain that a lot of the films of the time depicted their violent animal attack sequences in shadowy darkness or under cover of the night—something that on many occasions is an obvious indicator that the picture lacked the elements necessary to create effective special effects sequences. A perfect example of this not only happens once but throughout the entire movie *Claws* (a killer bear movie), whereas, with *Kingdom of the Spiders*, the movie monsters (mighty, bird-eating tarantulas) are in clear sight, jumping onto the human cast and crawling all over their cadavers!

Set in the vast glory of the Arizona ranges, *Kingdom of the Spiders* explores the disastrous effects of man's treatment of the natural world. Multiple nests of deadly tarantulas start popping up in farming communities and soon spread throughout the entire county. These spiders attack aggressively, killing off many residents. We learn that a new insecticide has killed off the spiders' natural food supply, so they have started to improvise, turning man and beast alike into hearty meals!

The opening shows off the glorious Arizona canyons as a country crooner moans out a strange, unnecessary song to accompany the credits (unnecessary since the musical score for the film is so good, evoking the majesty of the movie Western). Instantly the movie lets us know what we're in for—a warts'n'all horror show with killer spiders! The first spider attack (on a prize-winning calf owned by a struggling farming couple) is quick, well shot and completely engaging. The mesmerizing, spider p.o.v. articulates sheer terror as the poor, defenseless calf is brought down by one single bite. The farmers (incidentally they are black farmers in a very white community, playing on the recurring theme of displacement that occurs throughout the movie) call upon local veterinarian William Shatner to look at their calf. Shatner is at a loss here, and even though he is a vet dealing with ranch animals and related illnesses to which they are prone, he cannot determine what has killed this calf.

Into the picture comes Tiffany Bolling, an absolute delight. She is an entomologist who understands spiders and the effects of their venom. Her connection to the creepy crawlies (that we the audience are so hardwired to fear) is summed up in one great scene where this ethereal nymph prepares to shower to wash away any

Tiffany Bolling, connected to the natural world, explains all things arachnid to Shatner in *Kingdom of the Spiders*.

displacement she is experiencing from being an educated, sophisticated woman called upon to help an isolated, small Southwestern town. A large tarantula finds its way into her motel room and her instant reaction is both calm and calming to the arachnid. She connects straight away with it, her understanding condensed into this serene scene, but this connection is then put to the test as the film progresses. Her affinity with these insects is put under great strain when she (along with Shatner) discovers that these once shy creatures are about to aggressively attack and kill everyone in town!

Bolling spends some time trying to convince Shatner that it is spiders to blame for the death of the calf, and her dislocation in this small rural town is heightened by her initial isolative diagnosis as well as her antagonistic relationship with the town's councilmen. These councilmen are, of course, responsible for the insecticide that has caused the spiders to behave in such an aggressive manner. These town leaders (much like the officials on Amity Island in *Jaws*) are obsessed with their county fair going on uninterrupted. The fair is the main source of income for business owners and a little incident involving spiders cannot be allowed to affect commerce (once again, this can be very much likened to the 4th of July celebrations as seen in *Jaws*).

Shatner is a leftover cowboy (played to perfection) haunted by his brother's death. He explains to Tiffany Bolling's character that his brother was killed in Vietnam on the second day he was there. It comes across that Shatner and his brother had a loving, close relationship and somehow we get the feeling that Shatner's character is a casualty of war too—if not physically then emotionally. Shatner's own battle—his personal war—is struggling with alcoholism and the feelings of his brother's widow (Marcy Lafferty) who, in a state of desperation and loneliness, falls madly in love with him. However, Shatner just cannot commit himself to her; he has an undying loyalty to his dead brother that ultimately causes him to keep his distance. Marcy Lafferty's loneliness and Tiffany Bolling's professional isolation (trying to convince the councilmen of the county that their insecticide is doing more harm than good) is splendidly juxtaposed in *Kingdom of the Spiders*. In the middle of these two women's feelings, emotional strengths and turmoil is a man trying to do what he can to help fix the situation at hand. The spiders in this film are more than an aggressive army infesting a town, banding together to eat; they are a tangible reminder of desperation as seen in characters whose lives have become completely empty, devoid of any satisfying connection becoming emotionally displaced.

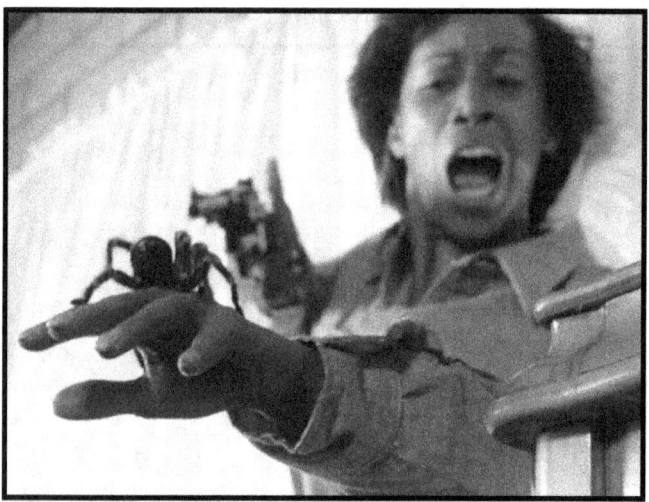

Altovise Davis prepares to blast off her own hand rather than be bitten by a creepy tarantula in *Kingdom of the Spiders*.

Ultimately, this film is a treasure. The spider attack sequences are beyond brilliant. The black farmer drives along the highway, his eyes fixed on the road ahead of him. Slowly, creeping upon his shoulder, appears a large furry tarantula that is soon joined by many others, paralyzing him with fear and sending his car reeling off the road. The aforementioned farmer's wife, cornered in her bedroom by a mass of deadly spiders, has a firearm and shoots at them to no avail. One suddenly hops onto her hand, and without even thinking, she shoots at the spider blasting several of her fingers away in a bloody mess. Come the exciting climax, Shatner's little niece is out on her swing surrounded by spiders. Marcy Lafferty sees this and screams in terror, racing out to rescue her little girl. She manages to save the child but succumbs to the wrath of the deadly spiders. The film says bucketloads about human pollution and the influence it has on the environment. These spiders have turned aggressive and attacked en masse simply because a man made insecticide has caused them to do so. An entire town is destroyed, and spiders that have been denied their natural food supply kill hundreds of people.

Townsfolk cloaked by tarantula webbing in *Kingdom of the Spiders* demonstrate how easily monstrous insects can devour sleepy backwater towns and all inhabitants.

Much like George A. Romero's zombie opus *Night of the Living Dead* and more on the same par in the eco-horror world as *The Birds*, *Kingdom of the Spiders* ends with the surviving community members, including Shatner and Bolling, barricading themselves inside a cabin and locking out the deadly spiders. It's a maddening frenzy staged beautifully. It plays wonderfully against the entire town falling victim to the thousands upon thousands of spiders that have encased civilians in webbing, bled them dry and bitten them dozens of times. The havoc that happens in the small town—children are dropping like flies, the elderly are completely overrun by spiders, a water tank crushes a policeman—is chaotic and tense; director John "Bud" Cardos delivers these sequences flawlessly. The final shot shows the entire town enveloped by thick masses of spider webs, a virtual living tomb. In this movie the spiders have won.

The Steven Spielberg-produced *Arachnophobia* is a fun ride; an affectionate nod to 1950s B movie nostalgia (and it borrows a lot from *The Kingdom of the Spiders*) with biting humor, nicely constructed characterizations and well-staged scares. The film opens in South America where spider specialist Julian Sands ven-

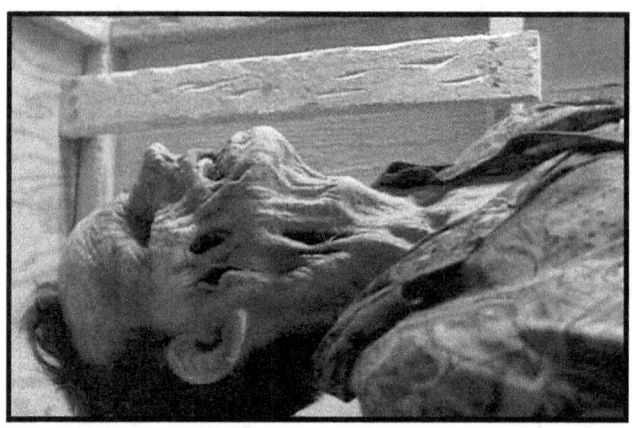

What the newly discovered South American spider can do to a person in a short time is demonstrated in *Arachnophobia*.

tures out on an expedition to study a brand new species of spider that has remained hidden for millions of years. Sands travels with a photographer who is bitten by one of these deadly spiders and instantly dies. The photographer's body is flown back to his home in small-town U.S.A. and, along with his quickly decaying corpse (the spider that killed him also drained him of his blood), the sinister arachnid comes along for the ride.

Into the Norman Rockwell-esque world of sleepy town Canaima we go and here Spielberg gives us a sweet portrait of a saintly little hamlet uninterrupted by major atrocities. Spielberg has so often given us his glorious romanticism of American suburbia as seen in *E.T.: The Extra-Terrestrial* and *Close Encounters of the Third Kind*, and here Canaima is a lot like the town in the Spielberg-produced *Gremlins* where everybody knows one another very well. Even though the characters are cordial to each other, the town is plagued with secrecy and unsaid feelings boil just below the surface that make this postcard-perfect slice of Americana not all that it is cracked up to be.

Jeff Daniels plays a young doctor who has left San Francisco with wife Harley Jane Kozak and two children to start up practice in Canaima, and from the beginning he is faced with a number of problems, problems that can only arise from the insular tight knit conundrums associated with small towns. The town's former doctor is an ancient old grouch who, just as Daniels arrives, decides that he doesn't want to retire from his profession in fear that he may lose a zest for life. This therefore renders Daniels without any patients until a kindly, widowed, ex-school educator shows Daniels sympathy and decides to be his one patient, even though she is perfectly healthy. What she does offer however is a feeling of usefulness for Daniels and she gives him an insight into the old doctor's slight malpractice and misdiagnosis of some of the citizens of Canaima,

Arachnophobia makes a solid note about small-town America. The picturesque and quaint serenity of a halcyon utopia is hiding something sinister, something creeping up on the unsuspecting and slowly killing them off. The film also scrutinizes small-town dilemmas and the interpersonal connection each community member has with one another, making up an interesting and complex web of people.

The cast serves the movie beautifully, but the film belongs to Jeff Daniels who shines. He is given such a meaty role as the frustrated but dedicated doctor who is stuck in the middle of a rut, the rut being a town that won't listen to him. The spiders are also a delight to watch and are truly scary, while the tone and direction by Frank Marshall is interesting and focused. Playing a small part as a bug exterminator, John Goodman really embraces the film's comedy and does a great job. Yes, *Arachnophobia* is most definitely a clear hybrid of two genres—horror and comedy—and it plays with both beautifully. A great moment that showcases the dry wit of the screenplay (while also serving the plot) is where Daniels and his wife (the husky-voiced Harley Jane Kozak) decide to christen their new house by making love on their first night, rather than continuing with their unpacking. The film dissolves from the human coupling to the South American spider (now living in Canaima and specifically in Daniels' barn) and a local spider locked together in a romantic embrace. This of course will beget the thousands of deadly mongrel spiders that will soon infest the sleepy hamlet.

Arachnophobia **shows the graceful elegance of an arachnid.**

Kozak's character is a photographer. Because she is someone in the arts, she is instinctively attracted to the beauty of the natural world. Unlike her husband, she has no fear of spiders and initially finds the web they have built as something beautiful. In the beginning of the movie she insists that her son doesn't kill the spider that has found its way into their house (soon to be the South American spider's mate), instead she suggests they give it a home in their barn. Once again the movie's leading woman is an animal sympathizer and this connects her to the natural world, and the specialist (who is the male Julian Sands) is a cold, compassionless professional who, although he points out that spiders are an extremely important part of the natural world (after all, they eat hundreds of bugs that otherwise would cause massive distress for the human population), remains distant and cynical to the situation at hand. He has no real sympathy for the people who are dropping like flies.

Jeff Daniels suffers from acute you know what in this intense sequence from *Arachnophobia*.

The spider attacks are lovely and subtle to begin with. An elderly woman reaches to turn her light shade off and, as she pulls the string, a spider leaps onto her hand; a young footballer grabs hold of his protective helmet just after a spider has crawled inside; and as the movie hits the middle of the second act, the spiders infest the town and everybody must fight for his or her life. The spiders are ultimately killing off a dying town, cleaning up a place that is scared of change. By the end of the picture, Jeff Daniels and family leave the place and decide to move back to San Francisco. The final scene shows husband and wife resting up over a bottle of wine as an earthquake hits—better an earthquake than deadly spiders (or the unfriendliness of supposedly friendly small-town America).

Spiders once again feature in more contemporary movies as the number one threat to humankind as seen in *Spiders* (2000), *Arachnid* (2001) and *Webs* (2003), where entire communities are at the mercy of deadly eight-legged terrors, but these web-spinning menaces aren't the only creepy crawly to cause the human race great distress.

Bees are the monsters of many ecological horror films and it's easy to see why. They travel in swarms; they are naturally aggressive if provoked, especially during spring; they have a leader (their queen) that makes for a good plot device; their buzzing is a marvel of sound effects for filmmakers exploiting the dangers of these pollinating nuisances; and, of course, they have a stinger that can do some major damage.

Disaster movie maverick Irwin Allen (*The Poseidon Adventure*, *The Towering Inferno*) gave the world an extremely exhilarating roller coaster of a ride in his 1978 film *The Swarm,* where millions of deadly African killer bees have migrated to North America. With its impressive cast including Michael Caine, Olivia de Havilland, Richard Widmark, Fred MacMurray, Lee Grant, Henry Fonda, Richard Chamberlain, Patty Duke Astin, Ben Johnson, Slim Pickens and genre favorites Bradford Dillman and Katherine Ross in the leads, *The Swarm* is a solid example of how well an ensemble gels so beautifully under wonderful direction, vibrant cinematography, a great script, genuinely frightening sequences involving massive swarms of killer bees and a marvelous score written by award-winning composer Jerry Goldsmith, who used French horns to replicate the sound of buzzing bees.

A young boy watches his parents stung to death in *The Swarm*.

Although the film did badly at the box-office and critics were extremely harsh, calling the film one of the worst disaster movies of the decade, Allen's film is a testament that 1970s audiences were obsessed with a diversity in character types (the gruff sheriff, the hapless romantic matron, the smart little boy, et al.) being terrorized by something beyond their control. In *The Poseidon Adventure* the fear of drowning shook audiences, and in *The Towering Inferno* the fear of being burned alive or falling to one's death scared them out of their wits. Here in *The Swarm*, African killer bees (extremely aggressive bees) invade Texas with great ferocity, which made fans of the eco-horror genre scream with delight!

Irwin Allen of course was the man responsible for some of TV's most wonderful series, such as *Voyage to the Bottom of the Sea, Lost In Space* and *The Land of the Giants*, all of which at one point in their runs featured killer insects, fish and other creatures, so it makes sense that the man was a fan of the ecological disaster subgenre and has lots of fun here with *The Swarm*.

The entire ensemble gives the movie everything they've got, their hearts firmly planted on their sleeves. Fred MacMurray (in his final film performance) and Olivia de Havilland (who made a career out of making a number of horror films since *Hush...Hush Sweet Charlotte*) head the cast of seasoned professionals from the Golden Age of cinema, and the beautifully and warm Katherine Ross and rugged Bradford Dillman come to represent the new Hollywood. The look and feel of the movie is something to behold; beautifully shot slow motion majestically captures the killer bee

In *The Swarm* even children fall victim to the deadly bees' fatal stings. No one is safe.

Olivia De Havilland watches hopelessly as her students are killed by sinister bees in *The Swarm*.

attacks with great style and vivid colors, especially during the sequence involving the Texan town's annual flower festival (why this movie was only nominated for Best Costume Design by the Academy is beyond me).

The film employs a dual narrative. It jumps from the military base to the small Texan town that is under the threat of African killer bees. A grim Henry Fonda and a stubborn Richard Widmark head the military base, with Michael Caine (who sadly claimed this to be the least favorite film he ever worked on) playing an English entomologist who is stoic and headstrong. He constantly gets worked up when he tries to convince the U.S. army that the threat of African killer bees is nothing to trivialize. The town is much like the small town in *Arachnophobia*, clean and polite, a postcard haven where only decent people live. But as soon as the bees swarm overhead, real human nature surfaces and rears its ugly head. The chaotic mass attack of bees sets the entire town into a foaming frenzy and the deaths are plentiful. A wonderfully scarily game of guessing who will survive (in other words, which Hollywood A-lister will survive) becomes the film's major buzz!

An interesting note to be made about *The Swarm* is that the film has a little message in the end credits saying that the American honeybee is our "friend" and that this film did not intend on giving all bees a bad rap. This clearly indicates society's changing attitudes towards once feared animals and insects that of course benefit the human populace. A few years later *Roar* (at the request of animal activist and actress Tippi Hedren) featured a laundry list at the end of the final film credits of what we the public can do in order to help our animal friends.

Bees are once again the main instigators of destruction in two gloriously garish movies that deserve noteworthy attention. The first stars one of Hollywood's most famous silent movie stars (made even more famous near her career's end starring in a movie that examined the nightmarish reality of the shift in Hollywood from silent film to talkies), and the other is a movie written by the man who gave us *Psycho* and directed by one of the greatest cinematographers in Hollywood history—*The Killer Bees* (1974) and *The Deadly Bees* (1967).

Both these movies make a connection between swarms of menacing bees and a character either coldly driven as seen in *The Killer Bees* or hard done by as seen in *The Deadly Bees*.

The Killer Bees is a made-for-TV horror film directed by the talented Curtis Harrington, who had a lot more fun making this film than he did four years later with his next venture into the natural horror film subgenre, *Devil Dog: Hound of Hell*. The ABC Network seemed to keep out of his hair during production of this killer bee gem and let him employ his chosen writers, who were the married team of Joyce and John Corrington. The script is great and reads like a play, one involving very few characters and keeping the tension just at bay. Signed on to play the lead was Hollywood legend Gloria Swanson, who got along famously with Curtis Harrington, and the pair remained great friends for years to come.

Gloria Swanson will of course forever be remembered as Norma Desmond, that decrepit, monstrous leftover from the silent era lost in the world of the "new" cinema in Billy Wilder's *Sunset Boulevard*. (a film that beautifully married film noir with horror movie archetypes). But her character here in *The Killer Bees* is not far removed from the grandiose theatrics of the aging screen star Norma Desmond in Wilder's film. Here she plays an intensely driven mad woman named Madame Von Bohlen, who owns a picturesque vineyard and runs a rather successful wine business. Not only does she control her business and her family (except for the outsider, played by Kate Jackson, who has come to disrupt familial affairs and cause change), but also this glamorous, grand dame controls a swarm of killer bees that have multiple hives in her vineyard. Swanson has a psychic control over these bees and will use them if Kate Jackson questions the way in which the Von Bohlen family goes about its business. This connection made between sexually aggressive predatory women, swarming buzzing bees and angry wasps pops up in wonderful B picture outings such as the very saucy and sexy *Invasion of the Bee Girls* and the monster-on-the-rampage classic *The Wasp Woman*.

The Deadly Bees was an earlier film written by *Psycho* author Robert Bloch. Bloch had originally intended horror legends Christopher Lee and Boris Karloff to star in the film, but their schedules clashed, prompting the

studio to enlist a secondary writer to develop his own ideas and inject them into Bloch's script, which caused great conflict for the production team. The movie has a lot of heart and some great sequences, but it does suffer from continuity errors, bad plotting and uninspired characterizations. The film tells the story of a maniacal beekeeper living on Seagull Island who has trained a swarm of bees to kill a fellow scientist and the rest of the small island town. Suzanna Leigh stars as an exhausted rock 'n' roll singer, badly in need of a holiday, who goes to rest on Seagull Island, only to be the sole survivor of these nasty bee attacks. She also uncovers the truth regarding the demented scientist and ultimately outwits him and his frightening bees. The direction by former ace cinematographer Freddie Francis is not among his best.

Of course, when movie lovers discuss killer bugs, more than often they think of the giant bug movies of the 1950s like the iconic *Them!* The giant-sized subgenre was successfully resurrected in the '70s with thrilling movies like Bert I. Gordon's *The Empire of the Ants*, but many movies appeared that depicted insects in their natural state (or more accurately, their natural size) and this made for stylish and sophisticated character study pictures—movies that dissected family, societal values and the world as we know it.

Ants and insects that are completely social and community minded feature in the sci-fi horror gem *Phase IV* (1974) and the seldom seen made-for-TV classic, *Ants* (1977). Parallels made between human society and ant society is the focal point of *Phase IV* (the only movie directed by movie poster artist and opening movie credits designer Saul Bass) where ants, due to unknown cosmic phases, have developed higher intelligence that pits them against humankind in a battle to see who can override the other.

Meanwhile, ants cause much panic in the delightful *Ants* (aka, *It Happened At Lakewood Manor*), starring horror movie regular Lynda Day George who stars alongside Suzanne Sommers and an aging Myrna Loy, far removed from her glamorous horror movie days as Boris Karloff's lascivious daughter in *The Mask of Fu Manchu*. In this movie, ants ingest a powerful insecticide and develop a taste for human flesh, causing chaos at a world-renowned hotel.

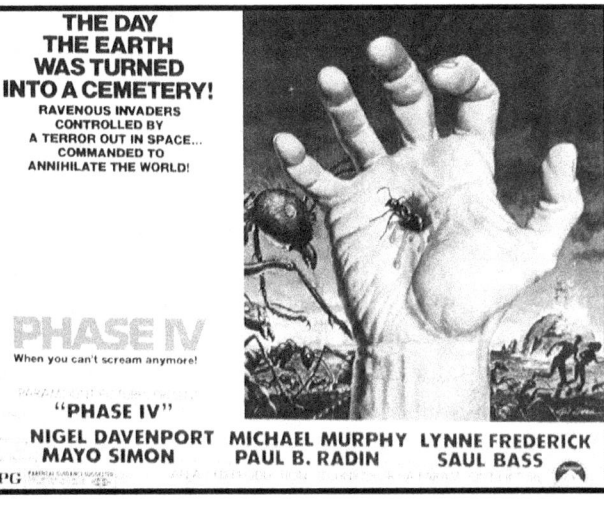

George A. Romero's *Creepshow*, written by the talented Stephen King, is a great anthology movie crafted in the vein of the E.C. horror comics from the 1950s. In the last story "They're Creeping Up On You," E.G. Marshall plays a xenophobic, obsessive-compulsive recluse (similar to Howard Hughes) whose absolute disdain and fear of cockroaches reflect his hatred for ethnic people and germs. His horrible nature is something so despicable that it is almost laughable, and Marshall's performance is so marvelously over-the-top that it works splendidly. When his fear of these roaches hits a height that becomes something completely out of his control, Marshall's breakdown is final and the sight of his limp body becoming a nest for thousands of bloodthirsty roaches is just pure gore-fuelled brilliance. Make-up master Tom Savini creates an extremely violent image of a man completely consumed by his own fear in a blood-soaked finale that is simply breathtakingly beautiful. The wrangler hired for the beetles and roaches used in *Creepshow* is the same person that worked on *The Silence of the Lambs*, where beetles, cocoons and but-

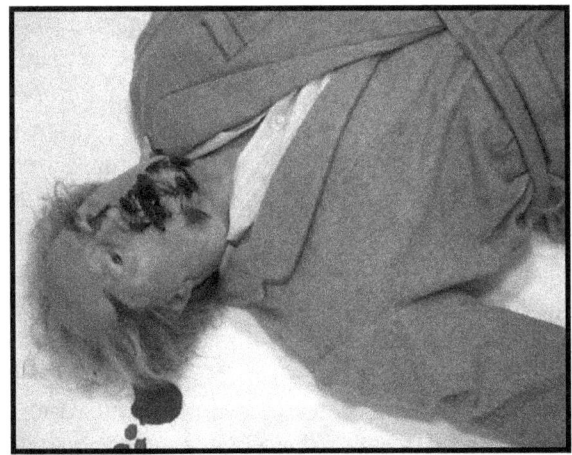

E.G. Marshall, consumed by his own xenophobia, as he appears in one of the great anthology movies, *Creepshow*.

terflies were masterfully used as a symbol of change and transition in a movie dealing with a transgendered character. But years before Jonathan Demme's controversial yet ultimately successful Oscar-winning slasher film rejuvenated the horror genre for the 1990s, two movies that defined the 1970s ecological horror movie fad adopted the insect as primary movie monster and became great unpretentious cult hits.

Bug (1975) and *Squirm* (1976) are perfect movies. Their stories are strong, the characters are interesting and both movies have a gorgeous, sumptuous visual style. Everything about these two movies defines the full essence of what quintessential 1970s ecological fright fare should be.

Enigmatic and legendary film producer William Castle, the maestro of showmanship who employed novel gimmicks in his movies throughout the 1950s and 1960s, took hold of writer Thomas Page's book *The Hephaestus Plague* and turned it into a fine film simply called *Bug,* which also became his final film. Castle made a career out of giving audiences fun-filled scares with amazingly thrilling horror movies such as *The Tingler,* starring Vincent Price, and *Strait-Jacket,* starring Joan Crawford.

Bug demonstrates the frightening intelligence of the creepy crawly.

He then made the big time with the extremely popular box-office smash *Rosemary's Baby,* which he wanted to initially direct. However a European auteur by the name of Roman Polanski was handed the reigns of director. Three movies after Polanski's satanic-themed chiller, Castle enlisted French director Jeannot Szwarc and writer Thomas Page to give life to *Bug.* The movie starred eco-horror go-to guy Bradford Dillman (who faced *Piranha* and *The Swarm*), accomplished theatre actress Joanna Miles, handsomely young Richard Gilliland and the extremely talented Patty McCormack, star of the classic suspense thriller *The Bad Seed.*

Bug begins with an earthquake eruption that causes a swarm of large roach-like beetles to emerge from the ground. However, these bugs are not like any ordinary creepy crawly. Instead these critters can start fires by rubbing their cerci together! Jeannot Szware has a masterful control of visual style. Much like his delightful *Jaws 2* that came out a few years later, Szware manages to capture captivating visual compositions that feed the audience information on more than one level. A perfect example of this is when a bug is positioned in the foreground of the frame and looks as though it is watching its handiwork—a burning truck that is completely engulfed in scorching flames. This beautiful *mise en scene* is reminiscent of the shot in Hitchcock's *The Birds* where the sinister gulls hover over a burning Bodega Bay.

Once a bad seed, the electric Patty McCormack succumbs to the fiery wrath of the hephaestus plague in *Bug*.

Aside from the outstanding visual style and genuine creepiness of these fire-starting beetles, *Bug* says something profound about science in a world still trying to understand religious conviction and the education system as an institution that remains distant and cold to those who want to learn. Besides this social commentary, *Bug* scrutinizes one man's descent into madness, driven by personal repression.

The eerily quiet opening of *Bug* involves Joanna Miles leaving husband Bradford Dillman to go to church. Dillman mocks Miles by telling her that she better hurry and get into church or she'll miss the "show." Even though Miles smiles at his snide comment, this cements Dillman's disinterest (and possible disbelief) in religion and the world of Christianity. He is a man of science and his wife is a woman clutching at the importance of religious faith and the strengths of fundamentalism. The scene in the church is a clever critique on the role Christianity plays in America during the Age of Aquarius. The reverend's sermon is all about the notion that God is dead (something that comes up in the William Castle-produced *Rosemary's Baby*) which (thanks to an issue of *Time* magazine, which brought the subject to the whole world's attention) was an important factor influencing the youth movement of the late '60s and early '70s. The reverend refers to the collective mindset of America's youth as "the questions rising from the hairy heads of our children," suggesting both long-haired hippie ideology as well as fluffy, airy-minded kids who have rejected their Christian upbringing in favor of more fulfilling spiritual or hedonistic enlightenment. Both the yelling reverend and the angry earthquake interrupt the quietness of the opening sequence, and as the church is completely demolished, the congregation is in turmoil—a clear statement is being made about the diminishing, crumbling mess of religious sentiment, yet at the same time, a concrete statement is made speaking volumes on the power of God and/or nature.

Nature is an important interest for Bradford Dillman's character as he is a biology teacher. He is compassionate and actively interested in the mechanics of life and has a great respect and understanding for animals and insects. He has a genuine bond with them (a rarity in this subgenre where usually a woman is more in tune with the natural world).

This connection to nature is all summarized in an early scene where Dillman is teaching his students about animal communication and telepathy, but his class is interrupted by the entrance of a squirrel that, after some coaxing, feels comfortable enough to climb aboard Dillman's extended arm.

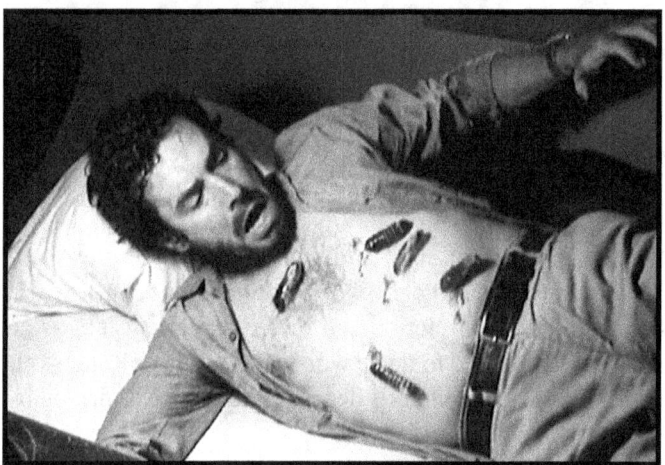

Bradford Dillman becomes dinner for the number one menace in *Bug*.

Although animals and insects are Dillman's specialty, *Bug* is quietly obsessed with the idea of communication between humans, something that is slowly eroding. Communication breakdowns run rampant in this film and the bugs attack usually at a moment during or just after one character tries to reach another. Examples include a young teenage girl on the telephone and a bug invades her ear, causing great bloody stress; after Joanna Miles talks to Patty McCormack on the phone (once again the telephone being a symbol of technologically-driven communication), Miles is burnt alive by terrifying bugs; and later in the picture, Patty McCormack goes to see an aloof Bradford Dillman (driven mad by his wife's death and now completely obsessed with figuring out what makes these evil bugs tick) to talk to him and give him his late wife's Bible, but she is attacked by aggressive bugs and killed.

Using the metaphor of the education system in ruins, screenwriter Thomas Page keeps Bradford Dillman's character detached from the rest of the world because of his work. He is obsessed with biological studies (a fact made clear throughout the movie by Joanna Miles, who keeps insisting he not work so hard) and it is his work that ultimately serves as his downfall. Being a man of science restricts his ability to learn about being human, and inadvertently, Dillman actually helps the bugs reign supreme.

Much like in *Kingdom of the Spiders*, the beetles in *Bug* reign supreme, killing off the major cast and ultimately developing wings (making the beetles look like demonic insects who have emerged straight from hell, setting everything and everyone on fire).

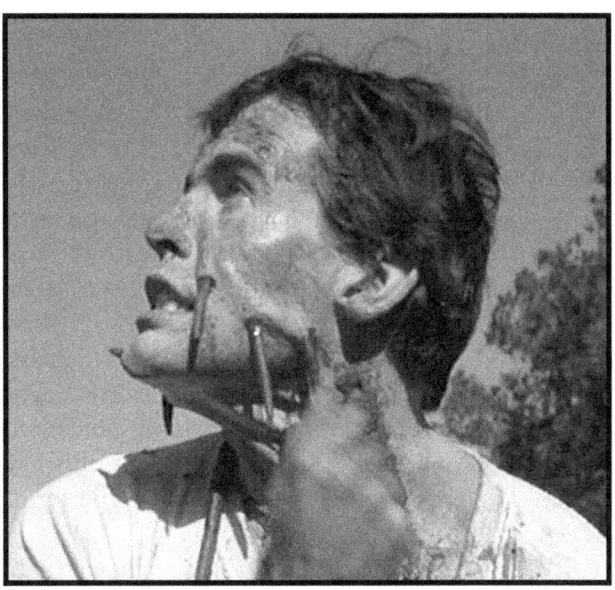

Nicknamed "Wormface" by horror aficionados, R.A. Dow's face becomes a home for bloodthirsty worms in *Squirm*, featuring make-up by Rick Baker.

The drug culture of the '70s also makes an impact on *Bug*, as the increasingly neurotic paranoia of Bradford Dillman becomes something derivative of America's youth culture's interest in hallucinogens like LSD. He finds the bugs feasting on meat (they only eat as a collective) and then wakes up to find them leeching off him, gnawing away at his own flesh—a paranoid vision of the effects of mind-altering drugs. He also notices that the bugs have started to spell out words, his name, letters of the alphabet and the sentence "We live," which pushes Dillman over the edge. His mental state now a shattered fragmentation of what once was controlled and comfortably conditioned.

The eco-horror cult hit *Squirm* keeps this theme of drug culture (particularly LSD and other hallucinogens) alive, but only subliminally. *Squirm* director, the talented and passionate Jeff Lieberman, has often stated that the idea of worms slithering inside one's face (which happens to one of the characters in his film) was born from a bad acid trip. His movie *Blue Sunshine* became a clear representation of America's mainstreaming of the hippie subculture and the subculture's obsession with drugs, but *Squirm* is more of an interpersonal character drama (featuring bloodthirsty killer worms) rather than a socially conscious movie like *Alligator* or *Bug*.

Lovers from two different worlds—the backwater hick Geri (Patricia Pearcy) and pseudo-intellectual Jewish New Yorker Mick (Don Scardino)—are brought together in *Squirm*.

Squirm is an absolute treat. Not only is the film a sleepy, strange oddity that oozes with slimy spectacle, but it also is a well-written and poignant study of a community haunted by repressed sexuality, domestic abuse, unrequited love, urban pretensions and small-town secrecy.

Jeff Lieberman's superb film is set in a small Georgian fictional town called Fly Creek, inhabited by Southern yokels who go about their day without any fuss. The opening sequence showcases a massive electrical storm hitting this sleepy backwater village, which eventually causes the earth-dwelling worms to turn into carnivorous monsters. Don Scardino, the out-of-town hero of the piece, gradually understands this scientific event. Scardino plays a New Yorker who arrives in Fly Creek with one thing on his mind—local girl Geri (Patricia Pearcy), in a performance straight out of a Tennessee Williams play.

Pearcy met Scardino back in New York at an antiques store and the two hit it off. Pearcy invited him to visit her and from the get-go Jewish New Yorker Scardino runs into trouble. The local sheriff despises him and doesn't trust him, a cantankerous worm farmer finds him obnoxious and, most of all, Pearcy's mother Jean Sullivan's hired hand (played by a sweaty, oafish R.A. Dow) is mighty pissed off at Scardino because Dow also has his eyes set on Pearcy.

R.A. Dow is amazing as Roger the lustful hick, and he rounds off the love triangle very well. Incidentally, Martin Sheen, Kim Basinger and Sylvester Stallone were all considered to play the three leads (Scardino, Pearcy and Dow) before their fame skyrocketed at about the same time that *Squirm* was made.

Much like Hitchcock's *The Birds*, *Squirm* follows the outsider who influences the course of nature. Don Scardino is a somewhat clumsy but bright pseudo intellectual from the big city that is forced to adapt to a world that is foreign to his sensibilities. Not only must he face aggressive sheriffs, dim-witted yokels and a jealous cretin who wants his girl, but he must also lead the way in defense against the bloodthirsty worms that have oozed their way into town.

Squirm shares as many narrative hooks (as well as distinct visual trappings) as *The Birds*, most notably in the characterization of a mother desperate to hold on to something that inevitably she will lose and the outsider being an influential force of nature. *Squirm* has its lead (a working class college graduate) face adversity in a clean, direct manner, whereas Hitchcock's heroine in Tippi Hedren (a rich and yet rebellious society girl) uses deceit and white lies to get to her man and make her mark in the Rod Taylor household, one dominated by an oppressive Jessica Tandy. Both movies rely on a quiet, repressed hysteria interrupted by the leads and mothers trying to protect and completely control their young (and not so young).

Jean Sullivan's performance as the mother of Patrician Pearcy (the object of Don Scardino's affections) is an overblown, theatrical, heavy-handed delight to watch. She delivers her breathy lines as if she were Blanche Dubois. And the actress is not the only thing Williams-esque here. The film has a spacey, not-quite-there vibe about it, and it really does capture and explore Southern repression (both societal and personal) where that repression seems to exist in full form just under the surface. A beautiful metaphoric connection here is made between human secrecy and the electric, bloodthirsty worms—both are hiding just under the surface, and when they decide to reveal themselves, all hell breaks loose. People get hurt, fights break out and worms devour those who aren't willing to move forward.

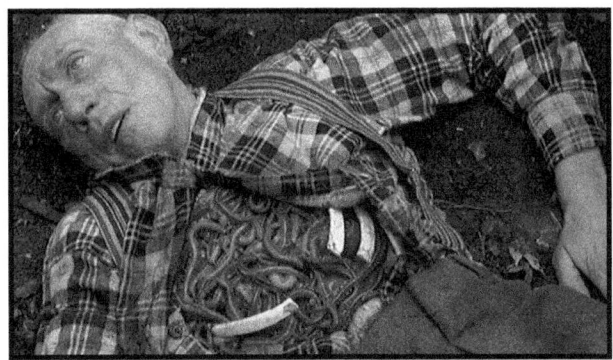

At the end of the day we are all food for the worms, a sentiment made clear in *Squirm*.

In *Squirm*, no one says what they really mean, and what they don't say speaks volumes; this is a movie for theater-lovers, a grimy character study as healthily, sickly delightful as *Suddenly, Last Summer* and *Baby Doll*. *Squirm* is a true American Gothic much like those Williams plays, and after watching it audiences will feel like washing off the slime.

The movie is a marvel of special effects as make-up genius Rick Baker (*An American Werewolf in London*, *Videodrome* and many, many more) gets to show off some of his early work here in *Squirm*. He vividly creates R.A. Dow's revolting worm-infested face so gloriously gory that it is an image that will stay with audiences long after they have seen the film. On the film's release fans everywhere called the R.A. Dow character "Wormface," which is a clear indi-

Yuppiedom is deconstructed and there's gore-a-plenty in *Slugs*.

cation that Baker's make-up effects left a lasting memory. The masses of squirming, repulsive worms oozing about the town is captivatingly beautiful as well as being repugnant. Jean Sullivan's yarn of wool gradually turns into a pile of worms that devour her (here it is a clear presentation of a woman not budging, not willing to adapt to change, who gets consumed), worms invade a bar and devour the only teens that live in Fly Creek (the youth are to be eaten whole, their dead-end lives wasted) and R. A. Dow becoming a human-worm hybrid of sorts, wriggling along and chasing the leads through the dark and grimy house. It is a sight to behold.

Once again, similar to *Kingdom of the Spiders* and *Arachnophobia*, *Squirm* is all about small towns eating themselves into non-existence, into oblivion, and Lieberman's film does this so beautifully that it can be compared to something completely different in style and content. If we compare Stephen King's *Salem's Lot* where doomed, small-town locals become soulless, bloodthirsty vampires one by one, *Squirm* does the same thing but in a totally distinct style. Much like Hitchcock's *The Birds* and the aforementioned *Salem's Lot*, Lieberman gives us a portrait of a town (interrupted by both the presence of outsider Don Scardino, who has come to rescue a local girl from being swallowed up by small-town boredom, and man-eating worms that have come to surface and devour all that cross their path) slowly swallowing itself whole.

Movies like *They Nest, Tarantulas: The Deadly Cargo, Insecticidal, The Bone Snatcher, The Hive, Damnation Alley, Black Swarm* and the gory *Slugs* (which makes very witty commentary on the burgeoning yuppie movement and its insincere connection to what should be positive trends like vegetarianism and veganism) revel in the angry insect-on-the-rampage mold, and thanks to production companies like the Syfy Channel, these movies will continue to entertain audiences for years to come. Of course, these movies do somehow belong to an era fixated on the complexities of community after significant political or social unrest (in *Bug* an earthquake stands in for the failures of once stoic institutions; in *Squirm* an electrical storm wakes up a town that is slowly eating itself), but in these more recent times, insects, for some strange reason, have taken a step back as the metaphoric monster for a period so dependent on technological advances. After all, bugs would make an obvious representation of the hidden gremlin in a society so reliant/obsessed with innovation in science.

Films like *Squirm* really rely on character interplay and social change; the worm turns as do the attitudes and dynamics associated with the human cast members occupying the space in Lieberman's smart film. Worms once again surface as a formidable foe to man in the extremely graphic yet intelligent *Slither,* where alien life forms take on the appearance of more earthbound worms feasting upon human flesh.

A town, already eating itself alive, faces the onslaught of killer worms in Jeff Lieberman's *Squirm.*

In his DVD commentary for *Squirm*, director Jeff Lieberman explains that at the end of the day we all become food for the worms. In our deep dark graves we are fodder for the earthworms to feast upon and this is a great condensation of what the insect-inspired ecological terror movie does. It makes us understand the true importance of such tiny creatures and forces us to comprehend the fact that A) there are far more of them in number than us (this is the way it has been for millions of years and will be for millions to come); B) that they aren't as helpless as we think they would be; and C) that under great stress these buzzing, flying, squirming, creeping, crawling bugs can become one of humankind's most deadly enemies.

Of course, as we briefly discussed earlier in this chapter, if the bugs were larger in size (genetically altered by science or leftover residents from prehistory), then we would be intensely frightened. Something mammoth in size would obviously be threatening as opposed to a miniscule creature hidden within the deep recesses of our backyards. We would have to flee for shelter from these oversized monstrosities, cowering from them and desperately taking cover! So let us take a look at those gigantic beasts most foul in the next chapter as we hit the halfway mark in our deep examination of all this ecologically scary natural horror.

Children of Kong, Spawn of Godzilla: The Super-Sized Animals of Hollywoodland

As discussed in the previous chapter, the 1950s saw a great shift in horror movies. Mammoth menaces on the rampage gradually replaced Gothic romanticism, a clear sign of studios exploiting America's growing anxiety over Communism and Russian influence. Cold War fears in the Atomic Age became a focal point in the development of American sci-fi and horror pictures like *Them!*, *Beginning of the End* and *Tarantula*. Making the monster a massive giant was a clear indication that writers and directors were drawing a comparison to the great power of something as terrifying as the Red Threat! However, science was just as scary as political and social unrest. Creatures that were usually tiny in scale (ants, spiders etc) and easily *controlled* by the human population became gigantic and truly frightening monstrous aberrations of nature—made this way through the advent of scientific breakthroughs (either man made and maneuvered intentionally or accidentally, or caused by a natural event).

One of cinema's most famous couplings, Ann Darrow (Fay Wray) and the mighty Kong, in the magnificent *King Kong* (1933).

A blast of cataclysmic proportions ushered in this new era of monster movies and the threat of Armageddon. The devastating forces that science unleashed, such as the power of the atomic bomb (which made people realize that entire countries can be destroyed instantly) and the possibility of being wiped out by science, fueled the fear in audiences who screamed at the sight of giant man-eating bugs and lizards!

Atomically mutated beasts owned center stage during this period. Obsessive and somewhat maniacal scientists who dealt with genetics or radiation created a world of monsters in their labs. Man-made monsters took a detour from the

Frankenstein mythology that dealt heavily with religion, birth and death. Instead, here in the 1950s, Hollywood monster movies were preoccupied with the dangers of science and the newfound abilities of man playing around with genetic experimentation that could go horribly wrong. Nuclear radiation became part of the subtext of these movies and proved to be more powerful than electricity, the power that helped in the creation of Frankenstein's monsters from the past.

The lovesick Kong, in the supposedly civilized world, climbs to the top of the Empire State Building as Fay Wray looks on, from *King Kong*.

Audiences during the 1950s consisted primarily of the baby boomer children of the working and middle classes, and they accepted the use of radiation as a plot device in the creation of these gigantic creatures. Teenagers were usually the primary target of such movies (independent American International Pictures dished them out like a factory line would dish out its latest nifty product) and this made sense both commercially and artistically. Teenagers were the ones going to see these movies, as young girls and boys flocked to watch them on dates and gangs of kids rushed out to see the latest big movie monster epic. Also, serving the narrative, the films spoke to these Atomic Age monsters swallowing up the young and killing off a new America (a theme that would be explored more graphically come the 1980s with the rise of the slasher film).

However, way before the 1950s, at the dawn of cinema, dinosaurs were already deemed movie stars as an obsession with these prehistoric monsters surfaced in the early days of celluloid innovation. For example, movies such as the silent *The Lost World* (1925) features the stunning work of stop-motion animator Willis O'Brien, who would go on to work on one of the greatest movies ever made, *King Kong*.

Directed by Ernest B. Schoedsack and Merian C. Cooper and written by James Ashmore Creelman and Ruth Rose, the majesty and glamour of the classic monster movie *King Kong* influenced generations of movie enthusiasts, remaining to this day one of cinema's most treasured films. And for audiences everywhere, those spellbound by its beauty in 1933 and for those who later discovered and embraced this mammoth monkey epic, *King Kong* stands strong as a staple for the nature-gone-amok subgenre, even though the animal in question is of unnatural size and, much like his prehistoric brethren, a left over of a

The Dino De Laurentiis production of *King Kong* (1976) featured make-up artist Rick Baker as the romantic simian.

bygone era and also a creature of myth and legend. But this does not mean this much-loved movie shall be excluded from a book dealing with animal monstrosities, for *King Kong* is the ultimate in monstrous monkeys! It also proved so popular that it spawned sequels—*Son of Kong* (1933 also), which featured a misunderstood white gorilla, and the much more benign *Mighty Joe Young* (1949), where the ape actually helps save children from a burning orphanage. It also inspired remakes; Dino De Laurentiis' 1976 remake of *King Kong* starred Jessica Lange in a breathy, sultry performance that cemented her as one of the '70s and '80s most important actresses (the film copped a lot of criticism, but it has loads of heart and a distinct style all its own); and in 2005, New Zealand director Peter Jackson brought back the great celluloid simian in his retelling of the beauty and the beast story, which for this writer's liking was far too long and ruined by an overkill of bland computer generated imagery. *King Kong vs.. Godzilla*, *King Kong Escapes* and *King Kong Lives* also hit the big screen, all of them charming in their own special way. Many movies dealing with a giant gorilla on the rampage existed, including the Korean film *A.P.E.*, which featured an amazing fight sequence between a great white shark and the featured giant monkey. And the Disney re-visioning of *Mighty Joe Young* (1998), although obsessed with making a very loud environmental message, does have some great moments involving a wonderful giant gorilla that is state of the art in animatronics.

The sexuality of these giant apes (most notably in the original 1933 outing) always seemed to influence the course of action of these movies—Kong's curious and instant attraction to the human fair maiden who, although tiny in scale, represented unashamed sensuality and beauty. Epitomized by the lovely Fay Wray who starred as the street urchin come wannabe starlet Anne Darrow in the 1933 classic, these girls and their gorillas became a staple in the monkey movie mold. The relationship between modern day human being and untamed wild beast from a time long, long ago is explored in later B picture greats like *Trog*, starring the sensational Joan Crawford, and *Konga*, featuring the wonderfully hammy Michael Gough.

Of course, movies set in prehistoric times also proved just as successful, resulting in cult movie status for many of them. One that comes to mind is the popular British Hammer production, *One Million Years B.C.* (1967). It starred the smart and beautiful Raquel Welch as Loana, "the fair one," who survives the clutches of a Pterodactyl and the angry wrath of an Allosaurus. The equally smart and beautiful Martine Beswick also appears as Nupondi, "the wild one," a fellow cavewoman who deals with the day-to-day struggles co-existing with menacing dinosaurs.

The lovely Raquel Welch is about to be fed to hungry pterodactyls in *One Million Years B.C.*

The marvelous special effects wizardry for this Raquel Welch vehicle was handled by auteur Ray Harryhausen, whose credits include *Mysterious Island* (featuring giant crabs and a large honeybee, among other creatures); *20 Million Miles To Earth* (featuring the Ymir, a monstrous creature from Venus) and *The Valley of Gwangi* (marrying the Western and the fantasy film by transporting dinosaurs to the Wild West). He also created the humongous octopus for *It Came From Beneath The Sea*, which really set the standard for giant aquatic menaces that terrorized entire cities. In *It Came From Beneath The Sea*, the octopus was made massive from radioactivity and this monstrosity destroys the Golden Gate Bridge in San Francisco. Such imagery suggests that the natural world, when placed under great man-made stress (that of radiation), will destroy whatever brings man together as symbolized by the famous bridge's destruction. The actual foundations of humanity will be brought down by the angry wrath of an animal done wrong.

Ray Harryhausen avoided the cheap but endearing advent of real lizards covered in make-up and costumed (immortalized in the original *One Million B.C.*, 1940) and as seen in the *Flash Gordon* serials produced from 1936 to 1940, where the actors were superimposed with the real-life decorated lizards, making these reptiles look humungous. Lizards of course were

A monster from Aztec legend in *Q: The Winged Serpent*

a popular choice of monstrous menace during the '40s and '50s, most likely because of their likeness to prehistoric creatures that captured human attention forever. The remake of *The Lost World* (1960) is infamous for featuring lizards as dinosaurs, as is the campy *Valley of the Dragons* (1961) that used reptile footage from the original *One Million B.C.*

Larry Cohen's *Q: The Winged Serpent* (1982) is a clever gore-soaked modern dinosaur movie with some memorable moments. It appeared at a time when fantasy movies about leftover dinosaurs were coming back into vogue.

Cohen makes interesting and socially aware horror films, as well as character driven dramas where horrific situations happen to the average person. His commentary on health food fads and consumerism was embodied in *The Stuff*; his take on parental fears in an age of social dilemmas, such as urban crime and drug abuse, was the basis of his film *It's Alive;* and his take on the notion of religious fanaticism being just as evil as government dictatorship was explored in the creepy *God Told Me To*. *Q: The Winged Serpent* is no exception. It is a film that belongs to both the subgenres of giant monster movie and cultist film (it is a movie about cults; here the Aztec cults that partake in human skinning and sacrifice in order to appease the lingering, winged dinosaur). This large-winged serpent has come to New York City terrorizing people in skyscrapers

Symbolizing Japan's fear of uncontrolled nuclear weaponry and the horrors of radiation sickness, Godzilla (Gojira) attempts to destroy Japan in *Godzilla* (U.S. release 1956).

and killing topless sun worshippers, construction workers and anybody that comes too close to the heights this serpent sweeps through. The film heavily draws from two more subgenres that really balance out this fine story. It adopts the heist/urban crime genre with Michael Moriarty playing a getaway driver who becomes an accidental and unlikely hero, and David Carradine as a no-nonsense cop, caught in the middle of the bloody carnage the serpent relishes, who has to rely on criminally inclined Moriarty.

Godzilla and his diminutive friend try defending themselves from an array of fellow Japanese menaces in *Destroy All Monsters* (1968)

It also takes from the religious-themed film with some wonderful moments of biblical destruction littered throughout the film. One of the best sequences includes a moment where blood literally falls from the sky as local New Yorkers look up and notice crimson raining down upon them (a reign of blood to end all unnatural phenomenon that is both religious in tone and brutal in execution).

Of course, these giant reptilians also surfaced in Japan for many years and made a huge impact on Western cinematic monster movie mayhem! These Japanese monsters were most clearly defined by Tokyo's greatest threat (and ultimate treasure) *Godzilla* (aka *Gojira*, 1954). This behemoth of a lizard has appeared in a number of wonderful movies and has gone on to become (much like his hairier cousin Kong) a staple in popular culture. *Godzilla* says volumes concerning Japanese widespread fear of uncontrolled nuclear weaponry and the horrors of radiation sickness. This overwhelming anxiety grew into very tangible fears involving the contamination of food and water supplies, playing upon the devastating results for a country so reliant on its fishing trade. The giant lizard's rampage across Tokyo is most definitely linked to the horrific nuclear attacks as seen in Hiroshima and Nagasaki leading to the end of World War II. With Japan being the victim of nuclear devastation and radiation poisoning, resulting in mass hysteria caused by such atrocities, Japanese monster movies almost always featured a threat in the guise of an animal of gargantuan proportions such as the graceful giant moth in *Mothra*, the oafish turtle in *Gamera* and the bird-like screeching *Rodan*. A generation after the release of *King Kong*, Toho and other Japanese studios ushered in the mutated horrors of atomic radiation for a new generation of giant monster lovers.

While the Japanese screamed with delight at their noisy but beautiful monsters, American drive-in audiences shrieked at the likes of *The Killer Shrews* and the *Attack of the Giant Leeches,* where oversized furry shrews ran rampant and gnawed on the body parts of civilians and big bloodsuckers lunged at poor unfortunate souls taking a midnight dip in a dark murky lagoon! But it was the insects (in a state of humungous proportions) that ruled America's cinematic big movie monster explosion. Films such as *Them!* brought to life mutated giant ants that caused chaotic distress for all those that got in the way. *Them!* was the initiator in Cold War fears as dished out by the horror/sci-fi genre and a film that embodies anxieties and hidden paranoiac attitudes toward the innovation in science. However, the film is not without its more existential leanings. The beautifully written piece of prose about biblical prophecies coming to life as spoken by one of the cast members at the end of *Them!* manages to marry the essence of a film driven by scientific explanation to a sense of religious/spiritual reasoning—something that was the usual case in the early Universal monster movies.

The Giant Spider Invasion magnifies the innate fear humans have of creepy crawlies—arachnophobia is a popular human fear and to have a mammoth-sized furry fiend on the rampage is something simply scary on a larger scale. The giant spider motif is not something that strictly belongs to a drive-in either, for the actual fear of such a thing pops up again in the witty, modern homage like *Eight Legged Freaks* and becomes the cumulative shared fear of the young child outcasts in the terrifying Stephen King adaptation of *It*. But two of the best big spider movies to grace the silver screen would have to be *Earth vs. The Spider* (directed by the iconic Bert I. Gordon) and the magnificent *Tarantula*!

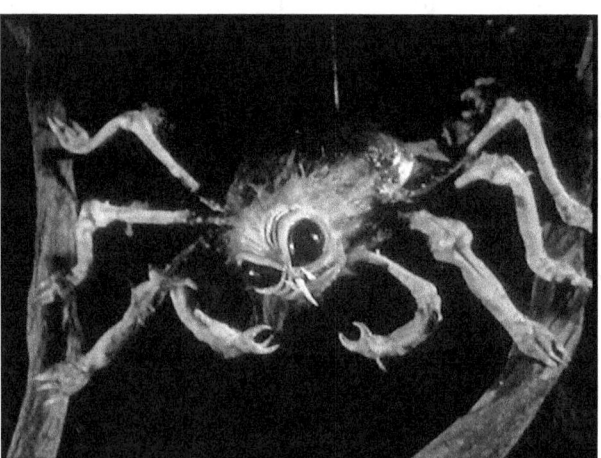

One of the violently aggressive spiders from *Horrors of Spider Island*

Most definitely one of the best of the giant spider films came from a studio that thrived mainly because of monster movies—the foundations of this motion picture company were built from the likes of *Frankenstein* and *Dracula*. Universal Pictures during the 1940s was an interesting place and at a tumultuous time of change. *The Wolf Man* and the many sequels adding to the legacy of the *Frankenstein* and *Dracula* movies (such as *Son of Dracula* and *House of Frankenstein*) raked in the cash and firmly cemented the studio as one of the major players alongside the likes of MGM and Warner Bros., but there was a sense that come the 1950s the movie monster of the classical period would start to backpeddle in favor of more contemporary threats. But this didn't deter the studio from adapting and taking on the current '50s fad by the horns.

The era of the giant monster movement had arrived and *Tarantula* (1955) was the result of this new movement. Jack Arnold, who directed Universal's number one 1950s hit *Creature from the Black Lagoon* (the only movie outside of the '30s and '40s to be regarded as one belonging to the classic monster films of the Golden Age), was at the reigns of this special treasure. The movie not only features a monstrously large Mexican red-rump tarantula, but it also features some stunning make-up execution (namely the effects of the gigantism caused by the disease acromegaly), a glorious musical score even more fully realized than the music from *Creature from the Black Lagoon*, some beautiful desert settings all shot in and around a lovely area called Dead Man's Point in the Californian Lucerne Valley (as seen in many great Westerns) and a spectacular cast headed by Leo G. Carroll, John Agar and Mara Corday.

Leo G. Carroll is the professor with good intentions in *Tarantula*.

The film tells the story of a well-meaning professor played by the forever-affected Leo G. Carroll, who is trying to deal with the world's food shortage problem by experimenting with nutrients. He has isolated a specific nutrient that can sustain an animal's survival without the need to consume food. Tackling the issue of food shortage is a common theme in movies featuring monstrous mutations (seen even in such late entries as *The Food of the Gods* from the 1970s and *Alligator* from the 1980s), but the thing that differentiates *Tarantula* from other big-animal-on-the-rampage movies is that this one features a professor who is genuinely kind hearted and not driven mad by his discoveries.

We feel for Leo G. Carroll; he is as sympathetic as Lon Chaney, Jr. is in Universal's earlier monster movie classic *Man-Made Monster* and *The Wolf Man*, and just like Chaney's lycanthropic Larry Talbot, Carroll goes through a monstrous transformation. In an early scene, he is injected with the same nutrient with which he is experimenting on mice, guinea pigs and spiders and, as a result,

The mighty monstser survives the gas bombs in *Tarantula*.

starts to mutate, growing hideously deformed! The make-up design is exquisite!

The sequence in Carroll's laboratory is especially spellbinding, as it closely resembles a scene straight out of a classic Universal monster movie. It is a terrific melodramatic piece of cinema that merrily includes the ingenious superimposition of giant test rats and guinea pigs that share frame with the gravel-faced Leo G. Carroll, as well as the intrusion of Carroll's former assistant who has injected himself with the same nutrient that is transforming the newly grotesquely-sized animals. The assistant's face is much like one of the titular characters from Universal's *The Mole People* and he frees the giant tarantula that will grow even larger in size and wreak havoc on the small desert town.

The film also features cool footage of a real life tarantula battling a wasp and a snake. What seems like a little lesson on tarantulas serves as a workable plot point for the audience to understand the creature more. The John Agar character (a small-town doctor thrust into a series of unfortunate events) learns what we the audience has begun to understand.

John Agar's inoffensively handsome small-town doctor oozes charm and takes the movie over with great ease and class, and the beautiful Mara Corday stars as the biologist who arrives too late on the scene.

Corday follows the glamorous line of Universal's women of horror—Helen Chandler, Mae Clarke, Evelyn Ankers and the rest—and just like many of them, Corday was a horror movie starlet as well as a model. Her famous *Playboy* shoot enhanced her cult status and Clint Eastwood (who incidentally has his first ever film role, a tiny part, in *Tarantula* as a jet squadron leader) used her in some of his movies many years later including *The Gauntlet*, *Sudden Impact* and *Pink Cadillac*. Mara Corday also starred in another giant-animal-on-the-rampage movie called *The Black Scorpion* (1957), a very fine movie that featured amazing work from a special effects team including Willis O'Brien, who of course created the superlative effects for *King Kong*.

Unlike the scenes in *Tarantula* where the arachnid looks as though it is crawling all over the Californian desert lands but is only being superimposed against natural backgrounds, many shots of the scorpions in *The Black Scorpion* play against a series of traveling matte paintings to make them look as though they are attacking Mexico City. In *The Black Scorpion*, a volcanic eruption unleashes giant scorpions into Mexico City, and these kinds of natural disasters are the cause for many more creatures to grow in size or be unleashed already mammoth in size. This is the general standard for many other larger-than-life movies of the same era. But when one discusses the advent of larger-than-life movie monsters making their massive mark on movie history, we cannot go past the man who made a career out of these divine films—Bert I. Gordon.

Bert I. Gordon (affectionately known as Mr. B.I.G and fans already understand how apt these initials are) is a movie lover from the get-go and from watching his endearing movies it's easy to see why. As a youngster he would watch everything from film noir and gangster movies to Westerns to romance movies—but it was the horror and science fiction films that really appealed to the young maverick-to-be, who grew up much like many of the monster-movie makers to come—on a healthy steady diet of horror movies. His movies generally dealt with a big lumbering monster that wreaked havoc on unsuspecting townsfolk, genetically mutated animals and insects that caused massive stress, or characters that have been shrunk down in size so they are forced to deal with the world literally at large!

Natural disasters often cause small creatures to grow in size. Such was the case of *The Black Scorpion*.

Even though some of his movies—*Attack of the Puppet People, The Amazing Colossal Man, The War of the Colossal Beast* and *Village of the Giants*—featured giant animals, the movies predominantly dealt with monstrously large human characters. These films are simply perfect, but it is Gordon's animalistic endeavors that truly deserve extreme high ranking in this book. Two of Gordon's films rejuvenated the subgenre and have come to be among the most treasured, ecologically scary movies ever

123

Mr. B.I.G., Bert I. Gordon, delivers his own oversized man in the form of *War of the Colossal Beast* (1958).

to grace the silver screen. But before those two '70s gems are discussed, let's first examine Gordon's response to the Atomic Age of the 1950s with a swarm of giant grasshoppers in *Beginning of the End* (1957) and a rock 'n' roll-loving arachnid in *Earth vs. The Spider* (1958).

Bert I. Gordon's films have so much heart and his passion comes across in these motion pictures through the writing, the production values, the storytelling and the way in which his actors give their all in each performance, and *Earth vs. The Spider* is no exception. In an age of rock 'n' roll rebellion, this giant spider gem tells the story of a spunky teenage girl (June Kenny) who goes looking for her missing father. Along with her boyfriend (Gene Persson), Kenny discovers the remains of her father, his blood drained, trapped in an enormous spider web. She and Persson try to convince skeptical officials that perhaps a giant arachnid may be the culprit and eventually a science teacher and his team of teens set out to capture and kill this beast. They paralyze the giant monstrous spider and, believing it to be dead, decide to bring it into town for research purposes. The spider is kept in the gymnasium of a nearby school, and during a local band's rock 'n' roll rehearsal, the spider awakens and causes havoc for everyone in its path! In Gordon's endearing classic, raucous rock 'n' roll awakens the giant spider, a beautiful commentary on middle-class values that the

Teenagers in peril were a staple of movies made at the peak of Cold War anxieties, such as *Earth vs. The Spider*.

rebelliousness of youth will be the cause of the destruction of the American family.

In Gordon's earlier movie *Beginning of the End*, he delivers a wonderfully charming B picture as the Atomic Age comes to bear horrific consequences for civilians in the Midwest. When local agriculturists experiment with radioactive material to help grow their crops, they inadvertently cause the grasshopper population to increase in size. These gigantic grasshoppers usher in the beginning to an end of biblical proportions and it's up to Peggie Castle and Peter Graves, as an intrepid reporter and a botanist respectively, to do battle with these hungry and violently vicious cretins. Just after he made *Beginning of the End*, Gordon also directed *The Cyclops* (1957) where a search crew, on the hunt for a missing test pilot, finds large snakes, lizards and other giant animals, all turned grossly huge thanks to radioactivity. Radioactivity, of course, endlessly proves to be the sure-fire plot device of the decade.

June Kenny and Gene Persson are the intrepid teenage couple that become entrapped by sticky webbing in *Earth vs. The Spider*.

The 1950s was clearly the ultimate time for movies featuring larger-than-life movie monsters—many of them being large insects and mammals as opposed to fictitious creations such as the Ymir in *20 Million Miles To Earth* or humongous humans such as the scorned, angry and mistreated Allison Hayes in *Attack of the 50 Foot Woman*. But by the 1960s horror took another turn as Alfred Hitchcock dished out his intricate character study with *Psycho,* and horror became internal and stealthily sinister. Lumbering giants no longer scared audiences, instead parlor room monstrosities dominated as seen in classics such as *Whatever Happened To Baby Jane, Peeping Tom* and *The Innocents.* A revival of glorious color Gothic horror films featuring the classic movie monsters rose from Britain's Hammer Film Productions, beginning with *The Curse of Frankenstein* (1957).

However, the 1970s arrived, and thanks to a huge interest in ecological terror, the mutated mammoth movie monster began to rear its ugly/beautiful head again. And thanks to a movie maverick that made his mark in everything B.I.G., this phenomenon was widely embraced by audiences who grew up loving the stuff in the '50s. So new audiences comprised of young girls and boys wanting to experience terror on a bigger scale emerged! And the older generation returned to see just how much the subgenre changed in 20 years.

Bert I. Gordon's love for these larger-than-life movie monsters was resurrected and he single-handedly brought those lost treasures of the Atomic Age back for a new generation of horror movie enthusiasts. Thanks to magazines like *Famous Monsters of Filmland*, these giant bugs, lizards and other creepy-crawlies enjoyed their day in the sun again. Theaters began to replay them as nostalgic trips down memory lane, while expensive toys depicting giant spiders and Godzilla began to over populate the collectors' market. Three new movies featuring gargantuan animals and insects made their mark on the natural horror movie movement. Two of them came from the master Bert I. Gordon, while an Australian novel with biting political and social commentary inspired the third.

Empire of the Ants (1977) begins with a documentary-style prologue depicting ants in their natural habitat behaving as ants would normally behave. A voice-over explains that ants are extremely intelligent and social, immediately making a clear comparison between these tiny creatures and humans. According to the narration, ant civilization is on a par with human civilization (a theme explored in *Phase IV* but made much more fun here); we share the same intellect and same roles in society—the builders, the soldiers, the teachers, etc. Bert I. Gordon's original screen story (with the actual screenplay written by Jack Turley) makes clear parallels between human characteristics and character types in relation to the nature of ants.

Giant ants watch potential food in *Empire of the Ants*.

After the prologue, a ship is seen throwing toxic waste into the ocean, where one of the tanks lands on the shore and becomes food for local ants. Of course, this radioactive waste turns these tiny critters into monstrous soldiers of destruction, but thanks to Bert I. Gordon's intelligent handling of the script, they are much, much more. It is established in the opening prologue that ants communicate by using specific pheromones that influence each other; usually a queen ant uses this aroma to tell her drones what to do. Later in this movie, the giant ants use this same pheromone to control the human race. It is a marvelous plot point and a beautiful pay-off so expertly executed.

Released by American International Pictures (Gordon's films were usually associated with the enigmatic moguls James Nicholson and Samuel Z. Arkoff), *Empire of the Ants* stars the fabulous Joan Collins as an assertive businesswoman, president of a Real Estate company, who leads a group of potential property buyers on a tour through a lush seaside resort. Her company is one of those investor traps selling condos to people who are promised a cruise, free booze and food in return. Collins is terrific as this high-powered diva and her characterization instantly draws parallels with the queen ant that will feature later in the movie. Collins has a young man that she uses for both professional assistance as well as sexual favors, and she has influence over the entire tour group, including an opportunistic elderly couple who come along on Collins' tours because they're free, a beautiful and young recently-divorced woman who is trying to restart her life and a handsome young man who jumped on board merely for something to do. Collins does however strike up an aggressive, antagonistic relationship with the stern, stoic Seabee boat captain, the two constantly arguing how to handle the disastrous events that take place.

The glamorous Joan Collins, equal in power to the queen ant, is under the influence of the mighty insects in *Empire of The Ants*.

The characters are nicely written and the dynamics are solid and always kept interesting, as Collins's future empire—a new housing estate complete with all the amenities including golf course, shopping district and theater—becomes an empire for the oversized ants that kill the tour group one by one.

The ants themselves are gorgeous creations; at times they are seen as stop-motion monsters traveling along with great fury, but in close-up they are big, furry, lecherous hand-held puppets that attack the hapless humans with great ferocity. Unlike Gordon's 1950s entries, plenty of bloodshed appears here for an increasingly bloodthirsty '70s audience!

As the ants begin to herd the humans like cattle, humankind's plight is trivialized and people soon become slaves to these gigantic, intelligent insects. These ants who now have power over people because of their size—a matter of size enabling them to grow dominant over those simians called humans—and by the end of the movie the human population has succumbed to the ants' pheromones and become their drones. When Collins and the surviving tour party arrive at civilization (free from the jungles and marshlands where they have been battling the giant ants throughout), they discover that mankind has changed and these once normal human beings want the disheveled group to obey the higher ant authority. Capable, independent-minded human beings have lost themselves to a kind of hypnotism, and one by one they face the queen ant (their new leader) and let her infect them with her pheromone. Collins is no exception. She stands face-to-face with her insect counterpart and becomes her slave. "We must

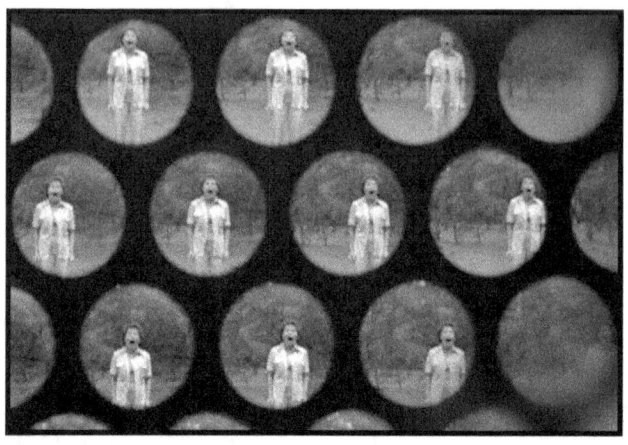

The p.o.v. shot of one of the colony members from *The Empire of the Ants*.

take care of them. And we must help them," she says. The queen ant's influence over the human population is nicely juxtaposed with Joan Collins's desperate attempts to control the people around her.

Bert I. Gordon's endlessly entertaining *The Food of the Gods* is loosely based upon the H.G. Wells story (and quite honestly, Mr. B.I.G. injects these classic tales with so much fun that they surpass the original science fiction Mr. Wells dished out those many year ago). In short, Mr. B.I.G. tells a story extremely well and adapts old ones to perfection, making *The Food of the Gods* quite simply—a perfect film.

The film is loaded with rich goodness that bursts with so much heart and clever wit that it becomes a breathtaking masterpiece. Bert I. Gordon's direction is crystal clear and he manages to paint distinguishable characters that not only serve their purpose to the story, but are also flawed in a way, haunted by a kind of human problem that makes them all the more interesting and fully fleshed out three-dimensional creations.

Gordon's direction is solid and he gets a wonderful performance from screen legend Ida Lupino, who not only worked as an actress (most notably in many

Giant rats terrorize Ida Lupino's log cabin in *Food of the Gods*.

film noir classics) but also made a career as one of the very few women directors in Hollywood. Alongside Lupino is horror starlet and go-to gal for the 1970s, Belinda Balaski, who of course went on to star in classics such as *Piranha* and *The Howling*. Former child preacher Marjoe Gortner just shines as the heroic protagonist with his wiry frame, thick locks of curly hair and snappy delivery of some wonderful one-liners.

Gordon also gets some amazing performances from live rats and chickens that have been made to look humungous thanks to the wonderful invention of superimposing imagery onto film. In my humble opinion, *The Food of the Gods* boasts some of the best superimposition ever put to screen. Rats crowd around a busted up motor home (some brilliant model work is also featured in this marvelous movie) as Balaski screams in terror, giant chickens parade in a dark barn as Gortner struggles with a maniacal giant rooster and massive wasps hover above the heads of Ida Lupino and company. This film is loaded with amazing moments. On top of the incredible shots of rats and other beasts running amok is Gordon's use of some spectacular puppetry! Giant rat heads are thrust into the faces of our human cast, tearing away at the less fortunate, ripping into their flesh and bleeding them dry. Earthworms the size of dogs lunge at Ida Lupino and chew away at her arms, and a giant rooster (with fiery crest and gorgeous feathers) dukes it out with Marjoe Gortner, who proves to be a worthy adversary for the charming chap.

Margoe Gortner, usually in charge, faces larger-than-life chickens and roosters that threaten his masculinity in *Food of the Gods*.

The film opens with Marjoe Gortner running around a football field. From the get-go we understand that Gortner is part of a winning team, a high achiever, and that he is a man who can overthrow adversity with one single blow. Under the advice of his coach, Gortner takes some time off practice to enjoy a relaxing weekend away before the impending big game. He takes along with him a fellow player and the personal relations manager of the football team, and these three set out to a remote island off the coast of Vancouver, Canada. They enjoy a spot of hunting but soon come into contact with giant wasps. These wasps are mighty big, and they do some mighty fine damage to one of the men, killing him in an instant. The make-up designs for the violent results of animal attacks are spectacular, and in this case effective use of prosthetic appliances give the gruesome aftermath of a wasp attack a sickly realism, similar to the make-up design for the doomed humans in *Frogs*. It is learned later that one sting from any of these massive wasps is the equivalent of 250 regular-sized wasps, so it makes sense that the poor sod went into shock and died instantly.

Marjoe Gortner wants answers and he sets out to find them. Remember, nothing stops this man from getting to the bottom of things; his character is a no-nonsense tough guy who aims to overcome any obstacle. Football is his chosen profession because it enables him to shine in a public arena. Later in the movie the female lead Pamela Franklin asks if he doesn't like women watching him when he takes on a problem. He simply responds with, "What's not to like?" He is a man of great substance and stoic steadiness. However, judging from his voice-over narration at the beginning of the film, Gortner's character is also haunted by the idea that nature is a far more problematical adversary than any other he ever faced. It is learned through this voice-over narration (which is only used to bookend the film) that Gortner's father had once told him that one day nature will rebel and it will be one hell of a rebellion. Gortner somehow understands that nature will seek vengeance over the people who do it harm, but unlike environmental sympathizers in previous films and films to come, Gortner in *The Food of the Gods* is ready to take on these mutated beasts the way he'd take on his football opponents—aggressively, head on.

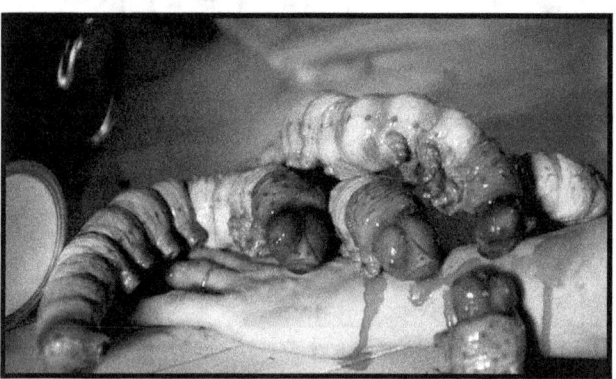

Ida Lupino's arm becomes food for giant Earth worms in *Food of the Gods*.

Gortner comes across a nearby farmhouse owned by a cagey Ida Lupino. From the beginning Lupino is painted as someone a tad shady and secretive. Her husband disappeared shortly after discovering a strange liquid matter that oozed from the ground. The husband thought it might make him and his poor wife instantly wealthy (much like striking gold), but this substance caused more distress than good. Lupino used it to help stretch the volume of chicken feed for her hungry fowl; however, it causes the young chicks to grow in size. Not just to a regular adult-sized chicken, but to the size of an elephant! These chickens (and one rooster) are not the only critters to consume this strange, unearthly substance—wasps have consumed it, worms too, but the biggest cause for concern are the local vermin, as the rats prove to be the greatest threat to the

Marjoe Gortner (holding the rifle) and Belinda Bakaski (holding the baby) are under attack by the massive rodents in *Food of the Gods*.

human stars of this picture, violently mauling many of them to death.

Lupino is endlessly ranting some religious banter and is convinced that it was God that sent this strange substance to her, to reward her for being such a good Christian woman. She bottles the stuff and calls it the food of the gods and will not part with it. Her religious fanaticism is nicely weaved into her character, but her dedication to protecting the God-sent ooze ultimately serves as her downfall, as she succumbs to the rat attacks!

Pamela Franklin's bacteriologist is a character that is possibly the most complex of the group and has the most with which to contend. Not only does she have a job to do (to study these strange occurrences on this remote Canadian island) but she also has to fend off oppressive misogyny as bought on by her money-hungry boss, played by the weasel-like Ralph Meeker. She gradually earns the trust of the driven Marjoe Gortner, who empathizes with a grieving Ida Lupino who fears the worst for her lost husband and nurse Belinda Balaski.

Balaski's character also has a nicely composed subplot written for her. She is noticeably pregnant but doesn't want to marry the father of her unborn child, whereas he does. Writer Bert I. Gordon nicely constructs a penetrative parallel here between societal institutions (such as marriage) cutting into natural occurrences (such as pregnancy and parenthood), all beautifully stitched into a tight fabric, primarily concerned with an environment in great turmoil, that has become the domain for animals who have been granted the opportunity to finally dominate the human race.

Rats of course make for great animal adversaries, with their beady eyes, their razor sharp incisors and their quick, jittery movement. They appear in many a great horror film, such as the extremely gory *Rats,* where they also grow in size, terrorizing the subways of New York City and slaughtering horny teenagers. And *Willard,* where rats become a metaphor for the human condition and the concept of the rat race is scrutinized and intricately examined. (But much more on *Willard* appears in the next chapter). Rats appear in the giallo Italian film *Rats: Night of Terror,* directed by Bruno Mattei, where he marries the ecological threat of a rat invasion with the culture of street thugs and biker gangs. In *The Food of the Gods*, rats have no problem in making meals out of people and, as their chief, a white, lean rodent leads them toward a promised land free of humans. The film delivers plenty of blood-soaked gore and viciously violent fun! An unofficial sequel to *The Food of the Gods* entitled *Gnaw: Food of the Gods Part 2* was made in 1989 and has nothing to do with Gordon's original fright-fest.

Bert I. Gordon's wonderful giant ant and rat programmers were not the only films to deal with gargantuan animals causing havoc for flawed human beings in the 1970s. A movie that became a cult classic, as well as a laughable joke for dullard cynics such as the people involved with the likes of *Mystery Science Theatre,* opened in 1972 to much criticism. However, as the years have gone by, its placement in the ecological horror film movement is well secured and the movie attracted an appreciative audience hopping with enthusiasm (bad pun completely intended).

From the very beginning, *Night of the Lepus* (1972) is obsessed with overpopulation. The film opens with a newscast and actual stock footage of rabbits running rampant in Australia during the 1930s. From what we are taught, these rabbits were introduced to the continent from England to increase the food supply; however, their introduction Down Under proves to be catastrophic. Rabbits have overpopulated and caused some serious damage. The newscast shifts closer to home, Arizona, in the early 1970s and the same situation is at hand—rabbits have

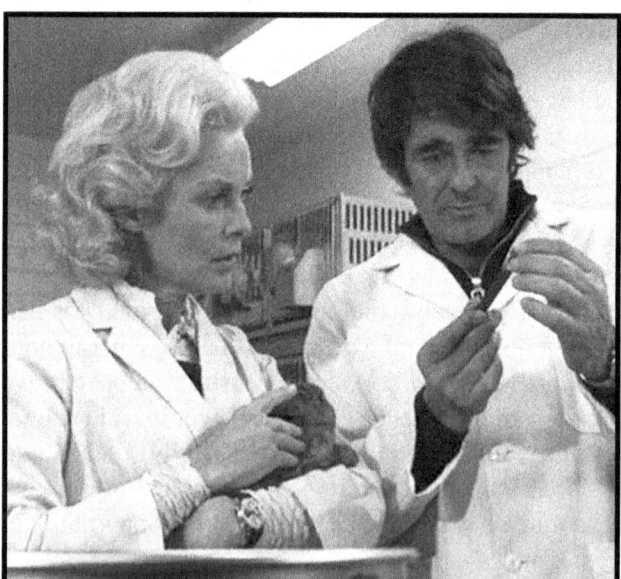

Janet Leigh and Stuart Whitman are about to inject a serum into one of the rabbits in *Night of the Lepus*.

bred like crazy and become the bane of the Southwest, even inadvertently killing off horses as we see right after the opening credits (in *Night of the Lepus*, the movie monster does not just kill off the human oppressor, it kills man's best friend in the Wild West, the horse!).

Giant rabbits terrorize a small Arizona town in *Night of the Lepus*.

Night of the Lepus is based on a 1964 Australian science fiction/horror novel called *The Year of the Angry Rabbit,* written by Russell Braddon. Braddon's great book uses science fiction motifs from the 1950s, where rabbits grow mammoth in size terrorizing Australia, to critique the stupidity of war, capitalism and oppressive nationalism—most notably the impending Vietnam War in which Australia was pivotally involved. *Night of the Lepus* downplayed these social themes and commentaries to primarily focus on the issue of overpopulation and how science can do great harm in response to birth control.

In this film, the destruction of the surrounding environment has all to do with the imbalance in nature—rabbits have come to overproduce, killing off every other living insect that helps in the ecological circle of life. Therefore rabbits need to be controlled. Directed by William F. Claxton (a director usually associated with Westerns and television), the film tells the story of a married biologist couple, Janet Leigh and Stuart Whitman, who have been enlisted by rancher Rory Calhoun and university president DeForest Kelley to help control the rabbit population in an Arizonan town. It is decided that poisoning is a bad idea and that a serum usually associated with treating birth defects will double as a hormonal control which, as Janet Leigh explains to her young, precocious daughter (Melanie Fullerton), will make Jack more like Jill and Jill more like Jack, hence influencing the rabbits' breeding habits and decreasing population.

Janet Leigh's daughter is promised a pet rabbit out of the control group, but she takes a liking to one that has been treated with the hormonal serum. She takes this treated rabbit calling him Romeo (a play on words as the lover in him will begin the spawning of all the mutated rabbits) and swaps him with one of the untreated control group rabbits. When Romeo escapes he transmits the growth disease to other rabbits; of course, this hormonal treatment causes these rabbits to grow in size and, soon enough, they terrorize the small rural town, killing many humans and doing major damage.

Claxton has a major task at hand with this movie—just how does one make cute fluffy bunny rabbits scary? Well, who knows? But he does a fine job. Being a director associated with Westerns and working with actors normally featured in Westerns, the film has the vibe of a Wild West romp the same way *Kingdom of the Spiders* and *Rattlers* do, and in comparison to a much championed movie like *The Birds*, the characters in Claxton's killer bunny movie trap themselves inside tight spaces, hiding from the outside menace. Here, much like in Hitchcock's epic, people become the caged animals, burying themselves down in the cellar. Humans burrow while rabbits reign supreme!

The movie may be laughable and the idea of rabbits being terrifying may not sit well with more critical audiences; however, it does speak volumes about the issues of birth control and overpopulation. Years later, the controversial, maudlin animated feature *Watership Down* (based on the novel by Richard Adams) featured rabbits as its stars and, much like *Night of the Lepus*, this dark cartoon scrutinized issues concerning human fears about overpopulation. Also, this movie came out in 1978 and really heightened public awareness to the problems associated with rabbit overpopulation and polygamy, making it a great allegory for plagues (note, 1978 was a few years before AIDS started to rear its terrifying head).

Emerging from the dusty plains, a big bunny is ready to kill all who get in its way, from *Night of The Lepus*.

In preparation for the release of *Night of the Lepus*, MGM wanted to underplay the rabbit angle, thus removing images of rabbits from the poster and downplaying the killer bunny theme in their campaign. But then it was decided that they had inevitably created a risible monster movie and had rabbit footprints painted around towns to promote the film. This seemed to work; the movie did wonders at the box office.

The extreme close-ups of the rabbits trying to look ferocious; the endless shots of the rabbits racing through miniature sets, shot in slow motion; the strange sounds the rabbits make as they race toward terrified, diminutive humans; the wonderfully gorgeous fake blood smeared across the bunnies' mouths; the large paws slashing at hapless human victims; and the extremely gory aftermath of the rabbits' rampage all contribute to this film being one of a kind. It is full of heart, warmth and furry fun! One of the best moments comes late in the piece where the desperate humans think of a way to kill these dangerous, giant rabbits. They herd the bunnies into the local drive-in, which is secured by an electric railway track, and the lepus are electrocuted! This imagery is a simple commentary on the kind of movie this is—a loud, brash, drive-in trash-fest and this is completely fine!

The beauty of the movie is its completely serious tone; some may argue the movie is made with tongue firmly planted in cheek, but this writer doesn't think so. The movie's played straight and that's what makes it work. It's disheartening when a movie audience is so jaded and cynical that they simply have to make mockery of a film like *Night of the Lepus*. Why isn't a film like this treated with the same amount of importance as *The Birds*? Sure Hitchcock is a great director (and everyone under the sun says that without even thinking), but what would Hitchcock have done differently with the mammoth-sized rabbits offered to him in *Night of the Lepus*?

This is why the likes of *Mystery Science Theatre* doesn't appeal to me, being a writer who respects, appreciates and, above all, loves these wonderful movies that have provided such joy throughout the years. These movies are escapist fun, monster movies made with heart and good intentions—what's not to love?

The giant animal and mutated menace movie is still doing healthy business to this day. Films like *Dinoshark*, *Sharktopus* and *Mega Shark vs. Giant Octopus* make loads of money for the their distributors and producers who release these high concept ideas straight to DVD. These films are remarkably entertaining and completely devoid of any self-serving irony. These CGI-geared monsters are a threat to the likes of singing sensations Tiffany and Debbie Gibson, as

Rabbits feast on the goods usually denied to them, in *Night of the Lepus*.

well as veteran character actors like David Carradine. Although audiences are clearly watching these movies for laughs, these programmers are played straight—no winking occurs at the audience, no direct referencing of earlier larger-than-life creature features and no room for the sardonic. These films are delivering exactly what the title suggests (audiences will see a shark/dinosaur hybrid and, of course, the monster's going to maim and kill more than likely sexy, fit and healthy young people wearing next to nothing) and doing a fine job of it.

From the leftover dinosaurs in *The Lost World* and *The Valley of Gwangi* to the giant love sick apes in *King Kong, Mighty Joe Young* and *Trog,* giant animals have forever proven to be a tangible threat to humankind, and their connection to something wild, primal or born from the advent of science (a human invention) has thrilled audiences for years.

Of course, most of these films dealing with the horrors of science, feature professors who, like the rest of the cast, eventually flee from their monstrous aberrations. But some movies, however, have the scientist or specialist form a bond with these giant celluloid critters and, soon enough, human/animal help/dependency emerges.

In *Konga*, Michael Gough's simian test subject becomes his most precious friend, and thanks to a serum that when injected into any animal, mineral or vegetable makes them grow in size, his ape became a formidable foe that could help him do battle with those who oppress, slander or hurt him. This bond is also shared more intensely for Mr. Gough in a wonderful dark horror movie, *The Black Zoo,* where the connection between humans and animals is a powerful force and something not to be trivialized.

Which brings us to our next point of topic—movies in which the featured monster is an extension of one of those simple simians we call humans. We will examine films such as *The Killer Bees* where Gloria Swanson controls the bees that live in her vineyard. Our next chapter is going to dissect human help in all its form, be they snakes, pigs or rats … our next stop will introduce us to a place where animals have become a loyal (and deadly) disciple to those poor put-upon chumps we like to call … people.

The Two Of Us Need Look No More: Human Help in the Natural Horror Film

A majority of ecological disaster films and natural horror movies depict nature's attack (both inexplicable or caused by man in some way) as a direct attack; in other words, nature targets humankind and humankind has to defend itself from this tyranny. In these films it's a case of man versus nature. However, some films exist where people are so in tune with nature that they become an extension of the natural world and play a major part in the evil and eventual harm it can inflict. In these movies, humans call upon animals as their familiars to work for them, to become their disciples of dirty goings-on; the human stars co-exist with these monstrous animals and usually their intense co-dependence ultimately serves as their personal downfall in the final reel. These bestial counterparts serve their masters and take heed of their direction, but often in the closing moments of the movie these once faithful beasts may rebel or just become too hard to control.

The films using this plot device are often solid movies and the characters that enlist animals or insects as their army of darkness vary in age and personality type. Most of these films come from a revenge angle—Bruce Davison as *Willard* is a much put-upon sad sod oppressed by those that surround him, Lisa Pelikan as *Jennifer* is an impoverished introvert alienated and abused by her peers, the lead in *Kiss of the Tarantula* is an ostracized girl who grows up wanting revenge on those who did her wrong. All of these characters call upon the help of deadly creatures. In *Willard* it's rats, in *Jennifer* it's snakes and in *Kiss of the Tarantula*, well, I'm sure the title says it all.

The other element of animal/human interaction is the metamorphic picture or the

The wonderfully hammy Michael Gough leads an animal worship cult in *Black Zoo*.

Diminutive character actor Elisha Cook, Jr. is attacked by one of Michael Gough's lions in *Black Zoo*.

shapeshifter subgenre. Much like the werewolf movie, the ecological metamorphic film uses the same kind of philosophy—a character is unfortunately cursed with an affliction that causes them to transform into an animalistic abomination. In this chapter I want to discuss three favorites of the eco-horror film—*Sssssss*, *The Bat People* and *The Beast Within*. But before we look at those oddities, we will start at possibly the first of the animal/human help films, a gorgeous, sumptuous diddy known as *Black Zoo* (1963).

Starring the always-wonderful Michael Gough, *Black Zoo* is a glorious movie that centers on Gough's connection to large jungle cats such as lions, leopards and panthers. He also shares a strong affinity with a large ape, played by the magnificent monkey actor George Barrows. All these animals are part of his private zoo, and not only are they well loved and looked after by the obsessive Gough, but they are worshiped too—literally. Yes, this movie is about animal-worship cultists and it is a glamorous ride all the way through.

Captivating in color, this strange little movie was the third and final collaboration between producer Herman Cohen and Michael Gough. The other movies they worked on were *Horrors of the Black Museum* and *Konga*. Gough is just so much fun to watch in this movie, audiences can clearly tell he is having a ball with this material. His hammy over-the-top antics are more of a spectacle than the lions and cheetahs that tear apart the folk who get in his way. The film offers some great performances from character actors such as Elisha Cook, Jr., Virginia Grey and Ed Platt. And the animals are just a sheer delight to watch as they obey every command Gough makes, taking heed in what he says and slaying those who do him wrong. The animal training is perfectly executed; sometimes it looks far too real when a large powerful cat lunges at a hapless victim. *Black Zoo* very much set the standard for many more ecologically themed, animal-to-human relationship horror movies to follow.

But the ultimate movie that deals with a human being's connection with the natural world and shaping it to suit their needs comes from a very clever, creepy motion picture that hit a nerve with audiences in the 1970s. Based on the atmospheric novel *The Ratman's Notebooks* written by Stephen Gilbert, *Willard* is a divine movie—flawlessly plotted with swift precision and marvelously acted. *Willard* precedes superlative horror movie outings such as George A. Romero's vampire classic *Martin* and Brian De Palma's iconic *Carrie* as a dynamic character study, where the horror grows from someone who is tormented for who they are. It is also a cautionary tale about the dangers of wish fulfillment and a modern

Bruce Davison finds solace in the company of rats. Here he observes his favored rat, Socrates, from *Willard*.

American Gothic set in the world of the humdrum mundane. In *Willard*, work and unemployment, home ownership, financial woe and the anxieties brought on by becoming a responsible adult in a cruel and unforgiving world are all contributing factors of a very tangible horror. And the rats embody these very real fears.

Bruce Davison's Willard Stiles is a likeable loser. Angry and edgy, moody and stuck in a permanent rut, the boy is a pathetic sod with a domineering but ailing mother, a menace of a boss and the ghost of his dead father forever haunting him. To the manic rat race, Davison's Willard is a lost cause. He is an unremarkable nobody whose tomorrows will bring him only more sorrow. But all this changes when he meets Socrates, a white rat who takes a shining to the young human loner. Socrates proves to be a charming companion and soon enough more rats appear and the rodent enthusiast forms a special bond with these Los Angeles-dwelling vermin. But then along comes Ben, the black independent rat. Ben is not one to be led by those accursed with no fur, no tail and only two legs.

The one-sheet poster for *Willard* features Ben, the black, rebellious rat.

Bruce Davison is perfect in the role of Willard. He moves with awkward twitchiness that at times resembles the jittery nervousness of rats. His convulsing with

The only glimmer of hope in Bruce Davison's life is Sondra Locke, but she too is bullied by the ruthless Ernest Borgnine, from *Willard*.

uneasiness and his inoffensive good looks complemented by his doe-eyed sadness are all perfectly realized in this wonderful characterization of a young person who goes from pathetic man-boy, to brooding victim, to vengeful, golden-haired warlock.

Davison's supporting cast is just as spectacular. Elsa Lanchester (most notably remembered as the monster's mate in James Whale's *Bride of Frankenstein*), in one of her final movie roles, has fun with her kooky Mrs. Stiles. Her shrill voice echoes through the empty, decaying mansion in which she lives; her loneliness dries up her weak son emotionally; and her declining health becomes a sorrowful burden on him. Sondra Locke (pre-Clint Eastwood and in one of her first roles) plays Davison's lovely co-worker and she is such a delicate beauty with her elfin features and her spindly frame. Her character is the only glimmer of hope for Davison's conflicted Willard, while Ernest Borgnine as Davison's oafish boss Martin has not one iota of humanity.

Borgnine is completely devoid of any sympathy whatsoever in the role of the head honcho of the factory. We learn that the factory was once co-owned by Davison's deceased father, but Borgnine's Martin weaseled his way to the top and threatens to never let Davison take his rightful place as co-owner. Borgnine's manipulative and sleazy Martin is somewhat a horrendous caricature, but this works fine for the film. It would complicate matters if the screenwriter decided to give Borgnine's character external interests, complexity or compassion for a son or wife who were completely oblivious to his malicious nastiness. The smart script shows us that Borgnine's Martin and Davison's Willard are both capable of true evil, one driven by greed and malice and the other by revenge.

Davison's Willard Stiles is the Pied Piper of Hamlin turned malevolent. However, he doesn't start out sinister at all; his descent into unhealthy co-dependency on his furry friends is made all the more terrifying by Davison's electrifying performance. We feel his frustration as Willard; he could be attractive and self-possessed but instead he is a grown man-child in ill-fitting suits. He is surrounded and oppressed by elderly busybodies (the kind of people you would find living next to Rosemary Woodhouse in Polanski's 1968 classic *Rosemary's Baby*) who think they know what's best for the sad sap.

Davison's relationship with the rats becomes the focal point of the movie, but does it? The central theme explores the human rat race where a drowning young man is frantically kicking to keep his head above water, avoiding the grimy sewer waters below. The rats do the same. They are living in and around Elsa Lanchester's large house and cause her great alarm. Davison attends to them and, instead of killing, he trains them—they soon become his only friends.

After the rats, the one shining light (and genuinely healthy escape) is Sondra Locke. She represents everything good in the world, a world Davison's Willard might enjoy. But she is pushed aside, first dismissed by the manipulative Borgnine who turns on her as soon as he notices that she is showing genuine sympathy for the poor boy and then she is rejected by Willard to make way for his furious furry friends. By the end of the picture, his own companions have run Davison out of town. The rats have taken over his home, his life and, when Davison learns that these rats will have their way with Locke, he insists she leave him alone. It is his one noble act, saving the girl who had shown him kindness.

Willard's mother Elsa Lanchester spots a rat in her living room, from *Willard*. What she does not know is that her son is friends with the vermin.

The film boasts several magnificent scenes. First, Willard unleashing his precious rats at a party Borgnine is hosting, the filthy rodents landing in cake, chewing through walls and racing along the plush environment causing havoc for the party guests. In movies like *Alligator* and *Frogs,* the ugly rich are disturbed and killed by critters that cause great distress, and these beady-eyed, grubby rats scurrying at the feet of L.A.'s wealthiest are much the same. Another wonderfully scary moment is where the rats spill out of Davison's leather briefcase and creep into Borgnine's office. Gleefully Davison orders them to, "Tear him up!" Borgnine's expression is memorable here. He understands that Davison's relationship with these rats is all about obedience and he fully realizes that this

Ernest Borgnine's horrific demise, as rats plague his office at the command of Bruce Davison, from *Willard*

young man, whom he has oppressed for all these years, has trained these ferocious rats to do his bidding. Borgnine's amazing expression of both terror and realization seems just perfect.

Davison's central character Willard uses these rats to cope with the problems life dishes out, but sadly for him, they prove to be too independent to control. The rats, led by the rebellious Ben, decide to turn on him, trap him in his manor and eat him alive. The outcome of *Willard* is similar to a film made a decade later. John Carpenter's *Christine* (the story of a put-upon boy and his genie-in-a-lamp car) warns us that possession can prove deadly, as those who supposedly own or control certain assets can somehow gradually be owned or controlled by these same assets. *Willard* explores this notion with masterful insight. The *help* may start to manage on its own and desire to turn the tables on the situation, controlling the master and taking over. But ultimately, *Willard* and similar movies to follow (namely *Jennifer*, *Kiss of the Tarantula* and *Stanley*) rely heavily on the audience's sympathy for the loser. If we didn't care about Willard Stiles, we'd hardly find his antics involving deadly rats charming. But we do care about his plight and revel in Borgnine's demise.

Willard was successful both critically and at the box-office. Audiences who at the time were flocking to see Francis Ford Coppola's *The Godfather*, Bob Fosse's *Cabaret* and Peter Bogdanovich's *The Last Picture Show* wholeheartedly embraced it. The film's appeal is cleverly connected to an audience's keen devotion to the underdog rising above adversity, a theme that would soon be embodied in movies like *Rocky* and in horror movie fare such as *Carrie* and *Christine*.

A remake of *Willard* was released in 2003, one of the first in a plethora of inferior and unnecessary remakes of classic horror movies, but it was one of the best (the remake of *The Texas Chainsaw Massacre* from 2003 was also pretty good). Willard's remake is a warts and all Gothic horror starring the witchy Crispin Glover as Willard Stiles. The film works as a gloriously decadent extension of the Grand Guignol and Glover's character, with his scarecrow-like stringiness, works beautifully. He is devilishly delectable as the twisted and tormented rat boy. He embodies an updated Willard Stiles and makes the character his own, injecting Willard with personal flair and finesse. Much like great thespians Charlton Heston, Jack Nicholson and Christopher Walken, Glover is his own actor. His delivery and nuances are his and his alone. So if audiences like Glover the artist, they will love his performance, one filled with skittish flamboyance.

In the 2003 remake of *Willard*, the scarecrow-like Crispin Glover has a little help (and much needed sympathy) from the loyal Socrates, perched on his shoulder.

R. Lee Ermey's characterization of the malicious, loutish boss is a marvelous updating of Borgnine's Martin. Ermey has great command as a viciously unsympathetic asshole. Glover's depressing alienation is made all the more painful with the right elements working in unison. The movie's horror and black humor are all the more effective thanks to Shirley Walker's beautiful score; amazing animal performance (especially good is a scene where a cat is terrorized by the hoards of bloodthirsty rats); and Elsa Lanchester's character recast as a monstrous, oppressive ghoul deliciously played by Jackie Burroughs. Most definitely not as good as the original 1971 motion picture, but this retelling of *Willard* is a beautifully composed dark fantasy for a cynical audience looking for demented nastiness with heart.

Ben's new human friend Lee Harcourt Montgomery reads about the rats' escapades in *Ben*.

The original *Willard* ended with the doomed anti-hero being eaten alive by rats, and so the sequel *Ben* (named after the large black rat that refused to listen to his human oppressor) begins from those final terrifying moments.

Ben (1972) is an oddity, a strange film that lacks the compassion of its predecessor but also most notably lacks the creepy malice. *Ben* leaves

143

Ben and his friends tear away at the legs of Lee Harcourt Montgomery's bullying enemy, from *Ben*.

you wondering how a very strong precursor can have such a benign follow-up that creates no real tension whatsoever. However, it is not without its charms, and despite the lack of intellect, *Ben* does maintain heart and an interesting premise.

After the rats are seen killing the previous film's lead (and yes, it is footage from the original), a detective investigates but is not entirely certain that an army of rats are to blame. Ben, the head honcho of the rat pack, escapes the Stiles' manor and makes his way to a quaint suburban house where he meets a little boy named Danny, played by terminally cute Lee Harcourt Montgomery.

Montgomery's Danny is a lonely boy who has a heart condition. He is in a fatherless home with a doting mother (Rosemary Murphy) and fashion-designer-in-training sister (Meredith Baxter, incidentally, was in an eco-horror TV movie, *The Cat Creature,* an eco-horror film directed by Curtis Harrington) but chooses to isolate himself playing alone, working on his puppets and composing music. He is also the target of bullying from a local tough. The loneliness and lack of a male role model hovers like a pendulous black cloud and heightens the importance of his newfound relationship with Ben the rat. Many horror and science fiction movies that followed feature houses marked with an absent father (*The Exorcist, Carrie, E.T.: The Extra-Terrestrial, Close Encounters of the Third Kind*), bringing the plight of mother/protector to the surface (i.e. *The Exorcist*). Such films also highlight the need for little boys to have a companion that can replace the absentee father.

A sensitive boy, Montgomery's Danny keeps himself locked up in his room away from the rest of the world, but after forming a special bond with Ben, things start to look better for him. He becomes more social, more interested in his mother and sister and less frightened of the local bully. Of course the faithful Ben, by this time becoming far more humanized through his friendship with Montgomery, attacks the local bully and, along with his army of rats, rips apart this obnoxious kid's legs. Ben's army of rats have been causing great stress for the city, killing people in sewers and supermarkets, as a detective tries to make sense of all the bloodshed.

Where *Willard* was an amazing character study, *Ben* is a safe film with a strange made-for-TV feel. The standout feature in this strange, sleepy movie is Lee Harcourt Montgomery's ode to his furry friend, a song made famous by a young Michael Jackson. Simply called "Ben's Song," the song received an Oscar nomination for Best Song that year and captures the connection between a lonely child and a misunderstood animal.

The misunderstood animal is a staple in horror cinema. Much like snakes and spiders, rats are commonly associated with the fear of death and archetypal horror (remember their inclusion in Draculean mythology?), and rats feature in many more horror movies, such as the Stephen King adaptation *Graveyard Shift*, *Deadly Eyes* (aka, *Rats*) and many more.

Their counterpart the snake has also featured in many horror films, and two of these horror films are perfect examples of the human help branch of the natural horror movie tree. *Stanley* and *Jennifer* both deal with snakes. They also deal with people on the fringe, marginalized individuals who enlist the help of slithering serpents. Snakes and spiders have been noted as being the two most feared creatures on the face of this planet. Many a survey have found that these two most hated critters have struck terror into the hearts of people everywhere, so it makes sense that a movie like *Rattlers* or *The Kingdom of the Spiders* has such an impact. When these creatures are the minions of a disenfranchised, abused or vengeful human they may be even more terrifying. After all, the human race is capable of more damage than any other mammal on Earth, and to put man or woman in cahoots with these creepy creatures is a sure-fire way to get an audience to scream!

A film like *Rattlers* paints the slithering menace of snakes as the "other," a wild thing that does damage on its own, whereas both *Stanley* and *Jennifer* connect the world of snakes to two characters completely out of touch with humanity, characters who are completely obsessed by the world of reptiles.

Stanley (1972) tells the story of a partnership between a Seminole Indian named Tim and his friend Stanley, his faithful rattlesnake. Tim (Chris Robinson) has recently returned to the U.S.A. from his tour in Vietnam, serving in America's most notoriously unsuccessful war. Robinson's Tim is completely disinterested in relating to his fellow man and lives in isolation deep in the everglades with his only friends the snakes, including the large and super-supportive Stanley. Robinson's efforts in the war have obviously shattered his opinion of the entire human race so the company of slimy serpents is far more appealing. Also, the fact that he can communicate and shares a beautiful bond with snakes is something to treasure. Robinson's loner Native American has found solace in the company of snakes. He is a man ruined by the system and who is no longer a part of society. Even his own people, the Seminole Indians, do not understand his misanthropy and worry about him.

Chris Robinson as Tim prefers the company of Stanley the snake and Stanley's bride Hazel over people, from *Stanley*.

The film sets up some magnificent plot devices. Robinson's main adversaries are local reptile poachers who are not only a direct threat to his snake friends but also horribly racist and malicious in everything they do. Robinson has a passionate but somewhat stinted relationship with a stripper who uses one of his pet snakes in her act, the film making a wonderful parallel between a woman who takes her clothes off for a living and a snake that sheds its skin. Both are sympathetic, open and honest creatures that care about our leading man. Also, the truth behind the death of Robinson's father is not dwelled upon but instead becomes the catalyst for the snakes to act on their master's anger. These snakes, magnificent and well trained, revel in their service to their master and they kill those who do him wrong.

Stanley presents a satisfying portrayal of a man bent out of shape because of the evil of an unjust system and the devastating results of war. Although director William Grefe claims that he made the film in response to the success of *Willard* (based on the idea that the newest, most profitable movie monster are unremarkable animals like rats and snakes), the movie was made at a time when Vietnam's horrific happenings had a major impact on young artists creating their initial works. The war did leave a lasting influence on diverse pieces of film and theater, from the innovative rock musical *Hair* to strangely quiet movies like *Coming Home*. The terrors from Vietnam echoed throughout Hollywood and the ecologically themed horror film was not exempt from this influence. *Stanley* is a perfect example. If *Willard* dissected domesticity and vocation, *Stanley* had something biting to say about the state of the human condition post-war. In Grefe's intelligent movie, the snakes shed their skins all the while the human cast is stripped of their humanity. The tagline for *Stanley* reads: "Tim has a pet rattlesnake … when Tim gets mad, Stanley gets deadly"

Chris Robinson has a deeply meaningful chat with his snake in *Stanley*.

This effective marketing ploy sums up *Stanley* perfectly, and it could well have been used for the next movie we explore.

The only difference in our next movie is that instead of a hardened, bruised and down-beaten misanthrope as the protagonist, the central figure is a delicate, hopeful, doe-eyed beauty that only wants to be loved and respected. *Jennifer* (1978) was released right after the hugely successful *Carrie*. It has been called a *Carrie*

Lisa Pelikan as *Jennifer* unleashes her beloved snakes onto her tormentors in this ode to Brian De Palma's *Carrie*.

rip-off, much like *Orca* and *Piranha* were pigeonholed as *Jaws* clones. However, much like De Laurentiis's killer whale movie and Dante's socially aware killer fish flick, *Jennifer*, although it borrowed from basic narrative principles that were established in a classic like *Carrie*, holds up on its own merits and is a slick, sophisticated and emotionally stirring ride.

In *Jennifer*, a lowly, bullied teenager is bestowed with the gift of communicating with snakes. She uses the reptiles to do her bidding when the going gets tough. When life gets too hard for this poor backwater innocent, she summons her slithering serpent friends to unleash terror unto her tormentors.

Lisa Pelikan plays the troubled Jennifer Baylor to perfection. She is beautiful much like Sissy Spacek's Carrie White is beautiful, but her beauty is restrained by her low self-esteem. Pelikan plays the role with soft, sweet sadness, a perpetual melancholy that is both heartbreakingly painful as well as downright pitiful. The film shares another similarity with Brian De Palma's horror classic *Carrie* in that the lead has an intense relationship with a parent. In *Carrie*, Spacek's relationship with her mother is a horrific and abusive one, whereas in *Jennifer*, Pelikan and her widower father share a loving relationship. However, it is a strong bond in which a dark secret hovers over their relationship, something that only father and daughter completely understand. As a child Jennifer had an innate connection to snakes. She could communicate with them, instruct them, train them and make them do whatever it was she pleased, and the only other person to fully comprehend this talent was her father. In the small-town where she lived, Pelikan as a young girl had the snakes kill the local preacher's son, a boy who was tormenting her. This is something from the past that she just doesn't want to remember. When her father found out he decided to pack up and take his little girl away. The two move and decide to start a new life together; Pelikan vows never again to turn to her snakes to cope with life's problems. Pelikan's father, who is mentally disabled, owns a pet store and relies on his daughter to help him out. As his mental health deteriorates he begins to encourage his daughter to communicate with snakes once again and to use her talent. She remains hesitant and continues without their help.

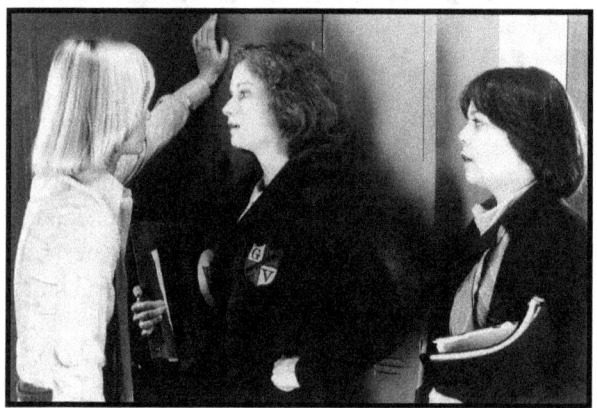
Bullies Amy Johnston and Louise Hoven pick on poor Jennifer, not knowing about her special power over snakes, from *Jennifer*.

The hardworking Pelikan receives a scholarship to an extremely upper-crust private girls school and her father insists she go and follow her dreams. Eventually she takes up the offer, promising she will return home to her father on school break. When she arrives at school in her secondhand clothes and with tattered books, she is the target of mockery. She becomes a social misfit for the other girls to torment. These vicious girls (reminiscent of Nancy Allen and company in *Carrie*) despise Pelikan simply because she is poor and different. Many cruel tricks are played on Pelikan and the nastiness just grows unbearable. But Pelikan befriends some sympathetic people who soon, in turn, also become the targets of her violently hateful peers. These peers are truly revolting—they try to drown her, steal her clothes kidnap her, put her in the trunk of a car and attempt to run her over at a car rally.

Finally, Pelikan, now pushed too far and wanting to protect her fellow bullied misfits, calls upon her friends the snakes to help her out. The film turns into a wonderfully scary Greek tragedy where these slithering, sinister serpents seek out these nasty rich kids and kill them all! *Jennifer* is a satisfying revenge flick and a gloriously visually stunning one. It's not up to *Carrie*'s standards, but it is a perfect movie featuring a stunning musical score by Porter Jordan.

Snakes are the menace as well as the misunderstood in one of the strangest and yet most endearing movies ever to come out of the 1970s. It is the first of three movies we will be discussing that deals with an animalistic metamorphosis, a common theme in the natural horror film. Even the title of this movie is a spectacle—*Sssssss,* and it is a gem of a picture!

Sssssss (1973) is a senSsssssational movie, an absolute treat. The spectacle of the young man turning into a human-snake hybrid is just superb. It is

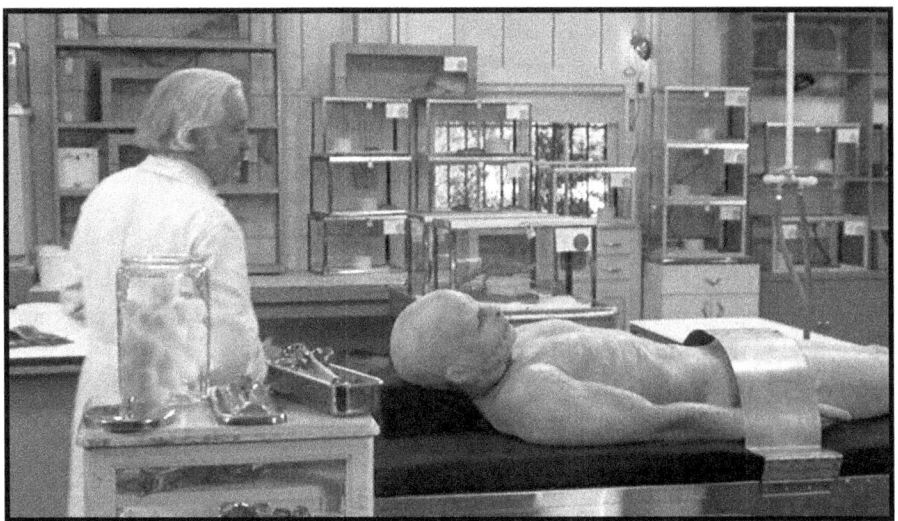

Dirk Benedict is hardly recognizable as the human/cobra hybrid made possible by the deranged Strother Martin in *Sssssss.*

a charming little movie with a lot of heart and good intentions and should not be written off as just another exploitation horror movie.

This visually sumptuous film is about a zealous student, played by handsome Dirk Benedict, who is enlisted as an assistant to the charismatic Strother Martin, a reclusive and obsessive ophiologist (the specific study of snake behavior and its natural history). This makes Benedict the target of bullying by a local football-playing meathead who ostracizes him from the rest of his peers. His relationship with Martin is solid from the beginning and he is quite happy to be the old man's assistant. Benedict's trust in Martin's scientific research involving snakes and their venom is evident when he openly lets the old scientist inject him with serums that he claims will protect him from venomous bites. Unfortunately, for Benedict, this serum is a formula that Martin is secretly working on that will eventually turn the young college student into a human/cobra hybrid!

Dirk Benedict is now a full-blown cobra and brings about a fateful end for villain Strother Martin in *Ssssss*.

Spunky Heather Menzies plays Martin's daughter and she is the epitome of the nature-loving specialist, so common in these films. She is lovely, intelligent and deeply connected to the natural world; her relationship with the snakes that live with her and her father is a beautiful one. She also takes a shine to the boyishly good-looking Benedict and the two have a blossoming romance. However, this romantic union is something that worries Martin and he does everything he can to stop his daughter from falling in love with him.

Benedict starts to feel the changes happening in his body. He has vivid dreams of slithering through grasslands, his skin beginning to peel. When fighting with the local thug, Benedict attacks him the way a snake would attack and his senses start to sharpen and become more serpent-like than human. Menzies struggles to understand these changes but is kept in the dark by her cagey father. The climax of the movie has Benedict finally morphing into a large cobra while a mongoose savagely kills him as Heather Menzies watches on, screaming in terror, finally realizing what has happened to her love interest.

The beauty of *Ssssss* is that it does not borrow entirely from werewolf movies. Instead of simply being a film about a man's transformation from man to beast, it is a staple eco-horror movie that enlists snakes as its monstrous animal. A great scene occurs where Strother Martin lets his poisonous asp kill the football jock that broke the neck of one of his most prized boa constrictors. He stealthily creeps into the oafish buffoon's bathroom and lets the spindly serpent bite the naked beefy brute!

The make-up design for the transitioning of man to snake is well done. It's a stunning example of glorious prosthetics and sharply utilized grease paint. The effects are breathtaking and evoke memories of the memorable *The 7 Faces of Doctor Lao* where the magical Tony Randall plays the snake from the Garden of Eden in his traveling sideshow. The concept of snakes being linked to something ancient and evil is explored in *Sssssss*, but this theme is not heavy-handed and does not get in the way of a terrific story.

The film is masterful. Universal really delivered the goods with *Sssssss*. The ad campaign included a stunning poster with a girl's mouth opened wide showcasing a gorgeous cobra hissing inside, and a theatrical trailer featured a determined voice-over insisting that we not say the name of this movie but *hiss* it! This is this kind of fun showmanship that makes *Sssssss* a super-fun movie!

American International Pictures produced two beautiful metamorphosis pictures in the 1970s, one dealing with someone being bitten and therefore accursed with a monstrous affliction and the other featuring its bestial lead as a victim of circumstance.

The Bat People (1974) is a nice little film with good performances and early special effects make-up executed by the master, the late Stan Winston. Unfortunately the wonderful make-up design by Winston is somewhat wasted in this film. Filmed in darkness, *The Bat People* at times looks as if it has been shot during a permanent blackout. However, the performances, tight script and the great cinematography (particularly during the dream sequences) make up for the lack of monster visibility. The film in essence is a werewolf movie where someone is bitten by a beast and goes through transformations, having to deal with a newfound monstrous existence.

A young doctor (Stewart Moss), recently married, decides to take his lovely wife (Marianne McAndrew) on a romantic trip that includes a visit to beautiful caverns, where a bat bites him. After be-

Husband and wife Stewart Moss and Marianne McAndrew are soon to become were-bats in *The Bat People*.

Shifty police officer Michael Pataki is slaughtered by crazed bats in *The Bat People*.

ing treated for rabies, he insists they continue their romantic getaway and not let the unfortunate attack get in the way. On a skiing trip, however, Moss begins to have hallucinations and strange nightmares as he begins to feel the effects of the bite and believes that he too is a bat! This upsets McAndrew, but she desperately tries to keep her man sane and stable. When Moss is treated for these delusions and panic attacks, the meds start to aggravate his condition and his metamorphosis gradually gets out of hand. But his newfound monstrous self is not as menacing as that of a local police sergeant, played by a loathsome Michael Pataki, who not only takes an instant disliking to the poor bat-man but also attempts to rape McAndrew.

The movie ends quite romantically, complete with a Carpenters-style number playing hauntingly over the rolling end credits. Rather than have our monster Moss lynched by an angry mob or gunned down by the loutish Pataki, the poor bat-person is joined by his wife, and together they venture into the depths of the cavernous underworld of the Californian deserts. She too becomes a were-bat and the two retreat during the day, hiding from the sunlight, ready to re-emerge into the night. In many ways, this film could be the precursor to Mike Nichols' *Wolf* where lycanthropes Jack Nicholson and Michelle Pfeiffer race through the woods at the end of the picture as fully formed wolves free from a world that never understood them as people. Both films *The Bat People* and *Wolf* permit their monsters a happy ending, as long as the monstrous nonhumans live in darkness and outside of civilized normalcy. A suggested promise exists that life can be enjoyed in an animalistic state and this is true for *The Bat People*, as opposed to the doomed animalistic people in *Sssssss*.

The extremely inventive *The Beast Within* (1982) features some of the greatest prosthetic and bladder work ever put on film! Directed by Philippe Mora (who gave us *The Howling 2: ... Your Sister Is a Werewolf* and *The Howling 3: The Marsupials*) and written by Tom Holland (who penned *Psycho 2*, *Fright Night* and *Child's Play*), *The Beast Within* opens with a married couple, played by Ronny Cox and Bibi Besch, whose car has broken down in the middle of rural Mississippi. Cox goes for help and Besch is brutally raped by some hideous creature that has escaped from the basement of a nearby household. Besch falls pregnant to this monstrous creature but decides to keep the baby anyway, her husband Cox supporting her decision and blocking out the fact that he is not the child's father.

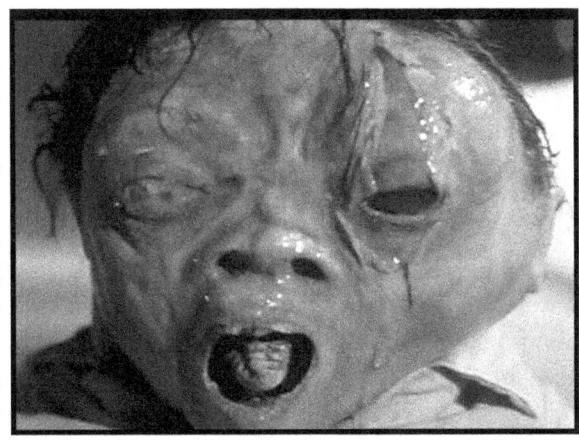
Paul Clemens goes through a painful transformation becoming a giant cicada in *The Beast Within*.

Seventeen years later, Besch's son (Paul Clemens), the product of rape, falls deathly ill. A physician informs the couple that their son may be a victim of a bad gene and asks if similar ailments appeared in the family history. Cox and Besch remain silent about their son's real father (both to the doctor treating their son and to their teenager himself); they decide to go back to the small Mississippi town where the rape occurred to see if they can find out more about the rapist and his health history. The town is made up of a secretive bunch and no one wants to give answers. Also arriving in town is the boy. Clemens has been suffering from intense, fever-induced visions where he sees the basement of the house where the rape occurred. He also hears the intense chirping of cicadas—those noisy insects that seem to inspire the likes of many poets.

After Clemens arrives in the same town as his parents, he somehow transforms into a demonic, bloodthirsty beast that kills a local newspaper editor. The way he kills the man is gruesome as he chomps down on the red raw flesh. The savage killing makes him feel better and, after succumbing to the urges of the beast, his health improves. Clemens also meets a young pretty girl (Kitty Ruth Moffat), whose family is connected with the rapist; she is related to the beast. What unfolds is a highly intelligent family-curse tale

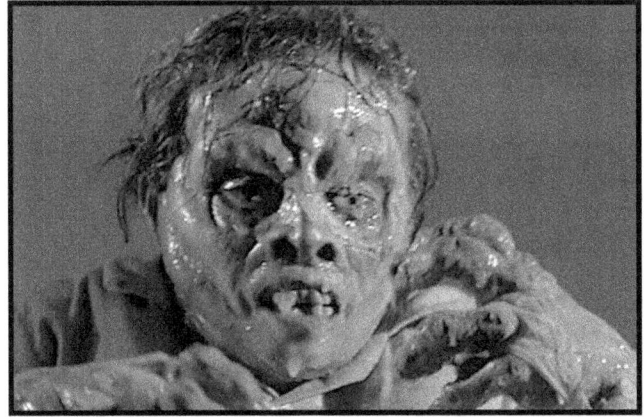
Beautiful prosthetics are used in the terrifying climax of *The Beast Within*.

153

mixed with the werewolf/shapeshifter motif, set to the mold of an ecological terror flick!

The best thing about this film is the climactic sequence where Paul Clemens morphs into a hideous giant cicada. The prosthetic and bladder work is just superlative and his transformation happens right in front of our eyes. I am certain this is the only horror movie ever to feature cicadas as its monster, a refreshing and truly scary outing.

Spiders (a creature commonly used in ecologically-themed horror movies) become the extension of a young girl's disdain for the human race in a beautifully composed grindhouse movie that played as the secondary feature among the likes of superior movies such as *Savage Weekend* and *Burnt Offerings*. *Kiss of the Tarantula* (1976) tells the story of a young girl who is ostracized by her peers simply because they think she's strange. It does not help that her parents own a mortuary. Her only companions are the spiders that she keeps as pets—large bird-eating tarantulas. They understand and help her get through the day; and yes, they even love her. But, besides her eight-legged companions, the little girl does have a strong bond with her father who is almost always busy dealing with corpses arriving for burial preparation. When this sad-eyed little girl finds out that her mother is having an affair with her uncle and plots to have daddy dearest killed, she lets one of her tarantulas climb into her mother's bed to scare her; but scaring her is not all this spider does. The sheer fright of seeing this furry arachnid causes the woman to have a heart attack and the little girl is scarred for life. But she also in that instant understands the power of fear. She comes to realize that the fear of spiders can be deadly for those not accustomed to their companionship. When the little girl grows up to be a teenager, now played by the sultry, sensual Suzanna Ling, she is continually ostracized by her peers and, yep, uses her arachnid army to kill those who torment her.

The beautiful Suzanna Ling as the misfit whose only friends are spiders, in *Kiss of the Tarantula.*

In *The Killer Bees,* examined earlier, Gloria Swanson uses her faithful, buzzing monstrosities to fight off people who get in the way of her ultimate success as a business woman and as a woman who wants to control an entire family. Swanson relishes her role and her conflict with outsider Kate Jackson is dynamic and twisted. Curtis Harrington's direction is terrific in this made-for-TV horror hit containing visually enthralling scenes including those of the bees terrorizing Swanson's large, extended family.

Suzanna Ling directs her arachnid friends to do her bidding in *Kiss of the Tarantula*.

Another film more like *Kiss of the Tarantula* than *The Killer Bees* (in that it is preoccupied with sexual tensions and unnatural connections between a young woman and her father) is a gritty picture called *Pigs* (1972). *Pigs* is a strange movie with an odd premise, a premise usually found in the action movie—the rape revenge film. In essence, *Sudden Impact* has more in common with *Pigs* than say the Ozploitation gem *Razorback,* which actually features a killer pig! It tells the story of a young woman, haunted by memories of her repulsive father who repeatedly raped her as a child, and now raises pigs at a rural piggery located behind a bar she tends. She seduces men that remind her of her loutish father and, after having her way with them, leads them out to her devoted piggies to watch the hungry swine ravage and eat them alive. The alternative title is *Daddy's Deadly Darling* and the tag line reads: "PIGS! They Eat Anything!" I think the genius of *Pigs* is that it actually makes audiences feel as though they've been rolling around in mud while watching this unpleasant exploitation gem. It's a sleazy excursion into uncomfortable territory. But it is possibly the most interesting

Toni Lawrence is the girl hell-bent on avenging her rapist father in *Pigs*.

A poster for *Phenomena* demonstrates how the youthful Jennifer Connelly has a positive communication with insects and animals.

of the rape revenge films that became quite popular during the '70s and '80s.

Of course, not all these human/animal horror movies featured young women hell-bent on revenge, using their ability to communicate with animals to do their dirty work. Much-loved Italian horror director Dario Argento's *Phenomena* (1985, aka, *Creepers* in an edited U.S. theatrical version) stars the lovely Jennifer Connelly as a young girl arriving at a very eerie Swiss boarding school where a series of malicious murders are happening. Connelly has the amazing ability to communicate with insects and animals and these compassionate friends help Donald Pleasance and others to figure out the identity of the campus killer.

The late great Michael Jackson sang the theme song to *Ben* and the opening lyrics went:

> Ben the two of us need look no more,
> We've both found what we were looking for...

This song embodies the soul of these aforementioned movies featuring lowly underdogs finding solace in animals. The compassion they find is genuine, but because these movies are horror movies, the relationships are tested and usually something unhealthy and somewhat demented results.

Unlike films such as *Old Yeller, National Velvet* and *Free Willy* where the relationship between humans and animals is painted in a loving light, these films are about unhealthy co-dependence and obsession; they also involve sadistic revenge, although warranted, and may prove to be the undoing of people who are completely out of touch and who lack healthy behavior.

From the introverted and abused Bruce Davison in *Willard,* to the impoverished wallflower Lisa Pelikan in *Jennifer,* to the sinister grand dame Gloria

Swanson in *The Killer Bees*, human help in the ecological horror film is an interesting and bankable narrative type. Meek underdogs rising above adversity struck a chord with 1970s audiences, a decade that mirrored a celebration of the old E.C. comics of the 1950s where the put-upon and falsely accused got their sweet revenge in the final panel.

As this chapter has pointed out, animals have proven to be the right hand man to human outcasts. They have helped the unfortunate throughout cinematic history as their army of darkness, and in turn have become the embodiment of their human masters' demented wish fulfillment. These twisted, sinister characters are complicated, intricately conceived characters that truly deserve iconic recognition in the horror universe. Move aside those Freddy Krueger and Jason Voorhees dolls and let us have Willard and Jennifer action figures instead!

Now we come to the next chapter in this ode to the ecologically evil, a chapter entirely devoted to the human characters that populate these wonderful movies. From drunken anti-heroes, to sassy specialists, to ruthless renegades, to buxom babes with hearts of gold, these sharply concocted people make the natural and ecological terror film something more than an animal-on-the-rampage popcorn junk pile, as they are so unfairly dismissed by the unenlightened.

Stock Characters of the Ecological Horror Film: Haunted Loners, Left Over Cowboys, Environmental Sympathizers, Sassy Professionals and Wise Indians

The world of art and letters is made up of archetypes and stock standards. The natural horror film is no exception to this rule. The eco-horror film subgenre features regularly appearing stock characters that exist within the texture of these movies so effortlessly that sometimes it's hard to recognize them.

Stock characters are a staple in traditional film, theater and literature. From the sad clown, to the whore with a heart of gold, to the lascivious sissy villain/coward, to the loveable drunkard buffoon and to the doting good ole mamma, stock characters are essential in creating a universal collective, a broad caricature that embodies everything associated with the classic archetype he or she represents.

In the horror genre there are many archetypal creations—the misunderstood monster, the innocent beauty, the mad scientist, the submissive servant, the romantic leads, the wise shaman/gypsy/professor, the angry villagers and so forth. In subgenres pertaining to the horror realm such as the slasher film and cinema demonica, new iconographic archetypes come to fruition and dominate, such as the Final Girl and the very proud monster-in-the-house, such as Regan MacNeil (Linda Blair) in *The Exorcist*.

In the natural horror film a group often pops up to serve this kind of creature feature fare. Such standard characterizations are altered to serve story, place and time and are almost always extremely identifiable and relatable. Since most creature features are set in reality or in realistic settings, these character types are regular people who experience irregular happenings.

A common thread in a lot of these movies (especially those made in the subgenre's most thriving period, the 1970s) involved the male lead as a haunted loner with some kind of vice that keeps him weak and ineffectual (alcoholism being a very popular hindrance). But by about the 20-minute mark he is forced to man-up as soon as he is introduced to the female lead, usually a strong, intelligent and also beautiful professional of some kind. She is usually somebody who has earned her stripes and worked hard, usually coming from a very working class background. She has not only had to fight all her life as someone on the low end of the socio-economic ladder, but she is also someone who has had to constantly fight sexism in her chosen field.

The attraction between the haunted male loner and the sassy smart specialist is either instant or gradual, although sometimes (but rarely) non-existent. At first, the male protagonist is simply interested in the female counterpart's physical beauty, but soon enough he sees a fighter in her that he respects. As depicted in most of these movies, these strong-willed women are also great questioners of authority (political and social institutions of all types). The male lead admires this kind of inquisitiveness and determination and eventually he comes to assist her in whatever the plight may be.

The rogue male's appeal for the woman comes from the core of his inner strength and genuine but deeply hidden compassion that will eventually triumph by the end of the last reel. What usually grounds these loners is their ability to love, even though this compassion hides behind a gruff and stoic exterior.

Let us take a look at some examples of the haunted, drinking archetype and the beautiful, hardworking specialist that populate these marvelous movies.

Bradford Dillman in *Piranha*, William Shatner in *Kingdom of the Spiders*, David McCallum in *Dogs* and even to a certain extent Roy Scheider in *Jaws* all suffer drinking problems. Dillman drinks to dull his loneliness, Shatner drinks to cope with the death of his brother, McCallum drinks because he likes it (he does live on a university campus where the favorite pastime is consuming booze) and Scheider drinks to unwind and deal with the pressure of being a big city cop stuck in a sleepy New England town.

Charlotte Rampling in *Orca*, Tiffany Bolling in *Kingdom of the Spiders*, Robin Riker in *Alligator* and Katherine Ross in *They Only Kill Their Masters* are diligent and warm professionals. They all share empathy toward the destruc-

The three principals in *Orca* (from left to right): the wise Native American Will Sampson; marine biologist Charlotte Rampling; and Richard Harris, an old and rigid Seabee

tive beasts with which they must deal. Rampling, scientifically and spiritually, understands the behavior of the killer whale who was wronged, Bolling possesses a sensitive touch with the spiders that will eventually want to kill her and Riker and Ross's knowledge of reptiles/dogs intrigue the tough, no-nonsense coppers as played by Robert Forster and James Garner. These women are also all environmentalists dedicated to sustaining a healthy eco-system, but they find themselves (along with their male counterparts) at the center of a battle that has surfaced as a result of the rape of nature.

Gender roles are often explored in these films and the role of politically-bent feminism (the women's movement being extremely influential in the cinema of the '70s and became widely covered by the media at the same time that the environmental movement was taking shape) made its mark on the horror genre; *Rattlers* is one of these movies. In *Rattlers* (1976), a Californian town is under attack by dangerously aggressive rattlesnakes. We learn that the U.S. government is responsible for these snakes being so aggressive and it is up to a herpetologist (Sam Chew) and science photographer (Elisabeth Chauvet) to reveal the shifty goings-on.

Elisabeth Chauvet is a fiery feminist who enligthens Sam Chew, in *Rattlers*.

Rattlers seems to be obsessed with male/female relations—the Elisabeth Chauvet character is assertively feminist in her opinions about women in the workplace and her vocalization of her political beliefs is incessant throughout the film. This, however, does not make her character annoying or even repetitious, instead it heightens her motives and grounds her relationship (both professionally and romantically) with the male lead Sam Chew (the herpetologist). Her cool handling of heated situations shows the audience that this is a woman who doesn't let misogyny get in the way of her work, as she investigates the snake attacks.

Chauvet learns all there is to know about snakes while Chew learns something about the burgeoning women's movement. Sam Chew doesn't initially strike us as somebody intentionally painted as a sexist; instead, he is young and liberal, and yet he discovers his personal sexism through Chauvet's fervent feminism. Chauvet and her male counterpart learn together and *Rattlers* makes this point as its fundamental centerpiece. Chew gradually understands that the U.S.

government is a shady and sinister one, and for Chauvet, her suspicions are validated. But Chauvet learns that she is in danger if she doesn't take heed of the advice given to her by her male lead. He also eventually forms a union with her based on the foundations of respecting feminist theory. Chauvet's beauty and intelligence is a staple for these movies and her strength and integrity helps Chew grow as a character. During the course of *Rattlers* snakes cause great stress for locals, as Chew comes to appreciate the complexities and dynamics of male/female relations on the human level.

As Elisabeth Chauvet learns to understand the nature of snakes, Sam Chew learns to understand women, in *Rattlers*.

However, women are not always sympathetic characters who have compassion for the male lead or the focus animal of the film. Sometimes women can be the one detached from the natural world, making them violently aggressive and sickly maniacal.

In *Long Weekend* (1978), Briony Behets is a foul-mouthed, self-absorbed harpy that has a disinterest and distrust in the natural world. She and her husband, played by John Hargreaves, argue throughout the film—an argument that has failed to cease since he found out that she was having an extramarital affair. When they make up and fall into a passionate yet slightly hateful embrace, we feel that everything is just off a little bit—an unsaid disdain and distrust exists in their relationship; something sick keeps them together. As they scream at one another, a twisted passion thrives, but when they hold each other tight in a state of panic, it isn't genuine and seems downright unhealthy. Their ups and downs are witnessed by surrounding fauna that gradually turn on these unlikable humans.

Long Weekend is a masterfully shot piece, written with great precision and expertly executed. It is a perfect film and remains one of my favorite Australian movies. In a chapter devoted to character stock standards used in the ecological horror film, Peter Hargreaves' performance deserves mention. He plays a ruthless, leftover cowboy who not only wants to conquer the wilderness and bring nature to its knees, but he also wants to control his vicious, adulteress wife.

Hargreaves is a menace to nature as he fires his gun at everything he sees, throws beer bottles into the ocean and hacks away at a tree for no apparent

Peter Hargreaves and Briony Behets are the unlikable and eternally bickering couple in *Long Weekend*.

reason. This total disregard for nature is analogous to he and his wife's utter contempt for one other as a couple. Mother Nature in *Long Weekend* becomes the enemy of a warring pairing. Bickering couples are usually pitted against nature interrupted or nature under great stress, and this Australian gem is a perfect example of that. Here, human relationships, as seen in contemporary marriage (be it a perfect marital connection or a flawed one), are no match for the anger and perpetual struggle of the eternally single Mother Nature.

The film works its clever design for Briony Behets's character, demonstrating her ferocious grotesqueness in one specific scene. She finds a large egg and wants to safeguard it (the only inkling of humanity she shows through the film). But when an angry bird suddenly attacks her, she throws the egg against a tree, smashing it to smithereens. When Hargreaves comes to see what caused this violent attack, she screams: "It was a she! She was trying to protect her egg!" The imagery connects her in an instant to the plight of the angry mamma bird just seconds before, grabbing hold of the egg and destroying it. Later we learn that Behets had an abortion without her husband's knowledge (the baby a product of her illicit affair). Her killing the eagle's unborn eaglet links her abortion to her anger towards a creature that relies on prospering through its young. Her resentment toward motherhood lingers like a dirty secret.

Behets' denial of motherhood is once again reflected in a movie that opened the following year. However, in this movie the link between motherhood and the natural world is something woven in a positive light and makes its central character an admirably strong one.

Prophecy (1979), starring Talia Shire, explores female unity with nature while at the same time exploring the notion of male disconnection from it. Shire's imagined association between her unborn baby and the mutant bear in *Prophecy* is

Dealing with nature the only way he knows how, Peter Hargreaves takes aim at a dugong, while Briony Behets looks on, in *Lost Weekend*.

The child as victim in *Jaws*

an ingenious story element that instantly connects her to the natural world and the natural world gone wild. Unborn babies are alien beings, growing inside their mother, developing teeth and nails instead of fangs and claws. The connection between women and nature is almost always clear and strong; the disconnection between man and nature is just as palpable and believable.

Children are also given a plan in ecologically-themed horror fare. Sometimes they are precious innocents that deserve to be protected by flawed parents as seen in *Cujo*; at other times they are victims of a menace that propels the protagonist to take action as seen in *Jaws;* and they are also witnesses to the carnage dished out by Mother Nature as noted in *The Swarm*. In the latter of these examples, children are more than often depicted as diminutive messengers, informing adults, and sometimes the audience, of the horrors that are happening—or soon to be happening.

In *Frogs*, the Crockett children bring a large toad to the Independence Day celebration only to have Ray Milland insist they get rid of it; in *Rattlers*, two children stumble across a nest of snakes but, before they are able to inform their family, are bitten and killed; and in *The Swarm*, a young boy watches his mother and father get killed by African killer bees moments before literally crashing into town to warn the Norman Rockwell-type community about these deadly insects that are on their way to do serious damage.

Children can also be the inadvertent cause of great monstrous happenings as seen in *Night of the Lepus*, thus making for an interesting take on innocence playing a vital role in the monstrosities that will face mankind.

The family (and what threatens the family) is always at the heart of many American horror movies, and although eco-terror films tend to be more fixated on individuals (*Willard, Jennifer*), couples (*Prophecy, Long Weekend*), groups pitted together (*Day of the Animals, Frogs*) and communities (*Arachnophobia, Squirm*), the domestic nuclear family made up of mother, father and children seems to become a more popular archetype during the 1980s.

Before that turning point, movies like *The Mafu Cage* featured animals as a clear representation of familial insanity (and suggested incest). Carol Kane's unhealthy relationship with the orangutan in *The Mafu Cage* borders on the pseudo-sexual, one beset in emotional turmoil, abuse and domestic torment. But the leading lady in *Pigs* uses her swine friends to deal with her problems.

Movies like *The Amityville Horror* and *Poltergeist* brought horror home and planted it right in our living rooms. Incidentally, these two movies also presented the sins of the father in the mold of a modern day Gothic ghost story (also seen in *The Shining*). Around the same time, the eco-horror movie served up its own branch of living room monster movies with *Cujo*, a perfect example of domestic bliss turned upside down and scrutinized (plus reversing the sins of the father concept by presenting an unfaithful wife in Dee Wallace's Donna Trenton) and *Pet Sematary*, a film that tackles family turmoil and anguish plotted in a zombie movie guise.

Carol Kane's unnatural relationship with her pet orangutan is the narrative centerpiece in *The Mafu Cage*.

Another seldom seen film that explores domestic grief is a potboiler called *Claws* (1977). Opening a year after William Girdler's great *Grizzly* (many fans of that monster hit thought it was an official sequel), *Claws* tells the story of a young family living out in the woodlands of California who deal with the likes of a huge hungry bear ready to tear them apart. *Claws* pales miserably in comparison to Girdler's movie and ultimately is not a good film; sadly, the weakest element is its take on domestic unrest. Unlike the genius of *Cujo* and brilliance of *Pet Sematary*, *Claws* features a lackluster subplot involving a bickering couple coming together for the sake of their sensitive son's happiness. This restoration of marital bliss is juxtaposed with lots of Native American mumbo jumbo involving bear spirits, all in servitude for a dull film where most of the action happens in complete darkness. Yep, it's one of those movies where every action packed sequence happens in complete blackout. Ultimately, *Claws* is clumsy in its heavy reliance on Native American folklore and religion which can make for compelling viewing as seen in great pictures such as *Prophecy*, but this brings us to one of the most common stock characters in the eco-horror film—the wise shaman!

Unlike Christian-Judaic-based horror movies such as *The Exorcist* or *The Omen*, many eco-horror movies that dealt with a very American animalistic threat employed a Native American subplot that works exceptionally well and seldom gets in the way of great storytelling. In the superlative *Orca*, Will Sampson plays the wise Native American who warns Richard Harris about the vengeful killer whale (it should be noted that Sampson also played

Loggers and Native Americans come to battle in *Prophecy*. Robert Foxworth tries desperately to make peace.

the wise elder in *Poltergeist 2: The Other Side*, which dealt with Native American spirits and ghosts). Other wonderful movies that benefitted from Native American tribal folklore include *Day of the Animals* and *Bats*.

But one movie brings this indigenous folklore right to the foreground and makes it the heart of the film—1979's *Nightwing*. It is a spectacular gem that just shines as a dynamic piece of entertainment and becomes a different kind of killer-bat movie. *Nightwing* is a movie that really puts the wise native into the limelight, and not only does it shift this staple character from the supporting cast to the forefront, but the film's hero is a Native American as well.

Italian actor Nick Mancuso plays a Native American deputy on a Hopi Indian reservation in New Mexico who is investigating a series of cattle mutilations on local farms. The old wise Native American, the elder who raised Mancuso after his parents died, warns the young deputy that the world is in dire straits and that the wise Native American cast a spell to end it that night. Mancuso laughs this off, thinking the old man is high on datura root, but soon enough more cattle mutilations happen as well as human massacres. The culprit—killer, bloodthirsty bats! Reading much like a Western, *Nightwing* serves up a storm, and when it delivers, it delivers. One sequence that really goes for the jugular is an attack on a campsite where

Outside help comes from Brit David Warner who discusses the science behind the plague-carrying bats to Native American Hopi police chief Nick Mancuso, from *Nightwing*.

Bloodthirsty bats terrorize a campsite made up of Native American sympathizers in *Nightwing*.

the bats, designed by Carlos Rambladi (*E.T.: The Extra-Terrestrial, Close Encounters of the Third Kind*), swoop down and attack. Blood and gore flows and the bats looks great. Their frenzy is extremely well paced and great fun.

The film does rely heavily on Native American diatribe, religion and folklore, and some may find the film, at times, seems like a bit of a talkfest with the bats taking too long to surface, but the film is a great exploration of social change and race relations. Where *Stanley* painted a picture between Native American and white interplay in a black and white harshness beset in hatred from the white side of the fence, *Nightwing* complicates things with Native Americans not being completely holier-than-thou. Of course, in a world where certain groups (unfortunately still known as minorities) are thrown crumbs by Hollywood, an absolute need exists for the mirror of cinema to reflect stories as diverse, complicated and varied as real life. *Nightwing* director Arthur Hiller leaves Native Americans from *Nightwing* to see what he can do for the gays in his next movie, the dreary and long-winded *Making Love* from 1982. Ultimately, *Nightwing* is an interesting and smart movie, with killer bubonic plague-carrying bats! David Warner submits a standout performance in the movie and Henry Mancini's musical score excels.

Unsympathetic Capitalists also feature prominently in eco-horror movies. From nasty, malicious and neglectful human menaces as seen in *Alligator* and *Piranha,* to opportunist entrepreneur wannabes as seen in *The Food of the Gods* and *Tarantula*, these single-minded megalomaniacs are usually killed by the featured animal in grandiose and bloody ways.

Along with the wealthy, sleazy and corrupt upper

The wise but secretly sinister Native American shaman is spiritually connected to the bats in *Nightwing*.

crust, bowery-mouthed, downtrodden, working class bums feature as unfavorable characters, usually portrayed as abusive drunks or just plain mean louts. Ed Lauter's characterization of Joe Camber in *Cujo* is a booze-downing wife-beater. His drinking buddy is much the same. So, when the rabid St. Bernard mauls both men to death it almost seems okay. It heightens the horror of little Danny Pintauro, who all through the movie has done no wrong in getting himself trapped in the over-heated car, gasping for air. Characters who deserve to die always feature in over-the-top death sequences—their bodies brutally chewed to bits or cut to shreds (the no good doers in *The Uncanny*, the murderer of the killer whale's mate and baby in *Orca*)—whereas characters whom the audience wants to survive usually end up doing so, such as Marjoe Gortner and the "good folk" in *The Food of the Gods* and Sondra Locke in *Willard*. They may be changed forever much like the Final Girl in many a slasher film (completely transformed by the experience but all the wiser for it), but they survive nonetheless. If these characters we rally for are also killed, the film usually presents such deaths as a shock ending, happening quickly. If these sympathetic characters put up a fight, it is something thoughtfully elongated and fueled with tension.

The alluring p.o.v. image from the shark's eyes becomes either an image of sensuality or simply food; Susan Backlinie as Chrissie becomes the first victim in *Jaws*.

First victims in eco-horror movies start to mirror the victims in many slasher movies produced during the late '70s. Horny teenagers and healthy, attractive young people oozing sensuality became meals for many animals in the natural horror film. Susan Backlinie in *Jaws* enters the ocean naked, leaving behind a drunk and stoned young man on the shore who can't keep up (*Jaws*, preoccupied with male impotence, sets up its first featured male as someone who can't keep pace with nymphet Backlinie, becoming a masterful foreshadowing of Roy Scheider's inability to keep up with the Great White shark's killing frenzy until the third act). What starts off as a sensual and alluring water ballet turns into a bloody frenzy as Backlinie screams in fear, her body quickly torn to shreds; two oversexed teens are chomped to bits in the opening sequence of *Piranha*; nubile pretty young girls are the first to be mutilated by the rampaging bear in

Grizzly; and lean, muscular boys and thin, leggy girls are the first to be terrorized by fire-popping bugs in *Bug*. Strong-willed, beautiful, independent women are plentiful in the horror genre as a whole and they have featured prominently throughout the history of monster movies. The eco-horror subgenre is no exception. Interestingly enough, the eco-horror movie does give men a chance to sink their teeth into juicier roles usually occupied by women in other forms of horror cinema. These men are allowed to be vulnerable, fascinating and are permitted involving character arcs.

Performers are often used effectively in horror movies; their craft stretched out and exercised in the healthiest of ways. Their versatility is constantly on display in the subgenre, thriving continually, featured prominently in outings such as *Frozen, The Grey* (killer wolves), *Pighunt* (killer pigs) and *Piranha 3DD* (need I even bother?).

Of course, as much as the human cast is the most relatable in these great films, these pictures truly belong to the animals that humans are fleeing, battling or being killed by. Ecological horror movies are a profitable, fun and heartwarming excursion into scary territory—thank goodness for all these celluloid treats and magnificent monster movie memories!

The Animal Kingdom Reigns Supreme: Animal Attack Sequences, Interviews and Other Fun Stuff!

Scariest moment in *Cujo*:

Dee Wallace arrives at the abandoned Camber farm and gets out of her Pinto, which is in desperate need of repair. As she circles the car, she calls out, "Hello?" (a staple cry in many a horror movie), but her cry for assistance is interrupted by young Danny Pintauro, who wants help with his seat belt (it doesn't seem to work). Wallace, annoyed with his "mooooooom!" whine, goes back to the car and struggles with releasing him from the grip of this stubborn seat belt. The camera pans around her (Jan de Bont's masterful camera-eye in its full glowing glory) as if from an onlooker's p.o.v., but this tense buildup is suddenly interrupted by the growling, slobbering, rabid St. Bernard attacking from the opposite end of the camera's eye. This throws off the audience and startles everyone as we see in full demonic force the nature of this violently aggressive beast that wants to tear Wallace and Pintauro apart! When the dog finally backs off, we are left with Pintauro screaming in terror, "Monster! Monster!" Wallace tries to calm him (completely shaken with utter fear herself) by repeating, "It's not a monster baby, it's just a doggy!" and in an instant the sadistic canine leaps up onto the hood of the battered car and digs at the windscreen, eager to rip out their throats and devour their sweaty, tender flesh. This is beautiful stuff!

Dee Wallace is soon to come face to face with the manifestation of her fear and anxiety, as embodied by the rabid dog in *Cujo*.

A Chat with Dee Wallace:

Gambin: How did you get started in show business?

Wallace: I got started in acting very early. My mom directed all the religious plays at church; Dad built the scenery and Grandma did the costumes! I modeled quite a bit and did commercials. I got started in the actual business, being paid for the work, at 27 when I left Kansas City, Kansas and moved to New York. Within four months I had my Equity card and my SAG card. I danced in a lot of industrials and did over 200 commercials. After two years I moved to Los Angeles, baked cookies to get meetings and began doing day roles. The rest, as they say, is history. I actually wanted to be a dancer and was a soloist with a couple of dance companies, but I just didn't have the right build. So I turned my sights toward my next creative love—acting.

The sad face of *Cujo*

Gambin: Some horror fans may not know but one of your very first on-screen appearances was in the Ira Levin-adapted horror hit, *The Stepford Wives,* starring Katharine Ross. What were some of your earliest works?

Wallace: The first job I did was in *Lucas Tanner*. I happened to fit into the costume that the girl—who got sick—was supposed to wear! It was during cookie delivery! Then I did a couple of smaller parts and booked a religious film called *All the King's Horses*. That got me a good agent who sent me on *The Hills Have Eyes* audition.

Gambin: Ah, *The Hills Have Eyes*! What a cinematic gem! What was filming that like?

Wallace: Intense and hot! Very hot! It was very much like a Judy Garland/Mickey Rooney kind of deal! "Let's put on a show!" It was rewarding in the end and everyone on board was absolutely wonderful, especially Wes Craven. We all knew he was someone special who would go on creating genre masterpieces.

Gambin: And then you went on to Karen White, the TV reporter who ends up in a touch-me-therapy-style colony occupied by werewolves in *The Howling*. I'm guessing that was an amazing experience too.

Wallace: *The Howling* was a blast! And my all-time favorite film to do! My fiancé at the time, the late, great Christopher Stone, played my husband.

We were in love and working together!! It was once again like, "Let's put on a show"—everyone in one trailer, working ungodly hours—and having a *blast*. It was the true beginning. It was also the film that got me *E.T.: The Extra-Terrestrial*.

Gambin: How did you meet the very talented Christopher Stone?

Wallace: I hate to admit it, but we met on *CHiPs*! When I got home, two dozen roses were sitting on my porch. We were never apart after that. I suggested this guy for the part in *The Howling*. Chris booked it as his own audition. They found out we were engaged. Dan Blatt, the producer on both, hired both of us later for *Cujo*. Again, both of us were offered *Lassie* by Al Burton, producer of my series, *Together We Stand*.

Gambin: *Cujo* is superb, a perfect film. What was it like working with those big beautiful St. Bernards?

Wallace: They were fabulous—very sweet dogs. Yes, there were like five or six dogs used for different shots. One of the dogs was great at jumping great heights and the other had a good growl. We had to steal their toys and keep them inside the Pinto with us (Danny Pintauro and me) so that they would jump up to make it look as though they were attacking us. It was

Flawed heroine Donna Trenton (Wallace), from *Cujo*

a great film and got me a load of fan mail, clearly marking me as a scream queen for years to come! I really love horror films and these films have given me such joy throughout the years. Thank goodness for horror movies, I say!

Gambin: You worked with some of Hollywood's greatest character actors. John Carradine comes to mind. What did you learn from these people?

Wallace: I learned humbleness and professionalism from all of them. But the biggest thing I learned is to have fun! They had fun sitting around all day. That was a big lesson for me.

Gambin: And you also worked with a lot of child stars, some of them are doing great work today as actors and producers (a certain Barrymore comes to mind). Are there any favorites that stand out?

Wallace: I've loved them all, but Danny from *Cujo* and I grew so close during those long, difficult and emotional scenes. He was an amazing kid—full of trust and willingness. I was in awe of working with him. We still keep in touch.

Gambin: Now you run an acting school, both in person and online. What is your favorite style of performing and how do you go about getting yourself prepared for a role dramatically?

Wallace: I studied with an amazing man, Charles Conrad. He is my mentor. He taught this phenomenal technique of not studying and not over-preparing. It puts you totally in the moment. All the roles I've ever done are from this place of not knowing exactly what I was going to do. It's better than sex. Being engaging, exciting and moving audiences is what an actor lives for—to touch lives, to make people feel, laugh, learn, grow, touch places within themselves they couldn't go to alone.

Gambin: Any favorite directors?

Wallace: Geez. I've had so many, but I must say I adored Peter Jackson on *The Frighteners*. I loved him and his direction, his ease and his respect for all of his cast and crew. But I loved Joe Dante and Lewis Teague as well—you know. They all had unique gifts.

Gambin: What are some of your favorite horror films?

Wallace: Probably *Don't Look Now* and *The Exorcist*.

A Chat With Danny Pintauro:

Gambin: In the last act of *Cujo* Donna Trenton (Dee Wallace) and her young son Tad (played so raw with perfectly channeled energy), stuck in their disabled Pinto, have just realized they are not alone. A rabid St. Bernard, foaming at the mouth, snarling and insanely violent is ready to sink its bloodstained teeth into mother and son. When the dog disappears for a brief second, a distraught Tad screams: "It's a monster mommy! A monster!" Donna's reply is, "It's not a monster, honey—it's just a doggy!" Cujo lunges onto the trunk and goes in for another attack, mighty paws scraping at the window and crazed barking nearly shattering human eardrums. Something so poetically poignant occurs in this scene. Fabricated horrors are nowhere near as scary as the real nightmares that can materialize in real life and tear your face off with unapologetic malice. What do you think makes *Cujo* such a perfect horror film?

Danny Pintauro as the tormented Tad Trenton in *Cujo*

Pintauro: I think it is partly that there isn't anything impossible about the premise of the film. It could happen to anybody … you said it perfectly, the idea that the monster is actually real ... and not from some alternate universe or hell, not a murderer or something. Your dog could be *that* dog ... *you* could be one of those people and it keeps us grounded in a family that is having problems. You care about these people and you care what happens to them. And the music! There's this one underlying bass/drum thing that comes when something is going to happen that still scares me when I hear it.

Gambin How did the part of Tad Trenton come to you?

Pintauro: I was working in New York at the time on a soap opera called *As The World Turns* and the producers of *Cujo* saw my work on the soap and brought me in to audition. My mom and one of the producers swear that the reason I got the job was because of something my mom and I would do after every audition. She would ask me how it went, I would tell her, and then she would say, "Okay, what do we say now?" And I would always say if I get it, I get it, if I don't, I don't. Apparently one of the producers was passing my mother and me when I said this and loved how mature I sounded for a six year old.

Gambin: What are some fond memories of working with the many dogs used in creating *Cujo*? How many dogs were used? What did each dog do that differentiated it from the others?

Pintauro: Unfortunately I don't remember specifics of each dog or their personalities, and I was kept away from them most of the time when not on set, partly because they were always covered in slime, fake blood and dirt. Also the trainers wanted the dogs to stay focused. They were all very sweet, though, when not in killer dog mode. There were seven dogs—a man in a dog suit, a Doberman

Domestic unrest in *Cujo* (left to right): Dee Wallace as the adulterous Donna; Christopher Stone as the local handyman and Daniel Hugh Kelly as the ambitious advertising agent Vic Trenton, holding his young son Danny Pintauro

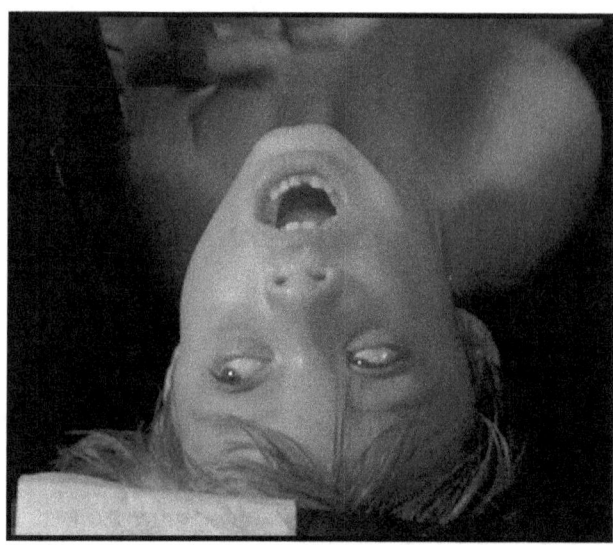

A dehydrated Tad convulsing from *Cujo*

in a St. Bernard suit, if you can imagine, and a mechanical dog head. St. Bernards are not really known for being that aggressive and they don't really bark much, so the Doberman was used in a few scenes where you just see the feet and hear him barking. What made them that aggressive though was a training device ... the trainers placed a tiny fake mouse in a small cage and covered it with some sort of scent the dogs recognized. Then they would put that prop inside the car in plain sight—it was this fake mouse that the dogs were so aggressively trying to get, not us. One time the dog actually got into the car. People were always on hand to pull Dee and me out should that happen, but the dog didn't care about anything but the mouse once it got in the car!

Gambin: Dee Wallace, an actress who has not only performed in many classic horror films such as *The Howling, The Hills Have Eyes* and many more, has also worked with many great child stars, notably Henry Thomas and the multi-talented Drew Barrymore in *E.T.: The Extra-Terrestrial*. But she has said in the documentary *Dog Days: The Making of Cujo* (which is on the special edition of the *Cujo* DVD release from a few years back) that she was very much impressed with your performance. What was it like working with such an amazing actress and how did the two of you feed off each other artistically?

Pintauro: Oh, it was amazing. She was just fantastic to work with, very focused and concerned for my safety and mental health. She, the director and others would constantly try to remind me before and after takes that none of it was real and that the dogs weren't really bad. I would laugh and say I know. But I think because I was so easily able to turn on that crazy, terrified screaming that they thought I might be scarring myself. No such luck, I was just acting. But Dee became a second mom to me really. With three months of filming, half of that in that damn car, we became family. That is how we fed off each other, just remembering the relationship and the situation. I mean, if you don't see a dog in the shot, there isn't one, so we would really need to get each other back to that emotional place with no help from a dirty, slimy dog. My favorite Dee story from the movie just shows the level of talent she has. Do you remember the scene in the movie where she breaks the window with the gun? I was lying in the back there but she was only supposed to bang on the window and try to open it. They hadn't actually put in the fake glass yet! But she was so committed that she hit the gun so hard on the glass she broke off the plastic butt of the gun and exposed the metal, which broke the window and cut a big gash in her hand. If you watch real close you can see the gun break and the expression of pain on her face as she gets cut. I freaked out and rolled in the foot area of the back seats to avoid the glass. It was crazy!

Desperately trying to save both her failing marriage and her son, Donna holds Tad close in *Cujo*.

Gambin: What was the most grueling sequence to shoot in *Cujo*?

Pintauro: You know, I was having so much fun being on this set and watching the crew rig the car and get the dogs ready and everything, so I can't say any of it was really grueling. But if I had to pick a sequence, it would definitely be the very end when Dee brings me into the house and tries to give me mouth-to-mouth before the dog comes in. It was freezing cold in that house and they would put heaters under the table, but I was so cold on that plastic and metal table ... and then Dee pours water on me! And of course doing the mouth-to-mouth bit over and over was difficult because we both had all this makeup on our lips to make them look dry and cracked, and she was pretty much actually breathing into my mouth, so it was challenging. If you look closely in the take they used there is a string of saliva when she removes her mouth from mine. My favorite part to film was the scene when my room elongates when I turn the light off. That was fun! They built this huge version of my room that was about half the length of a sound studio and I got to run through it. Fun!

Gambin: Director Lewis Teague has noted that he was attracted to the project because it dealt with real-life fears in juxtaposition with imagined fears—Donna's fear of growing useless and alone, Vic's fear of financial insecurity and your character Tad's fear of monsters in the closet al.l fears are all put on hold when a tangible threat, a violently aggressive rabid dog, attacks. Was this something Mr. Teague ran by you? What was his general direction for creating this effect?

Pintauro: I was six so it wasn't like he and I had long talks about motivation—like he did with Dee about the emotions and issues behind everything. For my character, it's pretty cut and dry—monsters in the closet or a scary dog

With his head stuck in the rabbit hole, the doomed St. Bernard is about to be bitten by a rabid bat in *Cujo*.

trying to get in. But I think connecting the two fears in the scene when I read the poem my dad wrote about the monsters to help me sleep was neat. My motivation was to try to make Dee and myself feel less scared. By reading the poem I was able to do that. And the scene when we are in the kitchen and Donna and Vic are quietly fighting and I break it up with the shark thing, that was probably the most adult emotional conversation on motivation with Lewis I had, you know? Why I was doing that, why I wanted them to be happy, etc.

Gambin: Some film theorists read *Cujo* as a study on the breakdown of the American family (as the St. Bernard's neurological condition worsens, the relationship between Donna Trenton and her husband becomes cold and distant as does the relationships in the Camber household). Other people see it as another fine example of the adulteress-left-in-the-storm subgenre. What are your thoughts on film analysis in cinema?

Pintauro: I think it gives people something to do. I studied a bunch of film theory classes at Stanford and really, there's 30 different ways to interpret any film. But to be a good director or writer requires having talent with relationships and dialogue. Plot and theory has nothing to do with any of that. I judge movies by how they make me feel, by what they leave me thinking about. I'll leave the analysis up to others. That's one of the reasons I would never be a good reviewer.

Gambin: Most pop-culture fans would know you from the long-running TV sitcom, *Who's The Boss?* How did *Cujo* help pave the way for that audition and do you remember understanding the distinct difference between feature films and television?

Pintauro: By six I had already been in over 40 commercials and on a soap opera for many years, but *Cujo* was my first film, so the experience stands out. But not necessarily for reasons you'd think. The props, sets, lights and cameras endlessly fascinated me. I would come to the set wondering which of the four or five cars we would be using that day. I'd wonder how they managed to get the engine out of the car so they could put a camera at our feet, or how they put a camera that spins on the inside roof, and how they would make me look sweaty or give me cracked lips. But then again, I was always fascinated by that stuff, even with *Who's The Boss?* We only went on location with that show once in eight years. So every single outdoor location was actually a set. I couldn't wait to see how they would make the forest or the beach or the snow-covered mountain. Also, if not for *Cujo*, I would not have done *Who's The Boss*?

Gambin: What are you most proud of from *Cujo*?

Pintauro: For me *Cujo* was by far my best work as an actor. And I think I'm most proud of the idea that it was rather easy for me to get there emotionally. There have been some unbelievable child performances since the dawn of film, but you'll be hard pressed to find many where the child spends half of the movie screaming, crying or convulsing. So I'm proud of that. I'm proud to have worked with Dee and I'm proud to be able to say I've been in a Stephen King movie. I think just getting the role is exciting too, that they could tell I would be able to deliver that level of intensity, you know?

The Trentons reborn! Dee Wallace, Daniel Hugh Kelly and Danny Pintauro from *Cujo*

Gambin: Were there ever any conversations being discussed on set or in pre-production that involved the character of Tad dying at the end of the film? Was anything filmed depicting this?

Pintauro: I've been told that we filmed it both ways, but I only remember filming the version that made it to screen, where I live. I think maybe for my mental health they sort of glossed over that I was dead while filming those scenes. I was supposed to be playing *almost* dead. So maybe I do remember filming them, but I'm not sure on this one. I've also been told that they screen-tested the dead version and audiences were really pissed off about it, so they used the upbeat version. But don't quote me as I don't actually know the whole story.

Gambin: Once you read Stephen King's novel years later, what would you have loved to see from the novel in a final cut of the film?

Pintauro: I've never actually read the book. I guess I could now ... but for years I wanted to remember the movie as the movie. It is all too often that reading the book makes you less happy about the movie because so much is cut out or changed. I mean, the Harry Potter movies are a perfect example. So I think I've just shied away from the novel for that reason. I'll have to give it a go and get back to you!

A Chat with Charles Bernstein (composer for *Cujo*):

Charles Bernstein was born to compose musical scores for motion pictures. He gave musical life to many a fan favorite: Nancy's dreams in *A Nightmare on Elm Street* came accompanied with Bernstein's eerily airy eight-note wonder, Tammy Blanchard's endless battle with her many inner-selves played against a truly emotive piano-driven score for the 2007 remake of *Sybil* and even George Hamilton's tanned Count Dracula in *Love At First Bite* benefited greatly from a bright, stringy composition that paid homage to Eastern European folk music. But for this writer, the stand out Bernstein score has always been that multi-layered, intense and equally touching music from that relentlessly raucous horror gem, *Cujo*.

Composer Charles Bernstein hard at work conducting in the studio.

Gambin: How did the job of writing the music for *Cujo* come about?

Bernstein: I had done a prior film for producer Dan Blatt. When Dan began *Cujo*, he asked me if I was interested in doing the music. I had already scored a number of horror and suspense films, including Sidney J. Furie's *The Entity* and several scary TV movies. As it turns out, I already knew the director, Lewis Teague. We had first met years earlier when I was scoring a feature documentary called *The Last Jews From Poland* for producer Burt Schnieder, and he was working as an editor. (Burt's brother Harold Schnieder produced *The Entity*). So, I told Dan that I would love to tackle *Cujo*, and I was especially happy that Lewis was directing and the great Dutch cameraman Jan De Bont was the cinematographer.

Gambin: Did you read Stephen King's novel before watching the first dailies?

Bernstein: No. I try to avoid reading a story before seeing the film. This way, the film gets to make the first impression on my consciousness. Much of the musical identity of a score comes from the way a film looks and feels, from choices the director makes when he or she interprets the story for film.

Gambin: By the time *Cujo* was to be adapted for the silver screen, other Stephen King novels had been turned into celluloid horrors. Some had very distinct scores, for example, Pino Donaggio's grandiose yet tender scoring for *Carrie*. Then we have Wendy Carlos' minimalist, creepy keyboard work for *The Shining*. Were you a fan of these scores and did their existence influence your work for *Cujo*?

Bernstein: No, I don't think those composers ever directly influenced me. However, I do recall being impressed with the many pieces of music that Stanley Kubrick used in *The Shining* (and other of his films) by the Polish composer Krzysztof Penderecki. His use of clusters of sound and closely voiced string textures influenced me, and I think this can be felt in parts of the *Cujo* score.

Charles Bernstein (left) poses with one of film music's finest, John Williams.

Gambin: From exploring certain themes that make up the fabric that is *Cujo*, such as real-life fears as opposed to imagined ones, including infidelity, a marriage in decay, childhood anxieties, bloodlust and disease driven carnage, what did you set out to do musically for this horror parable?

Bernstein: You are right that *Cujo* owes a lot of its effectiveness to the multiple layers of its story. The music does underscore these different elements. The family had its own musical themes and colors. Warm, sad, thematic, with strings and piano. The boy's material features a sort of sweet/plaintive piano motif, and this musical idea gets folded into the music for the parental conflict. Cujo himself has a theme featuring low French Horns over shadowy cello/bass clusters. The horn melody refers back to the ancient hunting, bloodlust heritage of dogs. It turns darker and more sinister with Cujo's transformation.

Gambin: After seeing the first cut of the film, what scene or sequence did you rush out to compose for first and why?

Bernstein: I like to start at the beginning of the film, and then double back to add and change things as needed. The family elements were written first. I was a third of the way through the film when I finally settled on Cujo's theme. Then I went back and worked it into the earlier scenes, like that moment when Cujo first appears in front of the rabbit in the opening sequence. Although I originally had something there for the dog, I substituted the horn theme once it was conceived. The violent action music that plays later in the film was among the last to be written.

Gambin: In the documentary *Dog Days: The Making of Cujo* you mention that you were somewhat influenced by fellow composer and close friend John Williams, who used menacing low end cello for the shark theme used for *Jaws*. How did you come up with Cujo's theme and what made you choose low French horns for him?

Bernstein: John is so terrific. As I mentioned, the horn idea for the dog was a reference to hunting. But I wanted a more murky hunting horn sound, and I thought about the horn-like sound that John used over the repeated bass notes for *Jaws*. At the time, I thought he had used a low French Horn, but I later learned it was a high tuba. In any case, I finally opted for the disturbing timbre of several low French Horns in unison. And, of course, what John had done for film music in his brilliant score for *Jaws* was to popularize the "off-screen" menace motif in the public mind (those trademark rhythmic bass notes that let us know that the shark was lurking). There's a scene in *Cujo* where the little boy actually jokes at the kitchen table as he sings the *Jaws* shark motif. That's how popular John's score had become by the time *Cujo* was made.

Bernstein poses with Quentin Tarantino

Gambin: The score for *Cujo* is a mosaic made up of an assortment of namely three musical themes. First we find a pleasant dreamlike wonder is epitomized in the Disney-esque opening. Then we encounter subtle melancholy tapped out by simplistic sad piano that is used mainly in assisting the quiet scenes between Donna Trenton and her husband, emphasizing Donna's loneliness and desperation. Finally full throttle horror carries the audience through to the third act of the film where the attacks by Cujo in the Pinto play out in violent spurts. What was your method in tackling this trinity of musical motifs and how did you map out this musicality so it flowed effortlessly without sounding like three different scores?

Bernstein: You have pointed out one of the main challenges presented by this film. Namely, to integrate these disparate elements so as not to sound like three separate scores were thrown together. All of these musical themes and textures were designed to flow together, either juxtaposed or superimposed. Also, they all had certain stylistic traits in common (such as common instrumentation or the raised fourth degree of the scale, etc.) So, the overall musical effect was very unified.

Gambin: What was the main factor that had to come into consideration when composing alongside a sound design that involved barking, growling, crying and screaming?

Bernstein: Well, the music always has to be mindful of the other sound elements in a film. Usually, this involves avoiding the pitch frequencies and rhythmic patterns already present on the soundtrack. An example of this occurs at the opening of *Cujo*. When the dog pokes his head into the bat cave, the bats are screeching in a fast pattern and in a very high register. As a result, I chose to place the music in a low register and a sustained texture. This way, the music and sound effects can compliment each other. The two sound elements can be heard together in the mix without one of them having to be subdued for the sake of the other.

Gambin: Are horror films fun to compose music for?

Bernstein: In a word … yes!

The Goriest moment in *Piranha*:

The attack of the hungry and severely violent killer fish is a sight to behold! Rob Bottin's beautiful work with latex, prosthetics and loads of fake blood just shines here. People swim in a state of panic as these insanely ferocious fish slaughter everyone in sight. Some lucky ones end up on the shore bleeding profusely and trying desperately to survive, shivering in shock and from loss of blood. This is a wonderful frenzy of a sequence that can be watched over and over again. The other great thing about it is the marvelous Dick Miller wandering around and trying to ignore the carnage that is happening right before his eyes.

SFX make-up maestro Rob Bottin shows off his killer fish used in *Piranha*.

A Chat With Belinda Balaski:

Every diehard horror fan instantly remembers that monster masterpiece directed by prolifically talented Joe (*The Howling, Gremlins*) Dante. Dante's fishy frightfest *Piranha* was unleashed into our waters back in 1978. Dante had an amazing way of collecting a troupe of gifted actors and using them effectively in many of his films, and one of them was the brilliant and beautiful Belinda Balaski.

Belinda Balaski offers comfort to little Shannon Collin's fear of the water in *Piranha*.

Gambin: This was your first film with director Joe Dante. What was he like and what was your initial reaction to John Sayles' script?

Balaski: Working with Joe is a joy! First of all he allows everyone his or her creative freedom. I just finished doing *Cannonball* with Paul Bartel and here we were on the set together in San Marcos, Texas. Paul and I had no scenes together and were joking around with Joe saying we wanted to be in a scene with each other. So Joe says, "Okay, just write one." So that night I wrote the moonlight scene with Melody Thomas, Paul and me and the next day I gave it to Joe and he loved it. We shot it! It's actually one of my favorite scenes in *Piranha*! As far as John Sayles and his writing, I just feel he is an absolute genius. He told me on the set of *The Howling* that he loved my Betsy character so much from *Piranha* that he created my Terry Fisher role based upon her! That was the day we shot the morgue scene where he got to be in a scene as the mortician in that werewolf gem. John is a great writer and had all these wonderful scripts up his sleeve just waiting for a break! As a playwright and screenwriter myself, John taught me to write screenplays "as if you are writing a silent film!" He is an absolute legend!

Gambin: Even though Bartel and you don't share any screen time together in *Piranha*, you appeared alongside the likes of horror icon Barbara Steele. Were you a fan of this legendary genre actress?

Balaski: It's impossible to not love Barbara Steele. She is such a horror icon from so many great movies like the Mario Bava pictures, to *Dark Shadows,* to being a great producer with *Winds of War* and *War and Remembrance.* There was no one like Dan Curtis, and the Barbara and Dan combination was amazing. Together they were true trailblazers opening up television mini-series to a whole new level!

Gambin: What was one of the most difficult scenes to shoot in *Piranha*?

Balaski: The underwater scene where it looks like the piranha are pulling me down! There were ten crew guys at one end of an Olympic size swimming pool holding on to a rope tied around my waist! They pulled me across the pool underwater and it looks like I'm going down deep!

Gambin: What do you remember about Rob Bottin's nasty fish and did you get to keep one after the shoot as a souvenir?

Balaski: They used gaffer tape to tie the rubber piranha to my skin! Then I'd get underwater and the fish would bobble around me and I would push them away. Because they were tied to me they'd come right back! All this was good fun till they went to take the gaffer tape off. Ouch! And sadly I didn't get to keep one to remember it all by!

Gambin: What are the strongest factors that make Joe Dante's *Piranha* a stylish film, and how do you think it compares with the more recent *Piranha 3D*?

Balaski: Joe Dante is an editing genius, which is something that sometimes goes unnoticed. He is also someone who has such social and political issues buried deep in his films that they lift the movie up to a whole new level without being preachy or distracting. He is also a huge movie buff and he injects his films with incredible film buff references and his sense of humor is to die for. His is a sense of humor that

Casting director Susan Arnold and director Joe Dante work to make *Piranha* one of the best killer fish movies.

only his audience can love for the wonderful roller coaster ride he loves to take them on! No remaking or re-imagining of his films will ever touch his magic, and this is most definitely the case for *Piranha 3D*!

Joe Dante Remembers Killer Whales, *Jaws* Spoofs and Werewolves:

With a healthy steady diet of horror and science fiction, young New Jersey-born Joe Dante spent most of his childhood and teen years living in the cinema, embracing monster movies of the 1950s and 1960s. "It would cost 25 cents to see a double-feature at the local movie house," says Dante, "but if you lined up early, the first girl and boy would get in for free." Struck down with polio as a child, Dante spent a lot of his time thinking and creating, becoming an avid cartoonist who expressed himself through his vivid drawings. Movie monsters and horror films were not only an escape for Dante but were also an inspiration, as filmmaking became a number one ambition very early on. "It was something I always wanted to do and was lucky enough to do it."

A young and enthusiastic Joe Dante on the set

Working for movie maverick Roger Corman opened doors for young Dante and it ultimately led him to co-directing the cult classic *Hollywood Blvd*. Then Dante graduated to the very clever and satirical *Jaws* spoof *Piranha*. It was those two movies that helped pave the way for *The Howling*, which became most definitely a milestone in Dante's career, as well as being a landmark film for not only the horror genre but for 1980s cinema as a whole.

"I used to cut trailers for Roger Corman's company," explains Dante, "then one day Roger asked if I'd be interested in co-writing *Rock 'n' roll High School* and co-directing *Hollywood Blvd*. This meant I was now a working filmmaker, which was great. After *Piranha* I got offers for all kinds of movies, lots of eco-horror fares such as *Orca The Killer Whale* and giant sea-turtle pictures until I signed on to direct a film called *Jaws: 3 People: 0,* a film Universal planned."

Jaws: 3 People: 0 was to be a co-production with the *National Lampoon* group joining forces with original *Jaws* producers Richard D. Zanuck and David Brown. "Zanuck and Brown wanted the piece to be a serious horror film with an R rating, whereas the *National Lampoon* people wanted it to be a comedy spoof with a PG rating." Dante was not very pleased with these feuding producers who never managed to see eye-to-eye.

"The worst thing you could do as a director is work for people who don't know what kind of movie they want to make." A producer friend asked Dante to take a look at a new film he was working on which needed a director, as the original director had been fired. It was described to Dante as an innovative and unique werewolf movie and Joe's ears pricked up. "I thought it would be great to once again work on an independent film," Dante goes on, "a film where I'd have complete artistic control rather than being at the mercy of a major studio like Universal. So I left *Jaws 3: People: 0,* which was shelved and made way for the legit *Jaws* sequel, *Jaws 3-D*. I went on to do *The Howling*, which was a superb career choice I must say!"

John Sayles Recalls Writing *Piranha*:

Piranha was also a rewrite for me as the original script was a bit too obsessed with the idea that there had to be blood in the water to activate the killer fish (young women menstruating, hippies attacked by a bear, etc.) and I felt that the basic premise—South American fish in North American waters wreaking havoc—was only an extreme example of some wrongheaded biological importation in real life. Whereas *Jaws* is based on a novel much influenced by *Moby Dick* by way of Harold Robbins, the subtext of *Piranha* is the excesses of the U.S. military-industrial complex coming home to roost.

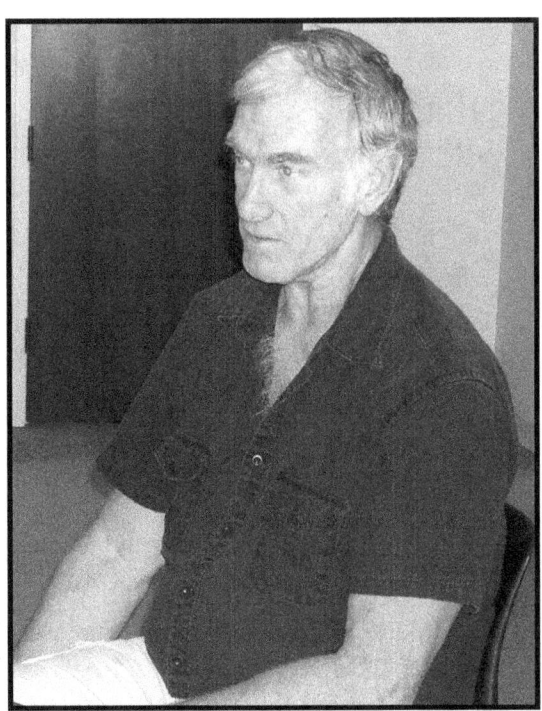

Screenwriter and director, John Sayles

I'd read of Army biological warfare tests and LSD dosing that affected U.S. citizens. I knew of big mistakes like the bringing of the kudzu vine, Siamese walking catfish, mongooses and cane toads to places where they choked off the native flora and fauna. And we're still dealing with the many depredations of the Army Corps of Engineers. All these things can have monstrous consequences, so why not work that scenario into a monster movie? Monster movies have a classic structure. The big whatever bumps off somebody without audiences seeing the creature itself, but then a protagonist sees it in action, escapes, but nobody believes him or her. And then the monster manifests itself in public, the Army tries to kill the beast with conventional weapons and fails, then the protagonist and the scientist's busty daughter figure out how to fight it. There is a climax where the beast is killed or driven into the sea to wait for a sequel (if it's a Japanese movie this happens in Tokyo, as all Japanese monsters are born knowing how to get there). The problem with the piranha, of course, is once people know they're present, people will stay the hell out of the water. So the trick was in devising a communication gap that could last most of the movie (much harder now with everybody carrying cell phones—even Superman has to use the bathroom at Starbucks to change outfits).

I drew a graphic of the plot—first a straight line representing the river the protagonists go down, second a line across it representing the dam they think will

A newspaper ad for the wonderfully sharp *Alligator*

stop the little buggers and finally a stream skirting around it that lets them get to the big circle at the end (lake) where all the campers are paddling around waiting to get nibbled to death. There was a bad drought in California that summer, all the rivers were way too low to shoot in, so they went to Aquarina Springs Resort (home of Ralph the Swimming Swine) near L.B.J.'s ranch in Texas. Roger Corman invited me down to play a small part, but I went there mainly to write some lines explaining why the supposedly new resort looked so second-hand. The perpetrators of the biological outrage get chomped in the last reel (today they'd just get a huge tax break) but the piranha are killed when the hero opens the floodgates of polluted water onto them—PCBs and dioxin turn out to be good for something. I later wrote a TV movie called *Unnatural Causes* about Vietnam vets who were Agent Orange victims, and I always thought of it as the real-world version of *Piranha*.

As I remember, the production had its own eco-meltdown when all the Karo syrup blood they were dumping into the USC pool (where Johnny Weissmuller used to wrestle rubber crocodiles) reacted to the plant life they'd put on the bottom for the underwater shots and turned the whole thing black with algae. They had to bring a specialist in to get the pool's ph level in balance and finish the shooting with burlap plant life below instead of anything organic.

I live near and swim in the Hudson River in New York, and we have a lot of tropical species that survive all year round near the influx of superheated factory water, but so far nothing with razor-like teeth that can strip you to the bone in seconds!

The Strangest Larger-Than-Life Beast in *Food of the Gods*:

A giant rooster is something amazing to see in a movie. I mean really! How cool is a larger-than-life cock-a-doodlin' gorgeously grotesque rooster pecking the shit out of Marjoe Gortner? Very cool! I love the ferocity of this foul fowl and only Mr. Bert I. Gordon could deliver such a beautiful mad rooster!

A Friendly Chat With Bert I. Gordon:

Gambin: Hollywood and your devoted fan base have come to know you as Mr. B.I.G. because you are the master of the massive threat! From amazingly huge colossal men to awesome empires of ants, you have ignited the silver screen with a lineage of movie monsters for which horror devotees

The giant rats have the human cast trapped in Bert I. Gordon's *The Food of the Gods.*

around the globe are forever thankful. How did all this start? Where did you come up with the notion that big Goliath monsters will make for good pictures?

B.I.G: I didn't consciously decide to make films with giant kids, men, spiders, grasshoppers, ants, pre-historic creatures because they would make good pictures. The ideas for the films came to me as stories that I wanted to see on the big screen. During the writing of my autobiography, now in print, I asked myself many questions like this one ... and the answers became gradually apparent. I loved horror, sci-fi, and action movies since childhood, and it became my lifelong ambition to make them.

Gambin: Among your movies are *Attack of the Puppet People, Beginning of the End, War of the Colossal Beast* and many more. Which of these gems were personal standouts?

B.I.G: As to personal standouts I think *The Food of the Gods, Attack of the Puppet People, Village of the Giants* and *The Magic Sword* are my personal favorites. Regarding films that I consider my best work to date, this is a difficult question for me because, except for a few of my films, I like them all.

Gambin: You have directed some of the most colorful people known to Hollywood; people who understand the true essence of showmanship and pure entertainment. Among them have been Maila "Vampira" Nurmi, Zsa Zsa Gabor, Joan Collins, Basil Rathbone, Ida Lupino and Marjoe Gorner. What fond memories do you have of these actors?

B.I.G: I remember Vampira as the witch in *The Magic Sword* portraying the role more realistically than any performance of a witch that I remember seeing. Zsa Zsa's performance before the camera and off stage was all Zsa Zsa ... right down to tossing the first lunch on the floor that she was served in her dressing room, making the comment, "Zsa Zsa does not eat from a paper plate. I want to see my director." After going to her room and telling her that she is the most

Marjoe Gortner and Pamela Franklin get ready to burn the giant rats in *The Food of the Gods*.

beautiful woman I've ever known, Zsa Zsa was as sweet as a kitten for the rest of the shoot. Joan Collins, star of *The Empire of the Ants*, filmed in the Florida jungle but wasn't too happy falling off the boat in an alligator-infested river, this according to the script, but she performed beautifully. Basil Rathbone couldn't have been nicer to direct. One take and it was a print in filming his scenes. Ida Lupino was great in her death scene with a giant rat the size of a jungle tiger.

Gambin: During your brilliant career, as well as relying on stop-motion, puppets and animatronics beasts, you have had to work with the likes of all sorts of real life insects and animals, from the mighty super-imposed arachnid in *Earth vs. The Spider* to the fabulous rats in *The Food of the Gods*. Which creepy crawly or furry beast was the hardest to train and work with and which were the easiest?

B.I.G: As I describe in my autobiography, the hundreds of rats that we trained for their scenes gave us a major problem when they were on camera. Of all the beasts I had in my films, the easiest to work with was the 20-foot python. He just did his thing wrapping his huge body around the Cyclops, squeezing it tighter and tighter with the intention of having our star for dinner. Of course our animal handler prevented it from happening by jumping into the scene after I shouted "Cut," unwinding the reptile in time before we lost the actor.

Gambin: *The Food of the Gods* is my personal favorite of your films. How did that come about and what was it like to shoot?

B.I.G: Being a fan of H.G. Wells, I bought the film rights to the story from his estate in England, and after writing the screenplay, my agent made a quick deal for the production. Upon its release, it was a top box-office hit in the theaters across our country. The film won first prize for fantasy films at a Paris film festival.

Gambin: What is happening now in Mr. B.I.G's world? Any new films we can look forward to?

B.I.G: I just finished writing a far out parody of the genre of the films I've made called *Colossal Kids, Big Bugs, and Giant Rats*!

The Most Tragic and Yet Most Satisfying Scene in *The Swarm*:
There was a period in horror movie history where children were just not really allowed to die … this is bullshit to me! I totally believe everybody should be up for inclusion in the horror body count, and when children are slaughtered, it is even more tragic and intense! Back in the mid-'70s, this was the case. Children, like every other human mortal, were up for the taking and a wonderful sequence in *The Swarm* occurs where little kiddies are stung to death by nasty African killer bees! Golden Age Hollywood royalty Olivia de Havilland watches as these aggressive insects kill her students. The lovely slow motion works a treat here and a great shot of a child still clinging onto his lollypop as bees congregate on his limp body still startles. It's a beautiful moment in this rather lengthy production!

The Most Unnerving Bit in *Pet Sematary*:
The story is so solid and devastating, especially for young fathers. The book and film really speak to young men who are new dads or daddies-to-be because the film really dissects the anxieties relating to not being able to protect your young. Just like *Rosemary's Baby* really played on the fears of motherhood, I believe *Pet Sematary* taps into the paranoia of young men being responsible for a human life. The scariest moment comes where Churchill the cat drops the dead rat into the bathtub, scaring the life out of the protagonist. Churchill's unholy eyes—gleaming with otherworldly disdain for his master—speaks bucket loads. His transformation into a zombie cat after re-emerging from the Micmac burial ground is nicely realized in Mary Lambert's movie adaptation of the beautifully written Stephen King novel.

The Best Example of Animals Trapping Humans As Depicted in *The Pack*:
Dogs that rip apart a cabin in the woods make for some exciting cinema! *The Pack* is a triumph of filmmaking and features some of the best animal acting ever.

The very hungry dog leader traps the likes of Joe Don Baker in *The Pack*.

The leader of the pack is such a charismatic villain. Its snarl, the bared white gleaming teeth, the eyes fixed with burning intelligence and cunning—this dog means business! Many natural horror movies rely on an animal closing in

on the human survivors and forcing them to barricade themselves inside a tight space, and *The Pack* does this with great ease. The dogs tear away at the wood panels, smash down doors, crash through windows—it's a wild, anarchic celebration of doggy demolition!

Screams of Fiery Terror in *Bug*:
Patty McCormack comes to visit the isolated Bradford Dillman character. She has his dead wife's Bible with her and is concerned about her widower friend. When she arrives at his strange little shack out in the vast desert lands of California, she finds that no one is around. She calls out and looks around, but no sign of him can be found. Suddenly, without warning, a rather large cockroach lands on her face and digs into her skin with its feelers. She screams in agony. The creature starts to ignite and burn her. She screams in a panic and runs for her life. More bugs seem to latch onto her and light up, her skin burning black and her flesh running red with raw, fresh blood.

Patty McCormack Recalls Shooting *Bug*:
Jeannot Szwarc was a great director and he demonstrates some terrific stuff. I especially enjoyed working with Alan Fudge and we worked together a couple of times after shooting *Bug*. I was sorry to see that he has since passed away. He was a gifted actor and someone I will truly miss. Working with the very talented Bradford Dillman was a great experience also.

My most Technicolor memory surrounding *Bug* involved the roaches being pasted on my face with spirit gum and breaking for lunch with a huge rubber creepy crawly still stuck to my face! I ate lunch with a huge bug on my cheek. It was annoying having to eat with this huge creature stuck to my face, but I think it was worse for my lunch mates who had to watch this gruesome thing sucking at my flesh! Producer William Castle was present on one of our locations in Riverside, California, but I cannot really remember him being there other than that. He seemed larger than life to me, like a classic old movie mogul!

More Bugs…

Cockroaches make another striking appearance in one of the *A Nightmare on Elm Street* movies. The extremely successful franchise exploited paranoiac fears of the creepy crawly in the fourth installment, *A Nightmare on Elm Street 4: The Dream Master*, where actress Brooke Theiss has a major phobia of roaches and in her nightmarish dreamscape morphs into one herself. But soon a demonic Freddy Krueger (as wickedly portrayed by the wonderful Robert Englund) crushes her.

A Chat with Brooke Theiss:

Gambin: You definitely get to have one of the most memorable and truly original death sequences of the franchise involving morphing into a human cockroach and being squished by Freddy. What can you tell me about this amazing SFX sequence?

Theiss: I would like to say that I had a blast working with Screamin' Mad George, who was the SFX make-up artist. Well, it was interesting to say the least. First off I love all things with one exception—cockroaches. Ewwww! So, it wasn't hard for me to act like I was grossed out. I started out in Screamin's (as I liked to call him) studio, getting full upper body casts taken. Screamin' was actually catching cockroaches in roach motels so he could study them. He would bring in this overflowing motel just to freak me out. So gross!! On set I spent about three hours in the make-up chair. His crew applied the mounds of flesh hanging from my upper torso and then meticulously airbrushed all of the skin. After that, I would slip into the cockroach arms that I would actually control just by moving my own arms. They were on hinges and very heavy. It was pretty cool and very physical at the same time. In the roach motel, I was actually inside a cockroach body with my camouflaged arms sticking out in front, so I could push up. We filmed that for hours in the middle of the night out in Valencia, California. It was some of the most physical work I've ever done. Looking back, I have some very fond memories of the whole SFX experience

Brooke Theiss from *A Nightmare on Elm Street 4: The Dream Master* featuring her insect costume.

Gambin: With the previous films already established as smash hits and instantly becoming part of horror cinema history, were you already a fan and what was your reaction when told you were going to be an Elm Street kid?

Theiss: I am a huge fan of horror films and love getting scared, so of course my BFF Michelle and I ran as fast as we could to see the first *A Nightmare on Elm Street*. We spent most of the movie sitting in each other's laps!!!! It was the scariest movie I ever saw and I loved it!!! Then, I just so happen to get cast alongside Heather Langenkamp on a TV show called *Just the 10 of Us*. I was quite tickled when I found out that she was the girl from *A Nightmare on Elm Street*. Joann Willette, who played my younger sister, had been in the second installment of the franchise. So, when I was cast as one of the Elm Street kids it was quite thrilling. So we started a running joke that everyone on the TV series at some point would be cast as an Elm Street Kid. Needless to say, *A Nightmare on Elm Street* was quite popular on our set.

Gambin: I've always believed that the horror genre is one of the only genres where women are almost always the protagonists. In horror films women run the show! As a young actress breaking into the industry, was this something that appealed to you?

Theiss: I have to be perfectly honest. Like you said, I was a young actor. So, I was just happy to book a job and a cool project at that. The fact that I would be playing a strong female character never crossed my mind. However today, that would be very appealing to me. I had so much fun shooting *A Nightmare on Elm Street 4: The Dream Master* and would love to do another horror film any time, any place.

R.A. Dow as Roger or Wormface in *Squirm*

A Chat with Jeff Lieberman About *Squirm:*

Gambin: What inspired the writing of *Squirm*?

Lieberman: As a youngster, my older brother Gary read a piece in *Popular Science* about a novel way to catch worms for fishing. It involved using a model train transformer, wetting down a dirt area at night, then zapping that area with electricity. Years later, add a couple of LSD trips, stir, and bingo, we have Squirm!

Gambin: Did setting the location in a small Georgian town (a town that is slowly eating itself into oblivion, captured perfectly with the onslaught of bloodthirsty worms devouring the locals) feed your writing?

Lieberman: Actually not at all, because the fact is I wrote it to take place in a small-town in New England. I was very much into Lovecraft at that point and I wanted it set in something akin to Innsmouth. By the time the production got together it would be too cold there and, more importantly, leaves would be off the trees. And I wanted that claustrophobic feel. So we moved the location to South Georgia, a place I'd never been, populated by people I knew nothing about, aside from what I had seen in movies.

Patricia Pearcy as Geri and R.A. Dow in Jeff Lieberman's *Squirm*

Gambin: *Squirm* shares similarities with many eco-horror movies where an outsider comes in and upsets the natural order or causes underlying stress for the locals. Was this a conscious decision in your writing?

Lieberman: I never saw the character of Mick (Don Scardino) as the cause for any of the events that happen, natural order wise. This being my first feature film script, I just applied a tried and true convention—the outsider, the fish out of water, whatever you want to call it, entering a setting after we already know something is rotten.

Gambin: *Squirm* is a wonderful Nancy Drew-like mystery movie that turns into a beautifully gruesome eco-horror film mixed with body horror. What are you most proud of regarding the SFX and make-up designs?

Lieberman: That one scene where Roger (R.A. Dow) gets worm-faced. Rick Baker told me right off the bat that we'd only get two shots at pulling this off because the budget only afforded two sets of prosthetic facial sections. That meant two takes. Period. And the idea of pulling those custom-made rubber worms through that flimsy stuff was a complete crap shoot because Rick cautioned me that it was created to emulate human skin. That it could easily just tear apart when we pulled the strings. But there was no way to test it unless we wanted to waste one of our two takes. Fortunately, some guy suggested using a machine shop fluid to coat the worms and that did the trick. We used that stuff on all the worm shots from then on.

Gambin: *Squirm* has that Southern American Gothic feel beset in deep-rooted oppression where hidden desires and small-town secrecy are like a plague. Are you a fan of Tennessee Williams and his plays?

Lieberman: Like I said previously, the Southern setting had nothing at all to do with my inspiration. And though I was not a fan of Tennessee Williams at the time, Jean Sullivan sure was and she just went off on it. Being my first movie, I really didn't have the confidence to tell her to fuck this Tennessee Williams shit and make this realistic. Which reminds me of something I instinctively felt on *Squirm* that has carried me till this day. When your premise is totally unrealistic, everything else in the movie needs to be as realistic as possible to make that premise work, and the behavior of the characters is front and center. Don Scardino and Pat Pearcy's humanistic performances grounded the movie in reality and that, in my opinion, is why we're still talking about it today. Oh, then, there are still those worms!

Matango (Attack of the Mushroom People in the U.S.) was a classic monster movie with an environment spin.

And Now We Shall Cross Over To John Sayles Who Recalls Writing *Alligator*:

Alligator was a rewrite for me. As I remember, the original was set in Milwaukee and the sewer gator got big by drinking run-off from the breweries—obviously not light beer. I changed the premise to stolen pets that had been experimented on at a laboratory and then they are thrown down the tubes ("Bring me more puppies!"). We decided that Ramon the alligator would, like most social problems, start off in the ghetto and work his way through the social classes and only be dealt with once he started eating the upper class. Killing him off was a bit of a problem in that the animatronics beast had already been promised to the University of Florida Gators as a mascot, and we couldn't destroy it (my early draft had him doused with gasoline and set on fire). Eventually there was just a big explosion. I think I had alligator bags falling from the sky just as they did in the cartoons, but Lewis Teague understood that was a joke. Robert Forster added the stuff about male pattern baldness because he'd just had some follicle replacement. This is a classic monster movie and many of those (especially the Japanese ones like *Attack of the Mushroom People*) have an environmental spin. We had a terrific cast of character actors (and characters) and Lewis really got the tone right. Plus they left in my scene with the 'gator poop. Can you imagine the scat Godzilla must produce?

Lawrence D. Cohen and Tommy Lee Wallace Remember Adapting Stephen King's *It*—The Monster Appears As A Giant Spider In The Final Reel:

Gambin: Was there a scene from King's novel that had to be in the teleplay but just proved too difficult to churn out? What kind of writing process did you adopt in order to flog out this troublesome sequence?

Cohen: Truthfully, adapting Steve in general—and in particular this huge book with its brilliant narrative idea and its grab bag full of goodies—was a joy. My biggest regret was to have to eliminate scenes for length. Gorgeous set pieces and sequences were expendable because the narrative could exist, strictly speaking, without them. There were a surfeit of riches, and it pained me to lose them. In retrospect, the only scene that proved difficult, not to write but to execute, was the final confrontation in which the identity of Pennywise, under all his multiple faces, is revealed to be a giant spider. Had I been on set during production, I'm sure I'd have said with all this time invested in the story, that's it or *It*—that's the best you've got? After all of Pennywise's ingenious shapeshifting manifestations, the actual reveal felt like a letdown. This was something Steve could get away with in the writing, but once it left the realm

Tim Curry as Pennywise the clown in *It*

The embodiment of The Losers' Club combined fears comes in the form of a giant spider in the Stephen King adaptation *It*.

of the reader's imagination and had to be actualized, and with only a meager television budget to boot, this super beast could never be on a par, say, with something like *Alien*. So much for regrets.

We asked the director and co-author of the screenplay a few additional questions.

Gambin: How did you and your writing partner Lawrence D Cohen set out to adapt Stephen King's mammoth book? What was decided early on? What are some examples of what was scrapped, what was altered to fit in a mini-series format and what were the essential elements that had to be maintained?

Wallace: When I came on board, Lawrence had already written a complete script adaptation. I got a call from my agent, showed interest, and the producers sent the script over. I started reading it and decided halfway through I wanted the gig, the writing was that good. It was set up as a two-night mini-series for CBS. I was deeply impressed with what Lawrence had done. The second part had some problems, but the first half was just about perfect. As fans of Stephen King know, *It* is a giant of a novel and there's enough material there to do a week-long movie-of-the-week, so to squeeze the script into three hours was a tall order. Lawrence had done a very clever thing with the first part. Avid TV watchers know that television networks divide their programs into units they call acts. By and large, this practice of segmentation has not evolved. Free television is paid for by sponsors who want their commercials shown as often and as advantageously as possible. In 1989, when this project was being set up, two-hour movies were typically interrupted six to eight times to sell products. Having your movie chopped up into little pieces is never what a filmmaker really wants, but in this case, Lawrence arranged the requisite act breaks in a way that, for the first and only time I know of in television, actually enhanced the drama. It was simple yet brilliant. Seven acts, seven characters. Each character received his own individual showcase, each of them presented as adults getting the big news that It has come back! This was all inter-cut with flashbacks of their childhood group trauma, a mosaic of events which, after seven acts, completes the picture of The Losers' Club back-story and sets the stage for the second part, which is their actual coming-together to re-engage with It. Just a brilliant stroke, an inspired way of structuring things, and a fine piece of writing on Lawrence's part. I filmed it pretty much as he wrote it. Achieving a coherent script for Part Two was more complicated. What happens in the book is, ultimately, an epic, supernatural face-off with an iconic force of evil, featuring a battle with a giant spider, and, finally, a cosmic competition ritual played out in some inner/outer space dimension within the mind of Bill Denbrough, or perhaps within the group mind of the seven characters. It read grippingly, stretches the imagination to the limit and was not filmable, even if the producers had a zillion dollars and all the time wanted. Hey, that sense of novel is one of the elements that made the book so pleasurable in the first place. It is, first and foremost, a literary experience, available in its totality only by sitting down and having a good read. Before I came along, Lawrence (with Stephen King's blessing, as far as I know) had decided to forego any attempt at all that cosmic stuff and keep things on the real, in the here and now. He had also scrapped any physical showdown with the spider, instead inserting a made-up episode in which Bev's nasty husband makes a surprise late reappearance as a pawn of It, tries to kill everybody and winds up impaled on the horns of a large moose head mounted on the wall. Or, something very similar to that. Some climax. Something gleaned not at all from the novel, and, in my view, not helpful or relevant to the drama at hand. I felt that as adaptations go, the second part was as lame compared to how brilliant the first part was, and I said so. It's one thing to simplify your source material, and it's inevitable you are going to be forced to cut a lot of stuff out, but I thought this interpretation went way too far in that direction, unnecessarily so.

Tommy Lee Wallace, the director and co-screenwriter of Stephen King's *It*

Author Stephen King, the creator of nightmares

I felt there was simply a lot more of the spirit of the book that was adaptable and belonged in the movie, and the climax was such a letdown it would disappoint general audiences just the way it disappointed me. Stephen King was not actually part of these conversations. Although he and I enjoyed a cordial exchange of letters after shooting, I have never met the man in person, much to my regret. During prep and shooting he was in Maine, and we were in California. I would love to have had him along as part of these discussions, but the producers made it clear that he was not in the loop. I didn't ask whose choice that was. Sometimes you simply have to play the hand that's dealt. I don't think the second part quite matches the first in its magic (the emphasis shifts, after all, to the adults, and, let's face it, even with great stars, grown-ups can't match that special world of childhood) and I have no doubt that another writer, perhaps Lawrence himself, could've improved on what I did, but I am proud of having captured a great deal more of the spirit of the book than had been there in the second part's script when I first came on board. I rearranged the narrative and introduced a voice-over, coming, of course, from Mike, the group's documentarian. I did the best I could with the seven-act structure, and, most of all, I feel I captured the heartfelt connective tissue that lies at the center of the story, about the bond among these seven people. Plus, though I couldn't do anything with the book's climactic battle-in-inner-space stuff, I provided a legitimate horror movie climax pretty much boiled down from events in the book, a rewrite that emotionally paid off the ultimate quest of the Losers' Club. Stephen King is celebrated for his horrific and often twisted sense of the macabre, but I think his secret weapon, in so many of his stories, is simply that he celebrates childhood—its rituals with the silly and simple kid things that take on iconic importance (magic stones, for example), the bonds of friendship that can last a lifetime and the secrets, even the scary ones. *Especially* the scary ones.

Gambin: Out of all the SFX used to make this mini-series (which included having blood spurt out of a basin as Pennywise emerges from a shower drain and a giant spider hell-bent on feasting on our misfit heroes appearing at the climax), what proved to be the most difficult to shoot?

Wallace: Anything involving fog, like the kid circle down in the Centrum, when It gets to Stan. Fog is always tough, but the "real" stuff is vastly superior to CGI, which, in any event, was not as readily available then as it is now. Also, that little boat was kind of tricky; not the monofilament pulling it so much as getting the camera follow-shot as the boat magically reaches its final destination. Ditto when Georgie was chasing the boat down the street in an early scene. It's frequently the subtler gags that prove hardest. Getting the balloon to come out of the drain and explode was easy, but getting the right amount of blood to splatter on Bevvie's face was not.

Grindhouse Legend William Grefe Sheds Some Light on *Stanley*:

Gambin: How did the impact of *Willard* influence the writing and eventual creation of *Stanley*?

Grefe: I was in L.A. when I picked up *Variety* and read that *Willard* was the biggest grossing independent film at the time. I figured animal horror movies were to be the next big thing. That night, I literally dreamt up the script for *Stanley*, just as if I had gone to the theater. Next morning, I went to see Red Jacobs at Crown International Pictures. He put up the money, and we started shooting within a month.

Stanley turned out to be one of the top independent horror films made at that time. Not only did it have a huge theatrical release world wide, but also it is currently in its 5th DVD release.

Stanley married racial prejudice and the effects of the Vietnam war to make one helluva eco-horror hit.

Gambin: The protagonist is not only a Native American Indian who gets berated consistently throughout the film, but he is also a veteran of war. Did you want to make a statement on racism and the devastating effects of Vietnam with this piece?

Grefe: The statement I was trying to make with the Indian being a veteran from Vietnam was that he saw the brutality of the human race and took his solitude in the Everglades, with creatures of the wild. If you listen to the title song, even though written in the 1970's, the lyrics are current today.

Gambin: What were the snakes like to work with?

Grefe: We had over a dozen rattlesnakes that were five to six feet long, but I had a great animal trainer. Being from Florida, I was used to the Everglades.

But my hat is off to Chris Robinson, the principle actor, who worked with them and created a rapport just as if they were another actor.

Gambin: What was the hardest scene to film?

Grefe: The hardest scene was with Alex Rocco, when he dove into the swimming pool. He did not want me to use real snakes, so I told him no problem, I will use rubber snakes. Little did he know, I had four handlers with real snakes and they threw them onto Alex when he hit the water. There was no acting on Alex's part, as he was truly panicked.

Gambin: Were there any major mishaps or accidents on set?

Grefe: Fortunately, no.

Gambin: The film is very successful in its beautiful pairing of an alienated figure and his animals. The animals in this case being the most misunderstood of all—snakes. What are your personal thoughts on snakes?

Grefe: My personal thoughts on rattlesnakes and poisonous snakes are quite simple. If they cross my path, it's either them or me, so I either avoid them or, if necessary, take drastic action!

Gambin: And what about *Mako: Jaws of Death*?

Grefe: Since *Stanley* was such a giant box-office success, I developed *Mako: Jaws of Death*, and since I could not afford million dollar mechanical sharks, like Spielberg, I used over a dozen 10 to 12-foot Tiger sharks. We had some close calls, but we all survived with our limbs intact!

Ellen Greene as Audrey in *Little Shop of Horrors*

Ellen Greene and Her Killer Plant: A Conversation With Someone Who On Stage Was Eaten Alive But In The Film Survived!

Gambin: From its B picture roots being one of the quickest films ever made at the hands of maverick Roger Corman, to its Off-Broadway incarnation as a raucous rock 'n' roll musical and finally to its filmic adaptation directed by the talented Frank Oz, *Little Shop of Horrors* is such an awesome creation. The story, of course, is a Faustian tale involving a poor schmuck, Seymour Krelborn, who buys an alien plant that has an insatiable taste for human blood! Along with Seymour and his killer plant are an assortment of wonderfully weird characters including a Greek chorus of Phil Spector-esque doo-wop gals, a

Rick Moranis, Vincent Gardenia and the lovely Ellen Greene take a look at the soon-to-be-bloodthirsty plant in *Little Shop of Horrors*.

sadistic demented dentist who loves nitrous oxide a little too much and an "Oi Veying" put-upon Jewish florist named Mushnick. But Seymour's favorite of these misfits is the sweet, petite blonde named Audrey, who is the beacon of hope in dingy Skid Row. Ellen Greene was Audrey on stage and in celluloid, and she is an amazing talent. Her singing style is the embodiment of everything fans love about musical theater and film; she can deliver silvery, comedic sweetness and heartbreakingly moving torch song devastation, as well as delivering the big, brassy, Broadway babe. Tell me how you came to create the character?

Greene: Audrey was one of the very first characters where I put lots of myself in and, luckily, I had the freedom to do that working with Alan Menken and the brilliant Howard Ashman. I got the script and I fell in love with the song, "Somewhere That's Green." It made me cry. Usually if something touches me emotionally like that I know it will touch the audience; I'm a very open and instinctual performer and I can tell if something has lots of heart because it instantly moves me. Creating Audrey was so much fun. I went in to audition for Alan and Howard, and Howard and I got each other in an instant! Audrey's voice just came out organically and I offered Howard suggestions on how the character should look and be played. I decided to make her blonde and suggested she be dressed in tight outfits that she had to continually adjust. And that her heels were so tall that she teetered around like a fresh peach just ripe for the picking! I offered alternatives to some of the lines and gags Howard had written. For instance, in the scene preceding the beautiful duet "Suddenly Seymour," Audrey mentions the Gutter, a seedy nightclub she and the demented dentist met at, and I said to Howard, the word "nightclub" isn't funny, so I suggested

Ellen Greene is about to become plant food in *Little Shop of Horrors*.

I say "nightspot" instead. He loved it straight away and changed it! It didn't matter that I was only making $50 a week playing Audrey; I had an absolute blast! I love *Little Shop of Horrors* so much. A lot of my own personality is in Audrey and I just adore her sweetness and the ability she has to see the beauty in everyone and everything. Of course on the flipside I had to channel a character who doesn't quite see the harsh realities of life for what they are. You see, for Audrey life could be or should be the way she envisions it in the number "Somewhere That's Green." She's such a sweet character and I love her so much.

Gambin: When you found out that the musical stage play was to be made into a feature film, did you have to re-audition for the role? Was there anything you changed about the character in order to down or upsize her for the silver screen?

Greene: Well, at first John Landis was going to direct it, and then Martin Scorsese was next in line as a potential director after Landis was dropped from the project. But things weren't working out for him either. One day I was hanging out with my boyfriend at the time—Marty Robinson, who was part of the wonderful Muppet crew and was working on *Follow That Bird,* puppeteering the beautiful Snuffleupagus. I met up with Frank Oz and said to him, "Frank, you should totally direct *Little Shop of Horrors,* the movie version!" The reason I told him this is because I was in love with his Grover from *Sesame Street.* I said to Frank, "Grover is so sweet and has a heart of gold but he also lives in such a fantasy world where he can't decipher what is real and what is make believe, and that is perfect for *LSOH*." A few meetings later, the amazing Frank Oz was on board to direct the film and the rest, as we say, is history! When I was told I got the part I nearly upchucked my lunch at the Russian Tea House in New York! I heard that everyone from Cyndi Lauper to Barbra Streisand was in the running to get the role. It's funny, most people who do the original stage production of a musical don't usually get the film role as well. I was lucky and extremely grateful.

Gambin: I remember reading something that legendary composer Richard Rodgers wrote in an autobiography that songs were about the simple things in life. Simple things that make a humble working class or poor person happy, like taking a walk, eating nice food, being outdoors, etc. He said that a song like "The Surrey With the Fringe On Top" from *Oklahoma* was one of those kinds of songs … a happy kind of sad. Howard Ashman and Alan Menken give you this sentiment in "Somewhere That's Green," that you embody so beautifully. Ashman's lyrics are superb. They really capture Audrey's simple dream of 1950s TV-style domestic bliss. What are your thoughts on this gorgeous number?

Greene: Originally I sang the number on a trash can in the stage version, and when Frank Oz told me that he had something else in mind, I was taken aback. I met up with him one day and he told me that he had worked out this brand new sequence that would involve Audrey's dream coming to fruition with the tract house, the lovely garden and I was like, "Oh no! I want to sing it on the trash can!" He said to me, "Trust me Ellen, you'll love it and the audience will too!" Also, the lovely piece of dialogue that sits in between the prologue of the song and makes way for the rest of the song was cut, but that was because it would not have worked in the movie. Frank's treatment of the song was extremely respectful of Howard's original intentions and my original treatment. It's a wonderful song and captures the essence of Audrey. She wishes for something modest, not at all out of reach, and Frank's beautiful sequence with her dream really is a testament to that ideology.

The demented denist Steve Martin inflicts pain on a patient during a lively rock 'n' roll number in *Little Shop of Horrors.*

Gambin: The late great Howard Ashman is one of the greatest lyricists of our time. Not only did he give Audrey her sweet wish for somewhere that's green, but he also gave Ariel her voice in *The Little Mermaid* and a beast his soul in *Beauty and the Beast*, two extremely important Disney features that ushered in the new Renaissance for the company. What was Mr. Ashman like in his vocal direction and what was the most meaningful piece of advice he ever gave you?

Greene: Howard was an amazing director and coach. Many directors tell you no, no no, but they never offer the reasons why. Howard wasn't like that; he would always explain what it was that he was opposed to in great detail, and he nurtured my performance during the run of the stage show in a wonderful way. We had a great chemistry, he and I, and he listened to me, which is sometimes extremely rare within the actor/director dynamic. For example, originally there was a high energy, high camp number between Audrey and the dentist somewhere in the second act, and it never sat with me and I explained to him why we didn't need it; he listened and it was cut. Its omission benefited the show and we moved on. He encouraged me to create which is something I will forever treasure. Not only was he a great director, he was a wonderful friend and sadly I lost him far too early; too many beautifully talented men (Peter Allen among many others) that I have worked with have passed away during the years way before their time, and it still hurts. Howard and I went to see *The Little Mermaid* premiere together and he was so nervous and I was so excited for him. When the film finished we were both blown away by its magic. Years later, when he was dying of AIDS during the great success of *Beauty and the Beast*, he told me to keep *Little Shop of Horrors* alive. He told me I was the torch that kept that show alive. What can you say about something like that? This is one of the many reasons the show and the movie mean so much to me.

A concerned Rick Moranis holds the blood-slurping plant from *Little Shop of Horrors*.

Gambin: What was it like working alongside the likes of Steve Martin and Bill Murray? And what was your relationship with Rick Moranis like? Your romance blossoms in the movie so organically, so beautifully; was this something that came easy to both of you during the course of shooting the film?

Greene: Steve and Rick were amazing! Rick was an absolute professional and I had followed his career on the Canadian comedy sketch show *SCTV*. He and I had a great working relationship on set. Our characters' love for one another was very much on par with how we were in real life. Bill Murray was of course in *Next Stop, Greenwich Village* with me in a very small part. He came into auditions for *LSOH* and sang "Tonight" from *West Side Story*! He really wanted a singing part! But instead he got the role of the sadist that Jack Nicholson originally played in the Roger Corman movie.

Gambin: What are you memories of the wonderful Audrey 2 puppet? What did you think of the design and the ingenious puppeteering?

Greene: Oh, I loved the Audrey 2 puppet! Frank Oz totally understood the monster of the piece inside out. He understood that the audience had to fall in love with Audrey 2 initially, then get a bit worried when it started to do bad things and then totally be scared of it all the while laughing at its twisted jokes and behavior! Not an easy thing to direct I can assure you. Marty Robinson built Audrey 2 for the stage production and operated the puppet also. For the movie, Frank had to understand the mechanics of this creature. It was part puppet, part animatronics and it was operated by a bunch of people who handled a different part of its body—its vines, its mouth, and we actors had to do everything in slow motion when we shared screen time with the plant. Frank discovered that when you walk you actually move a couple of millimeters backwards from each step and this shows up in film, so we had to walk slightly forward so we'd be in synch with Audrey 2! With its big red lips and big scary teeth I think it is one of the greatest achievements in SFX ever put to screen!

Gambin: I've always loved genre films. Horror movies and musicals are my all time favorites. I also feel that those two genres are extremely similar in that they embrace escapist ideas that really hit a pulse and entertain! Do you love the marriage of these two genres as showcased in such a perfect movie as *LSOH*?

Greene: I love horror films! All the Roger Corman ones are very close to my heart. But my all time three favorite horror movies ever are *King Kong, Son of Kong* and *Mighty Joe Young*. *Son of Kong* is such a spectacular movie; I just love that big ol' white gorilla. That movie inspired Howard and me to start writing a sequel to *Little Shop of Horrors*. It would have been our homage to all those wonderful horror movies Howard and I loved so much that featured a beauty and a beast.

I Do Not Understand the Human Race: An Ode to the Ecologically Evil

Rex Harrison sings a wonderful number in the movie Doctor Dolittle called "Like Animals" that he uses as his defense testimony in a court room scene in this glorious 20th Century Fox musical. Ultimately it is a list song, where Harrison comments on how we have drawn comparisons to animals in relation to certain human behavior or character attributes. It is a beautiful song and its sentiment is true. The sadness in Harrison's delivery as he sings (more so to himself, reflecting): "I do not understand the human race …" resonates so beautifully. Also, in the superb film *Sssssss*, Strother Martin recites a stunning poem by the much loved writer Walt Whitman, which really sums up my love for not only the animal kingdom but also for these aforementioned brilliant movies that I have hopefully made the reader love even more or have, at least, cordially introduced to the reader:

> I think I could turn and live with animals,
> they're so placid and self contained,
> I stand and look at them long and long.
> They do not sweat and whine about their condition,
> They do not lie awake in the dark and weep for their sins,
> They do not make me sick discussing their duty to God,
> Not one is dissatisfied,
> not one is demented with the mania of owning things,
> Not one kneels to another,
> nor to his kind that lived thousands of years ago,
> Not one is respectable or unhappy over the Earth
> I think I could turn and live with animals

Finally, a huge thank you goes out to those simians called people (also all of them animal lovers) who made the creation of this book possible. To them I dedicate this book:

To Natalie Papak, who was the first person I told I was to write this book. We were sitting in the cinema waiting to see Disney's latest offering *Tangled* (Disney animated features being another main love of mine) and I told her about the book … her words of encouragement led me to sit down and flog it out.

To Lisa Rae Bartolomei and Liam Jose whose fresh eyes helped shape this book.

To Cara Mitchell and Anthony Biancofiore who clearly love making lists.

Nature has triumphed and human kind must flee in the final shot of Alfred Hitchcock's *The Birds*.

To Anthony "Doovies" Davies, Justine Ryan, John "Graveyard Tramp" Harrison and Tristan Collings, who all helped in every possible way to get me some wonderful images for these here pages.

To the sublimely talented Dee Wallace who has been in five of my all time favorite movies: *The Stepford Wives, The Hills Have Eyes, The Howling, ET: The Extra Terrestrial* and of course *Cujo*.

To the massively magnificent Bert I. Gordon, who gave me some of my all time favorite movies: *The Food of the Gods, Earth vs. The Spider, Empire of the Ants* and many more.

To the forever glamorous Tippi Hedren who survived *The Birds* and befriended the lions in *Roar*.

To the wonderful Veronica Cartwright who also survived *The Birds, Invasion of the Body Snatchers* and *Alien*.

To the amazing Chris Alexander (EIC at *Fangoria*) who has single handedly made one of my most treasured periodicals one of the best things I have ever been part of and has supported my endeavors so fervently and passionately.

To everybody at *Fangoria* magazine; most notably Rebekah McKendry, Michael Gingold, Sean Smithson, David Ian McKendry, Marla Newborn, Thom Carnell, Lianne Spiderbaby, Justin Beahm, Lacey Paige, Sam Zimmerman, Debbie Rochon, Rod Labbe, David Del Valle and Susan Svehla—what a dream it is to be part of such an amazingly talented and passionate team!

To Gary Svehla, who responded to my endless emails so swiftly and with great words of wisdom—thank you so much for giving me this opportunity; it has been a pleasure working with you and the wonderful Midnight Marquee Press.

And a special thanks and dedication goes out to Anita Herrick, Tony Timpone, David Morris, Philippa Berry, Peter Savieri, Danny Pintauro, Joe Dante, Belinda Balaski, Dick Miller, Patty McCormack, Charles Bernstein, Richie Ramone, Alice McNamara, Hande Noyan, Georgina Tulett, Natalie Foreman, Mitch Clem, Harry Flynn, Ernest Borgnine, Jeffrey Schwarz and Automat Pictures, MoviePoster.com, *Famous Monsters of Filmland* magazine, Ki Wone, Keelan Gallogly, Lewis Teague, Jason "Stoney" Stone, Marcus Eastop, Dash Bourke, Sarah McKeown, Matt O'Neil, Sam Bowran and the Melbourne Horror Society and It's Only A T-Shirt.com, Ash Flanders, Declan Greene, Stephen Nicolazzo, Pip Edwards, Mark Fak, Jeff Lieberman, American International Pictures, Jack Callaghan and Sally Shanahan and Gretel, Penney Riches, Neslihan Noyan, Ellen Burstyn, Brooke Theiss, Maria Sokratis, Lotti Stein, Yunuen Perez, Antonio Gonzalez, Joan Collins, Zsa Zsa Gabor, Maila "Vampira" Nurmi, Cassandra "Elvira" Peterson, Bruce Davison, Amy Bell, Ash Pike, Coreen Haddad, Vanessa Ryan, Linnea Quigley, Alethea Belford, Mark Patton, Joe Zaso, Sarah Derum, Jennifer Blanc, Michael Biehn, Michelle Dellamarta, Ben Watkins, Cris Wilson, Ben O'Dowd, Matthew Hickey, Lara Bartolo, Louise Galofaro, Daren Hammer, Rutanya Alda, Nathalie Gelle, everybody who has been involved with Sissies and Sluts Theatre Company, John Caglione, Jr., P.J. Soles, William Grefe, Ellen Greene, Tommy Lee Wallace, Lawrence D. Cohen, Miko Hughes, Sissy Spacek, Ryan Clark, Screamin' Mad George, Carol J. Clover, everybody associated with the Tote Hotel Melbourne, Laila Costa, Adele Daniele, Bruce Milne, Dallas and Danae and Quinn, James Thom, Dale Bamford, Rachel Belofsky and Screamfest LA, Cameron Cairnes, Donald Bogle, David J. Skal, Molly Haskell, Shelley Duvall, Harry Benshoff, Melanie Schmidt, Kynan O'Meara, George A. Romero, Rudy Scalese, Linda Grant, Linda Blair and the Worldheart Foundation, John Carpenter, Tony Williams, Geoffrey Masters, Steven Spielberg, Stephen King, Capri Mollenkopf, Ian McAnally, Adam Devlin, Mitch Davies and Troy Varker and All Star Comics Melbourne, Steve McCredie, Sean Patrick Brady and the staff at Minotaur, DVD Collection Melbourne, the Night Crew podcast, the Shambala Preserve, the American Cinematheque, Fred Krampits, Alexandra Michaels, Andy Lalino, Welch Everman, Dotty, Scruffy, Budgie, my dad Charlie, my grandparents Tony and Maria, my mum Grace Gambin and sisters Gracie and Lisa and their families and to my dog Molly who loves watching all these animal horror movies along with her best buddy ... and to all the animals—be they dogs, rabbits, rats, birds or cats ... this book is for you!

About the Author

Lee Gambin is a Melbourne based playwright, screenwriter, film and theater essayist and journalist for famed U.S.A. horror film magazine *Fangoria*. He has been working as a writer for *Fangoria* magazine since 2008. He has worked in independent theater for many years as well as being Artistic Director of his own independent theater company. His rock musical *Oh The Horror!* was a major success in its initial workshop run in 2009. He has lectured for numerous film societies and film festivals including the Melbourne International Film Festival. Gambin's play *King of Bangor* was published by Stephen King associative publishing house The Overlook Connection and *Massacred by Mother Nature: Exploring the Natural Horror Film* is his first film analysis book published by Midnight Marquee Press, Inc. Currently Gambin is working on a book chronicling the making of Brian De Palma's *Carrie*. He lives in Melbourne, Australia.

Lee Gambin, with Molly, reflects about his love for the natural horror film.

Index

Page numbers in ***bold italics*** indicate pages with illustrations

20 Million Miles To Earth 117, 125
20ᵗʰ Century Fox 206
7 Faces of Dr. Lao, The 151

Abby 30, 55
Ackerman, Forrest J 29
Action-Adventure motifs 19, 20, 24, 26, 30, 31, 32, 33, 46, 56, 68, 155, 187
Adams, Richard 134
Addams, Neal ***54***
Addams Family, The (TV series) 44
Agar, John 121, 122
AIDS 63, 134, 204
Aliens 69
Allen, Irwin 100, 101
Allen, Nancy 149
Allen, Peter 204
Alligator 60, ***62***, ***63***, ***64***, 65, 109, 121, 141, 159, 166, ***186***, 194
Alligator 2: The Mutation 65
All The King's Horses 170
Allyson, June 85
Altered Species 27
Amazing Colossal Man, The 11, 123
American International 21, ***25***, 34, 54, 55, 70, 115, 127, 151
American Werewolf in London, An 111
Amicus Productions 42
Amityville 2: The Possession 35
Amityville Horror, The 34, 164
Anaconda 53, 65
Anderson, Pamela 45
Animal Liberation 22
Animal Rights activism 21, 25, 45
Ankers, Evelyn 122
Anti-War movement 21
Ants (aka *It Happened At Lakewood Manor*) 104, 105

A.P.E. 116
Arachnid 100
Arachnophobia 94, 97, ***98***, ***99***, ***100***, 102, 112, 164
Argento, Dario 17, 68, 156
Arkoff, Samuel Z. 25, 66, 127
Armstrong, R.G. 87
Arnold, Jack 121
Arnold, Susan *183*
Ashman, Howard 201, 203
As The World Turns 173
Astin, Patty Duke 100
Atherton, William 30
Atomic Age 18, 92, 114, 115, 119, 120, 125, 126
Attack of the 50 Foot Woman 125
Attack of the Giant Leeches ***18***, 120
Attack of the Mushroom People ***194***
Attack of the Puppet People 123, 187
Atwill, Lionel 77
Avalon, Frankie 25

Baby Doll 111
Bacon, Kevin 65
Backlinie, Susan 20, ***35***, 36, ***167***, 167, 168
Bad Seed, The 20, 91, 106
Baker, Joe Don 78, 79, 80, 81, ***189***
Baker, Rick 111, 112, ***116***, 116, 193
Balaski, Belinda ***61***, 129, ***131***, ***182***, 183
Bardot, Brigitte 45
Barracuda 70
Barrows, George 138
Barrymore, Drew 171, 174
Bartel, Paul 61, 182
Basinger, Kim 110
Bass, Saul 43, 104
Bat People, The 138, ***151***, ***152***
Bats 165

210

Bava, Mario 68, 76, 182
Baxter, Meredith 144
Beach Blanket movies 25
Beast Within, The 138, 152, *153*,
Beauty and the Beast (1991) 203, 204
Beginning of the End 11, 12, 18, *92*, 114, 124, 125, 187
Beghe, Jason 50, *51, 52*
Behets, Briony 161, *162*
Ben *143*, *144*, *145*, 156
"Ben's Song" 145, 156
Benedict, Dirk *149*, *150*
Berkley, Busby 16
Bernstein, Charles *178*, *179*, 180, 181
Besch, Bibi 152, 153
Beswick, Martine 87, 117
Beyond the Door 54
Birds, The *15*, 18, 19, 20, 21, 97, 107, 110, 111, 112, 134, 135, *207*
Black Christmas 60, 72
Black Scorpion, The 122, *123*
Black Zoo 136, *137*, *138*
Black, Karen 68, 69
Black Sunday 76
Black Swarm 112
Black Water 65
Blacula 30
Blair, Linda *17*, 45, 158
Blatt, Daniel 171, 178
Blaxploitation 25, 30
Bloch, Robert 30, 104
Blood Beach 53
BloodMonkey 52, *53*
Blue Sunshine 109
Blood Surf 65
Bloody Birthday 91
Body horror 17, 18, 19, 92, 93, 193
Bogdanovich, Peter 142
Bolling, Tiffany *95*, 96, 159, 160
Bone Snatcher, The 112
Bont, Jan de 44, 169, 178
Borgnine, Ernest *140*, 141, *142*, 143
Bottin, Rob *60*, 61, 181, 183
Braddon, Russell 133
Breed, The 76

Bride of Frankenstein 140
Brinckerhoff, Burt 82
Bronson, Charles 24
Brood, The 91
Brown, David 184
Bug (1975) 8, 61, 74, 93, *106*, *107*, *108*, 109, 112, 164, *190*
Bug (2006) *93*, 94
Burning, The 26, 74
Burnt Offerings 154
Burroughs, Jackie 143
Burton, Al 171

Cabaret 142
Caine, Michael 75, 100, 102
Calhoun, Rory 133
Cameron, James 69
Cannonball 182
Cardos, John "Bud" 97
Carlos, Wendy 179
Carpenter, John 76, 142
Carpenters, The 152
Carradine, David 119, 136
Carradine, John 77, 171
Carroll, Leo G. *121*, 122
Carrie (1976) 20, *24*, 25, 41, 64, 66, 86, 89, 139, 142, 144, 147, 148, 149, 179
Cartwright, Veronica *13*
Cassidy, Ted 44
Castle, Peggie 125
Castle, William 93, 106, 107, 190
Cat Creature, The 142
Cat People (1942) 20
Cat's Eye 43
Chamberlain, Richard 100
Chandler, Helen 122
Chaney Jr., Lon 121
Chauvet, Elisabeth *160*, *161*
Chew, Sam *160*, *161*
Children of the Corn, The 87, 91
Child's Play 152
CHiPS! 171
Chisum 31
Christine 89, 142

Cinderella (1950) 20
Cinema Demonica 16, 17, 19, 30, 86, 87, 106, 158
Civil Rights movement 22
Clarke, Mae 122
Claws 94, 164
Claxton, William F. 133, 134
Clemens, Paul *153*, 154
Clooney, George 33
Close Encounters of the Third Kind 30, 36, 98
Clover, Carol 73
Cohen, Herman 138
Cohen, Larry 118
Cohen, Lawrence D. 195, 196
Cold War fears 18, 21, 92, 114
Collins, Joan *127*, 128, 187, 188
Colossal Kids, Big Bugs, and Giant Rats 188
Coming Home 147
Communism, Cold War 18, 92, 114, 115, 119, 120, 125, 126
Concorde Pictures 55
Congo 52
Connelly, Jennifer *156*
Conrad, Charles 172
Cook Jr., Elisha *138*
Cooper, Alice 76
Cooper, Merian C. 115
Copolla, Francis Ford 142
Corday, Mara 121, 122
Corman, Roger 55, 69, 184, 186, 200, 205
Corpse Grinders, The 43
Corrington, John 103
Corrington, Joyce 103
Cox, Ronny 152, 153
Craven, Wes 17, 76, 170
Crawford, Joan 106, 116
Creature from the Black Lagoon 22, 29, 56, 121
Creelman, James Ashmore 115
Creepers (aka *Phenomena*) *156*
Creepshow *105*, 106
Cronenberg, David 17
Cujo 9, 10, *11*, 44, 64, 87, *88*, *89*, 90, 90, *91*, 163, 164, 167, *169*, 170, *171*, *172*, *173*, *174*, *175*, *176*, *177*, 178, 179, 180
Curse of Frankenstein, The 125
Curtis, Jamie Lee 41
Curtis, Tony 30
Cushing, Peter 42
Cyclops, The 125

Daddy's Deadly Darling (aka *Pigs*) 60, *155*, 164
Damnation Alley 112
Daniels, Jeff 98, 99, *100*
Dante, Joe 60, 61, 62, 65, 68, 83, 172, 182, *183*, *184*
Dark Shadows 182
Davis, Altovise 96
Davison, Bruce 137, *139*, 140, *141*, *142*, 156
Day, Doris 45
Dawn of the Dead (1978) 49
Day of the Animals, The 22, 30, *31*, 33, 34, *35*, *36*, 76, 164, 165
Day of the Dead 49
Day of the Dolphin 60
Day of the Triffids, The 23
De Havilland, Olivia 100, 101, *102*, 189
Deadly Eyes (aka *Rats*) 27, 132, 145
Deadly Bees, The 103, *104*
Death Wish 24
Deep Blue Sea 60
Destroy All Monsters 119
Devil Dog: Hound of Hell 86, *87*, 103
DeLaurentiis, Dino 66, 116
Demme, Jonathan 106
Dennis, Sandy 30
De Palma, Brian 24, 139, 147, 148
Derek, Bo 66, 68
Dern, Laura 33
Dillman, Bradford 61, 93, 100, 101, 106, 107, *108*, 109, 159, 190
Dinoshark *136*
Dirty Harry 24
Disney 20, 44, 48, 88, 116, 180, 203
Dog Days: The Making of Cujo 174, 180

Dogs 76, *82*, *83*, *84*, 159
Domergue, Faith 72
Donaggio, Pino 179
Donner, Richard 48, 76
Don't Look Now 172
Doren, Mamie Van 25
Douglas, Michael 44, 46
Dow, R.A. *109*, 110, 111, 112, *192*, 192, *193*, 193
Doyle, Sir Arthur Conan 77
Dracula (1931) 120
Dracula's Daughter (1936) 20
Dracula's Dog (see *Zoltan: Hound of Dracula*)
Draculean legend 145
Dreyfuss, Richard 21, 32, 57
Dr. Dolittle 206
Dr. Jekyll and Sister Hyde 87
du Maurier, Daphne 18

Earth vs. The Spider 18, 120, *124*, *125*, 188
Eastwood, Clint 24, 122, 140
E.C. Comics 43, 105, 157
Eight Legged Freaks 120
Elliot, Sam 27, *28*, 29
Elvira (see Cassandra Peterson)
Elvira: Mistress of the Dark 77
Empire of the Ants 11, 12, 104, *126*, *127*, *128*, 188
Enemy of the People 29
Entity, The 178
Environmental movement 21, 22, 25, 39
Ermey, R. Lee 143
E.T.: The Extra-Terrestrial 36, 98, 144, 166, 171, 174
Exorcist, The *17*, 19, 26, 30, 54, 55, 56, 58, 144, 158, 165, 172

Famous Monsters of Filmland 29
Farrow, Mia *16*, 41
Feminism/women's movement 22, 73, 160, 161
Film Ventures International 31, 58

Flash Gordon (Universal serials) 117
Flowers in the Attic 91
Fonda, Bridget 65
Fonda, Henry 70, 72, 100, 102
Food of the Gods 121, *128*, *129*, *130*, *131*, 132, 167, 186, *187*, *188*
Forbes, Ralph 77
Ford, John 16
Forrest, Christine 51
Forster, Robert 62, *63*, 64, 160, 194
Fosse, Bob 142
Foxworth, Robert 39, 40, 41, *165*
Francis, Freddie 104
Frankenheimer, John 39
Frankenstein (1932) 120
Frankenstein legend 114, 115
Free Willy 156
Freed, Arthur 85
Friday the 13th 17, 73
Friedkin, William 19, 93
Fright Night 152
Frighteners, The 172
Frogs 21, 22, 24, *25*, *26*, *27*, *28*, *29*, 53, 130, 141, 163, 164
Frozen 168
Fuller, Samuel 76
Fullerton, Melanie 133
Funicello, Annette 25

Gabor, Zsa Zsa 187
Gamera 119
Garner, James 84, *85*, 160
Gary, Lorraine 57, 72, 75
Gauntlet, The 122
Gay Liberation 22
Gein, Ed 30
Gender roles 19, 20, 21, 32, 33, 73, 158, 160, 161
George, Christopher 31, *32*, 33, 34
George, Lynda Day 34, 105
George, Susan 59
Ghost and the Darkness, The 44, *46*, *47*
Giant Spider Invasion, The 120
Gibson, Debbie 136
Gilbert, Stephen 138
Gilliland, Richard 106

Girdler, William 23, 30, 31, 33, 34, *35*, 36, 37, 66, 76, 164
Girls Nite Out 73
Glover, Crispin *142*, 143
Gnaw: Food of the Gods Part 2 132
God Told Me To 118
Godfather, The 142
Gods and Monsters 86
Godzilla (1956) (aka *Gojira*, 1954) *118*, 119, 126, 195
Goldman, William 44, 46
Goldsmith, Jerry 101
Goodman, John 99
Gordon, Bert I. 11, *12*, 25, 104, 123, 124, 125, 126, 128, 129, 131, 132, 186, 187
Gordon, Ruth *16*
Gortner, Marjoe 11, *129*, 130, *131*, 132, 167, 186, *188*
Gough, Michael 116, 136, *137*, 138
Grant, Lee 100
Graves, Peter 125
Graveyard Shift 145
Gray, Linda 83, 84
Great White 53, *58*
Greene, Ellen *200*, *201*, *202*
Greenpeace 22
"Greensleeves" 53
Grefe, William 147, 199, 200
Gremlins 65, 98
Grey, The 168
Grey, Virginia 138
Grier, Pam 25, 30
Griffiths, Melanie 14, 44
Grizzly 23, *30*, *31*, *32*, *33*, *34*, 47, 53, *54*, 164, 168
Grizzly 2: The Predator 33
Grover 202

Hair 147
Halloween (1978) 17, 41, 60, 72, 73
Hamilton, George 178
Hamilton, Murray 33, 57, 72, 74
Hammer Film Productions 87, 117
Happy Birthday to Me 26
Hargreaves, John 161, *162*

Harrington, Curtis 86, 87, 103
Harris, Richard 66, 67, 68, *159*, 165
Harrison, Gregory *38*
Harrison, Rex 206
Harryhausen, Ray 61, *72*, *117*
Hawks, Howard 16
Hawn, Goldie 30
Hayes, Allison 125
Hedren, Tippi *13*, 14, 19, *20*, 21, 43, 44, *45*, 102, 111
Henriksen, Lance 69
Hephhaestus Plague, The 106
Heston, Charlton 143
Hiller, Arthur 166
Hills Have Eyes, The 72, 77
Hitchcock, Alfred 14, *15*, 18, 22, 25, 36, 107, 110, 111, 112, 125, 134, 135, *207*
Hive, The 112
Hobbes, Thomas 29
Hoffman, Dustin 87
Hoffman, Philip Seymour 65
Holland, Tom 152
Hollywood Blvd. 184
Hooper, Tobe 17, 19, 77
Hopkins, Bo 70, 72
Horrors of Spider Island *120*
Horrors of the Black Museum 138
Hound of the Baskervilles (1939) 77, *78*
House of Dracula 120
Howling, The 61, 62, 63, 65, 83, 129, 170, 171, 174, 182, 184

Howling 2, The: ... Your Sister Is a Werewolf 152
Howling 3, The: The Marsupials 152
Hunter, Evan 19
Hush...Hush Sweet Charlotte 101
Huston, John 70, 71

Ibsen, Henrik 29
Imitation of Life 30
Innocents, The 91
Invasion of the Bee Girls *103*
Insecticidal 112
In the Shadow of Kilimanjaro 47

It 120, ***195***, ***196***, 197, 198, 199
It Came From Beneath The Sea ***72***, 117
It Happened at Lakewood Manor (aka *Ants*) 104, 105
It's Alive 118

Jackson, Kate 103
Jackson, Michael 145, 156
Jackson, Peter 116
Jacoby, Bill 89, *90*, 90
Jaeckal, Richard 31, ***32***, 34, 59
Jaws ***19***, 20, 29, 30, 31, 32, 33, 36, 46, 47, 53, 55, ***56***, ***57***, 58, 59, 60,62, 66, 70,72, 74, 75, 83, 96, 148, 159, 163, 167,180, 183, 184, 185
Jaws 2 72, ***73***, ***74***, 75, 107
Jaws 3D 60,75
Jaws 3: People 0 65
Jaws: The Revenge 75
Jennifer 43, 60, 137, 145, 146, ***147***, ***148***, 149, 156, 163
Johnson, Ben 100
Jordan, Porter 149

Kane, Carol ***164***
Karloff, Boris 104, 105
Kelley, DeForest 133
Kelly, Daniel Hugh 89, 90, ***173***
Kenny, June 124, ***125***
Killer Bees, The 103, 136, 154, 155, 157
Killer Fish 68, ***69***
Killer Shrews, The 18, 119
Kilmer, Val 44, 46, 47
King Kong (1933) 9, 48, ***114***, ***115***, 119, 123, 136, 205
King Kong (1976) 9, ***116***
King Kong (2005) 116
King Kong Escapes 116
King Kong Lives 116
King Kong vs. Godzilla 116
Stephen King 10, 24, 43, ***44***, 87, 88, 89, 90, 112, 120, 145, 177, 178, 189, 195, 196, 197, ***198***
Kingdom of the Spiders ***94***, ***95***, ***96***, ***97***, 109, 112, 134, 145
Kiss of the Tarantula 137, 142, ***154***, ***155***

Konga 116, 136, 138
Kozac, Harley Jane 98, 99
Kramer vs. Kramer 86
Kubrick, Stanley 179

Lafferty, Marcy 96, 97
Lake Placid 53, ***65***
Lambert, Mary 43, 189
Lanchester, Elsa 140, ***141***, 143
Land of the Giants 101
Lanfield, Sidney 77, 78
Lange, Jessica 9, 116
Langenkamp, Heather 192
Lassick, Sydney 64
Lassie (TV series) 85
Lassie (1980s TV movie) 171
Last House on the Left (1972) 73
Last Jews From Poland, The 178
Last Picture Show, The 142
Laurie, Piper 86
Lauter, Ed 89, 90, 167
LaVey, Anton 45
Lawrence of Arabia 47
Lawrence, Toni ***155***
Lebowitz, Fran 25
Lee, Christopher 104
Lee, Kaiulani 89
Leigh, Janet ***132***, 133
Leigh, Suzanna 104
Leone, Sergio 16
Letts, Tracey 94
Leviathan 29
Levin, Ira 170
Levine, Ted 76
Lieberman, Jeff 93, 109, 110, 112, 113, 192, 193, 194
Lifeguard 28
"Like Animals" 206
Ling, Suzanna ***154***, ***155***
Link 48, 48, 49
Little Mermaid, The 203, 204
Little Shop of Horrors (1986) ***23***, 200, 201, 203, 204
Little Shop of Horrors (stage musical) 200, 201, 202, 203, 204
Locke, Sondra ***140***, 141, 144, 167

215

Lockhart, June 85
Long Dark Night, The (aka *The Pack*) 76, 78, *79*, *80*, *81*, 82, 87, *189*, 190
Long Weekend 37, 161, **162**, 163
Lost Boys, The 77
Lost In Space (TV series) 85, 101
Lost World, The (1925) 115, 136
Lost World, The (1960) 118
Love At First Bite 178
Loy, Myrna 105
Lucas Tanner 170
Lupino, Ida *128*, 129, *130*, 131, 187, 188

MacMurray, Fred 100, 101
Madman 73
Mafu Cage, The **164**
Magic 46
Magic Sword, The *12*, 187
Majors, Lee 68, 69
Making Love 166
Mako: Jaws of Death 58, *59*, 200
Mancuso, Nick **165**
Manitou, The 30
Man-Eaters of Tsavo, The 46
Man's Best Friend 76
Marathon Man, The 46
Marshall, E.G. **105**
Marshall, Frank 99
Marshall, Noel 43, 44
Marshall, William 30
Martin 139
Martin, Steve 203, 204
Martin, Strother **149**, *150*, 151, 206
Mask 33
Mask of Fu Manchu, The 105
Mattei, Bruno 132
McAndrew, Marianne *151*, 152
McCall, Joan 31, 33
McCallum, David 83, 159
McCarthy, Kevin 61
McCormack, Patty 93, 106, *107*, 108, 190
McLean, Greg 65
McNeil, Kate 32, 51
Meeker, Ralph 131

Mega Shark vs. Giant Octopus 136
Menken, Alan 201, 203
Men, Women and Chainsaws: Gender in the Modern Horror Film 73
Menzies, Heather 61, 150
Mephisto Waltz, The 55
MGM 15, 85, 121, 134,
Mighty Joe Young (1949) 116, 136, 205
Mighty Joe Young (1998) 48, 116
Mikels, Ted V. 43
Miles, Joanna 106, 107, 108, 109
Miles, Sherry 78, 80, 81
Milland, Ray 27, *28*, *29*, 42
Miller, Dick 62, 181
Miller, Jason *17*, 56
Minnelli, Vincente 16
Misery 46, 88, 91
Miss Piggy 70
Moby Dick 32, 57, 66, 185
Moffat, Kitty Ruth 153
Mole People, The 122
Mongrel 84
Monkey Shines 32, 48, *49*, *50*, *51*, *52*
Monster Dog 76
Monster Shark 58
Montgomery, Lee Harcourt *143*, 144, 145
Moore, Juanita 30
Mora, Phillipe 152
Moranis, Rick *23*, *201*, *204*
Morheim, Louie 86
Moriarty, Michael 119
Morricone, Ennio 66, *68*
Mortimer, Emily *47*
Moss, Stewart *151*, 152
Mothra 119
Murphy, Rosemary 144
Murray, Bill 204
Musicals 15, 16, 20, 85, 205
Mysterious Island (1961) 117
Mystery Science Theatre 132, 135

Nalder, Reggie 85, 86
Nanny, The 91
National Lampoon Comedy Group 184

National Velvet 156
Native Americans and Original People 30, 35, 38, 39, 40, 67, 146, 159, 164, 165, 166, 199
Neilson, Leslie 34, *36*
New World Pictures 55
Nichols, Mike 152
Nicholson, Jack 143, 152, 205
Nicholson, James H. 25, 127
Nightmare on Elm Street, A 74, 178
Nightmare on Elm Street 4: The Dream Master, A *191*, 192
Night of the Lepus 132, *133*, *134*, *135*, 163
Night of the Living Dead (1968) 49, 97
Nightwing 29, 39, *165*, 165, *166*, *166*, 166
Nurmi, Maila 187

O'Brien, Willis 115, 123
Oklahoma! 203
Old Dark House, The (1933) 86
Old Yeller 156
Omen, The (1976) *48*, 55, 76, 165
One Million Years B.C. *117*, 118
Open Water 60
Orca 22, 29, 31, 32, 55, 60, 65, *66*, *67*, *68*, 75, 148, *159*, 165, 167
Ouspenskaya, Maria 39
Oz, Frank 200, 202, 203, 205
Ozploitation 37, 155

Pack, The (aka *The Long Dark Night*) 76, 78, *79*, *80*, *81*, 82, 87, *189*, 190
Page, Thomas 106, 109
Pankow, John 50, 51
Pataki, Michael 85, 86, *152*,
Pattern, Joyce Van 51
Patterson, Lt. Col. John Henry 46
Pearcy, Patricia *110*, 111, *193*, 194
Peckinpah, Sam 59
Peeping Tom 18, 125
Pelikan, Lisa 137, *147*, *148*, 149, 156
Penderecki, Krzysztof 179
Persson, Gene 124, *125*
Pet Sematary *43*, 164, 189

Peterson, Cassandra 45, 76
Pfeiffer, Michelle 152
Phase IV 104, 105
Phenomena (aka *Creepers*) *156*
Pickens, Slim 100
Picnic at Hanging Rock 37
Pighunt 53, 168
Pigs (aka *Daddy's Deadly Darling*) 60, *155*, 164
Pink Cadillac 122
Pintauro, Danny **88**, *89*, *90*, 169, 171, *172*, *173*, *174*, *175*, 176, *177*
Piranha 55, 60, 61, 62, 63, 65, 69, 106, 129, 148, 159, 166, 168, *181*, *182*, *183*, *184*, *185*, 186
Piranha 2: The Spawning 69, *70*
Piranha 3D 70, 183
Piranha 3DD 168
Platt, Ed 138
Pleasance, Donald 42
Pleshette, Suzanne 19
Polanski, Roman *16*, 106, 141
Poltergeist 39, 77, 164
Poltergeist 2: The Other Side 165
Poseidon Adventure, The 100, 101
Price, Vincent 106
Primeval 65
Prine, Andrew 31, *32*, 33
Prophecy 39, *40*, *41*, 42, 162, 163, 164, *165*
Psycho (1960) 16, 18, 30, 72, 102, 104, 125
Psycho 2 152
Pullman, Bill 65

Q: The Winged Serpent *117*, 118

Rambaldi, Carlos 166
Rampling, Charlotte 32, 66, 67, *159*, 160
Randall, Tony 151
Rank Organization 42
Rape revenge films 24, 59, 155, 156
Rathbone, Basil 77
Ratman's Notebooks, The 138
Rats (aka *Deadly Eyes*) 27, 132, 145

Rats: Night of Terror 132
Rattlers 29, 134, 145, 146, *160*, *161*, 163
Razorback 37, *38*, 155
Red Water 60
Remick, Lee 48
Riker, Robin 62, 64, 159, 160
Roar 43, *44*, *45*, 102
Robinson, Chris *146*, *147*, 200
Robinson, Marty 202, 205
Robinson, Peggy 14
Rock 'n' Roll 16, 25, 33, 76, 104, 124, 125
Rock 'n' Roll High School 184
Rocky 24, 142
Rodan 119
Rogue 38, 65
Roman, Ruth 34, 35
Romero, George A. 48, 49, 50, 97, 105, 139
Rose, Ruth 115
Rosemary's Baby *16*, 91, 106, 107, 141, 189
Ross, Katherine 32, *84*, 100, 101, 159
Rottweiler 76
Rubinstein, Zelda 39
Ruby 86

Salem's Lot 85, 89, 112
Sampson, Will 67, *159*, 165
Sands, Julian 97, 98, 99
Satanic-themed cinema (see Cinema Demonica)
Savage Weekend 154
Savini, Tom 105
Sayles, John 62, 63, 64, 65, 83, 182, *185*, 194
Scardino, Don *110*, 111, 112, 193, 194
Scheider, Roy 20, 21, 32, 56, *57*, 72, *73*, 74, 75, 159, 167
Schiffrin, Lalo 34, 35
Schnieder, Burt 178
Schnieder, Harold 178
Schoedsack, Ernest B. 115
Scott, George C. 60
Screamin' Mad George 191

Shambala Preserve, The **45**
Shannon, Michael 93
Sharktopus 136
Shatner, William *94*, *95*, 96, 97, 159
Shaw, Robert 21, 33, 46, *56*, 57
Sheba, Baby 30
Sheen, Charlie 33
Sheen, Martin 110
Sheldon, David 31
She-Wolf of London, The 85
Shining, The (1980) 164, 179
Shire, Talia 39, *40*, 41, 162, 163
Shue, Elizabeth 49
Silence of the Lambs, The 76, 106
Silva, Henry 64
Slasher films 16, 17, 18, 26, 30, 60, 72, 73, 106, 115, 158, 167
Sleepwalkers 43
Slither 113
Slugs **112**
Slumber Party Massacre 73
Snakes on a Plane 53
Snow White and the Seven Dwarves 20
Something Evil 30
Sommers, Suzanne 105
Son of Dracula 120
Son of Kong 116
Sound of Music, The 61
Spacek, Sissy *24*, 25
Spielberg, Steven 19, 29, 30, 33, 36, 46, 47, 53, 58, 60, 68, 94, 97, 98, 200
Spiders 100
Squirm 22, 93, 106, *109*, *110*, *111*, 112, *113*, 164, *192*, *193*, 194
Sssssss 61, 138, *149*, *150*, 151, 152, 206
Stallone, Sylvester 110
Stamp, Terence 49
Stanley 60, 142, 145, *146*, *147*, 166, *199*, 200
Steele, Barbara 62, 76, 182
Stepford Wives, The (1975) 46
Stone, Christopher 89, 170, 171, *173*
Strait-Jacket 106
Strasberg, Susan 30
Straw Dogs (1971) 59
Streep, Meryl 87

Studio One Productions 30
Stuff, The 118
Sudden Impact 122, 155
Suddenly, Last Summer 111
Sugarland Express, The 30
Sullivan, Jean 110, 111, 112, 194
Sunset Blvd. 103
"Surrey With The Fringe On Top, The" 203
Swanson, Gloria 103
Swarm, The 61, 100, ***101***, ***102***, 106, 163, 189
Swiss Family Robinson, The 44
Sybil (2007) 178
Syfy Channel 112
Szwarc, Jeannot 74, 93, 106, 107, 190

Tandy, Jessica 19, 21, 52, 111
Tarantino, Quentin 37
Tarantula 92, 114, 120, ***121***, ***122***, 123, 167
Tarantula: The Deadly Cargo 112
Taylor, Rod 14, 19, 21, 111
Teague, Lewis 44, 62, 64, 87, 172, 175, 178
Tentacles 55, *70*, 70, ***71***
Terminator, The 69
Texas Chain Saw Massacre, The (1974) 19, 72
Texas Chainsaw Massacre, The (2003) 142
Theiss, Brooke ***191***, 192
Them! 18, ***21***, 92, 104, 114, 120
They Nest 112
They Only Kill Their Masters 32, 84, ***85***, 159
Thing, The (1982) ***76***
Thomas, Melody 61
Three on a Meathook 30
Tiffany 136
Tingler, The 106
Tintorera 53, 58, 59
Titanic (1997) 69
Tobey, Kenneth 72
Together We Stand 171
"Tonight" 205

Towering Inferno, The 100, 101
Trog 136, 116
Tucci, Stanley 50
Turner, Janine 50
Uncanny The 42, ***43***, 167
Uninvited 43
Universal 8, 14, 15, 29, 39, 58, 60, 65, 85, 120, 121, 122, 151

Valley of Gwangi, The 117, 136
Vampira see (Maila Nurmi)
Van Ark, Joan ***28***, 29
Van Doren, Mamie 25
Vegetarianism, Veganism 22, 112
Vickers, Yvette ***18***
Videodrome 111
Village of the Giants, The 123, 187
Village of the Damned, The (1960) 91
Voyage to the Bottom of the Sea (1961) 56
Voyage to the Bottom of the Sea (TV series) 101

Walken, Christopher 143
Walker, Shirley 143
Wallace, Dee 10, ***11***, 65, ***88***, ***89***, 90, 164, ***169***, 170, ***171***, *173*, 174, 177
Wallace, Tommy Lee 195, ***197***
War and Remembrance 182
War of the Colossal Beast, The 123, ***124***, 187
Warner Bros. 15, 78, 121
Warner, David ***165***, 166
Wasp Woman, The ***19***, 20, 103
Watership Down 134
Wayne, John 31
Webs 100
Weir, Peter 37
Welch, Raquel 45, ***117***
Wells, H.G. 128, 188
Werewolf legend/Lycanthropy 16, 65, 76, 85, 121, 138, 150, 151, 152, 154, 184,
Westerns and Western motifs 15, 16, 20, 22, 95, 117, 119, 121, 123, 133, 134, 166

219

West Side Story 205
Whale, James 86, 140
Whatever Happened to Baby Jane? 91, 125
What's The Matter With Helen? 86
Which Lie Did I Tell? 47
White, Betty 45, 65
White Dog 76
Whoever Slew Auntie Roo? 86
Who's The Boss? 176, 177
Whitman, Stuart *132*, 133
Whitman, Walt 206
Widmark, Richard 100, 102
Wilder, Billy 103
Willette, Joann 192
Willard (1971) 27, 43, 60, 132, 137, *139*, *140*, *141*, *142*, 143, 144, 146, 147, 156, 157, 163, 167, 199
Willard (2003) *143*
Williams, John 35, 72, 74, *179*, 180
Williams, Tennessee 110, 111, 193, 194
Willis, Hope Alexander 78, 79, 80
Winds of War 182
Winston, Stan 151
Winters, Shelley 70, 71, 86
Wolf 152
Wolf Creek 65
Wolf Man, The 39, 120, 121
Wray, Fay *114*, *115*, 116

Year of the Angry Rabbit, The 133

Zanuck, Richard D. 184
Zebra Killer, The 30
Zoltan: Hound of Dracula 76, 85, 86

IF YOU ENJOYED THIS BOOK,
PLEASE VISIT OUR WEBSITE
WWW.MIDMAR.COM
OR PHONE OR WRITE FOR
A FREE CATALOG

MIDNIGHT MARQUEE PRESS, INC.
9721 BRITINAY LANE
BALTIMORE, MD 21234
USA

410-665-1198

www.ingramcontent.com/pod-product-compliance
Lightning Source LLC
Chambersburg PA
CBHW050149130526
44591CB00033B/1220